The Holy Spirit

The Holy Spirit

Setting the World on Fire

Edited by

Richard Lennan and
Nancy Pineda-Madrid

Paulist Press
New York / Mahwah, NJ

Cover images: Flame art by Artem Kovalenco / Shutterstock.com; Red background by Elena Ray / Shutterstock.com
Cover and book design by Sharyn Banks

Library of Congress Cataloging-in-Publication Data

Names: Lennan, Richard, editor.
Title: The Holy Spirit : setting the world on fire / edited by Richard Lennan and Nancy Pineda-Madrid.
Description: New York : Paulist Press, 2017. | Includes bibliographical references and index.
Identifiers: LCCN 2017010032 (print) | LCCN 2017025516 (ebook) | ISBN 9781587687136 (ebook) | ISBN 9780809153442 (pbk. : alk. paper)
Subjects: LCSH: Holy Spirit. | Catholic Church—Doctrines.
Classification: LCC BT121.3 (ebook) | LCC BT121.3 .H68 2017 (print) | DDC 231/.3—dc23
LC record available at https://lccn.loc.gov/2017010032

ISBN 978-0-8091-5344-2 (paperback)
ISBN 978-1-58768-713-6 (e-book)

Published by Paulist Press
997 Macarthur Boulevard
Mahwah, New Jersey 07430

www.paulistpress.com

Printed and bound in the
United States of America

*For all who minister in
the joy and hope of the Holy Spirit,
the Giver of Life!*

Contents

Acknowledgments

We, the editors, are particularly grateful to our colleagues at Boston College School of Theology and Ministry for their contribution of chapters in this volume. This book developed and matured by means of the generous investment of work by each author and their commitment to a genuinely collegial project. We acknowledge also the great contribution of Lakisha Lockhart, a Boston College doctoral student, who assisted the editors and the authors through her careful attention to detail and to James Dechant, a School of Theology and Ministry alumnus and now doctoral student at Fordham University, for his assistance with the indexes.

Toward the end of this project, a group of reviewers generously read the entire manuscript and then gathered together with the editors to offer their wisdom regarding how it might be improved. We wish to recognize and thank the following readers: Allison Cornelisse, Patrick Farmer, Mike Feloney, and Jacqueline Regan.

We greatly appreciate the Dean's Office of the School of Theology and Ministry for their material support of this book project.

We are especially grateful to Paul McMahon of Paulist Press for his support of this project.

Introduction

The Holy Spirit meets us where we are. In our experiences of joy and serenity, guilt and distress, wonder and awe, pain and anger, the Spirit is present. The Spirit remains present in all that comprises our life's journey; closer to us than we are to ourselves, and the source of strength for our "inner being" (Eph 3:16). What is more, the Spirit continuously invites greater life, animating our present. The Holy Spirit indwells our bodies and makes our very lives and living possible, empowering us with the grace of Christ. In being with us, the Holy Spirit is and remains sympathetic to our life situation and circumstance. For our part, we, like the prophet Elijah, need to learn how to pay attention, to deepen our awareness of the Spirit's presence.

Developing a heightened sensitivity is the first step. The Holy Spirit's movement in our lives, and in the world, is often elusive, not readily discerned. Much like Hagar, we may find ourselves wondering how God is moving in the events of our life (Gen 16:7–14): What does the Spirit want me to understand? How will I be able to survive? What am I called to be about? How might I practice greater fidelity to the Spirit? The Judeo-Christian traditions offer various responses to these questions. *The Holy Spirit* brings to the fore some of these many valuable responses, responses that have their foundation in the good news of Pentecost (Acts 2): that the Spirit has been generously poured out on all of us, personally and communally.

The liturgy for Pentecost includes a hymn in praise of the Holy Spirit. This hymn, which originated in the Middle Ages and is called a "Sequence," expresses a longing for the Spirit: "Come, Holy Spirit, come!"[1] That longing reflects the unique gifts that the Spirit brings: "You, of comforters the best…Grateful coolness in the heat; Solace in the midst of woe." Via poetry rather than prose, the hymn proclaims an unequivocal faith in the divinity of the Spirit: "Where you are not, we have naught." Consequently, the hymn pleads for the Spirit to effect what God alone can accomplish: "On our dryness pour your dew; wash the stains of guilt away. Bend the stubborn heart and will; melt the frozen, warm the chill; guide the steps that go astray." The gift of the Spirit is the focus of this book. Through this book, our awareness of the Spirit is nurtured by exploring the ways in which the Christian community has interpreted the Spirit's action, and by considering the responses that the Spirit evokes from those who receive this "most blessed Light divine, which can enflame us with the love of God."

The descriptions of the Spirit in the Sequence for Pentecost make clear that the Holy Spirit is not a substance that we can grasp physically, imagine fully, or understand definitively. The Christian community has more than two millennia of experience with the Holy Spirit, but that community can lay no claim to having control of the Spirit. Indeed, the Spirit retains today the characteristic that has been evident from the beginning of Christian reflection on this particular presence of God: the Spirit, like the wind, "blows where it chooses" (John 3:8). While that fact makes it impossible to provide a comprehensive analysis of the Holy Spirit, the Christian community has always understood that the Spirit's activity is not dependent on human knowledge. Similarly, the authenticity of the community's response to the Spirit is not measured by the depth and breadth of its capacity to account for the Spirit. Indeed, the goal of the Spirit's action is not to generate an understanding of the Spirit. Rather, the Spirit, reflecting the unity of God's trinitarian love, guides the disciples of Jesus Christ into the truth that is Christ, the truth that leads to the fullness of God's reign. With the Spirit, then, we come to Christ, in whom we have "the hope of glory" (Col 1:27).

Drawing on its relationship to Christ, the Christian community, without claiming ownership of the Spirit, has felt confident to affirm not only the existence of the Spirit, but the "shape" of the Spirit. Thus, the Christian community recognizes the Spirit as "the creative source of the power of nature, life power overcoming death; it is the power bonding humans together in the eschatological community that is the final destiny of human life; it is the prophetic power already working in history to achieve that relating of humans to one another in justice and peace that is the 'reign of God.'"[2] In short, the Christian community has always known that the Spirit is the present expression of God's love for God's creation, the love given flesh in Jesus Christ, the love that can enflame our lives.

The Holy Spirit does not present a comprehensive theology of the Spirit, a pneumatology, but it offers a wide variety of insights into the relationship between the Holy Spirit and the community of Christ's disciples. The book explores historical perspectives as well as numerous contemporary ones. In so doing, the authors seek to illuminate both the identity of the Spirit and the implications that faith in God's Holy Spirit have for life in the world and the church, implications that embody what it means to be empowered by the fire of the Spirit. This book is organized in three sections: *awareness*, *reflection*, and *commitment*.

The first part of this book—"Experiencing the Holy Spirit"— explores everyday experiences and practices that heighten our consciousness of the Spirit's generous, constant summons to *more* life. In the opening chapter of this section, Colleen Griffith draws on the rich imagery of the body found in the Pauline letters to explore the "indwelling Spirit" of God. Griffith focuses on living personal bodies and on the communal/ecclesial body as temples of the Holy Spirit, and thus, as the locus for encountering the closeness of God. She makes clear that as the one who vivifies, who gives life, the Spirit animates and compels all living bodies toward the fulfillment of God's reign.

Brian Dunkle turns our attention to the work of Irenaeus and Augustine, both of whom were theologians, bishops, and saints of the early church, and both of whom helped the early church better understand the triune God and the special role of the Holy Spirit. Through the lens provided by Irenaeus and Augustine, Dunkle explains that when we actively practice our faith, the Holy Spirit works through these practices, encouraging our participation in divine life, sanctifying us, and making us holy and more godlike. This process represents an ancient view of salvation referred to as deification.

Echoing Griffith's attention to bodies, Franklin Harkins considers a distinctive aspect of the relationship between the Spirit and the embodied reality of human beings. Harkins focuses on the medieval period, when relics were made from some fragment of a saint's dead body, clothing, or some other small artifact. He shows how these relics became a touchstone for the encounter between faithful Christians and the Holy Spirit, and so an opportunity for a deepening of faith. He reminds his readers that, even in their death, these saints remain living members of the Body of Christ through the power of Spirit.

The remaining two chapters in the section shift the emphasis to the church's worship and contemporary theology. With specific reference to the church's eucharistic liturgy, John Baldovin details how the Spirit is addressed in the church's worship. He demonstrates both how worship embodies the church's faith in the Spirit and how that same worship nurtures the church with the gift of the Spirit for its life in the world.

Richard Lennan and Nancy Pineda-Madrid complement the focus on spirituality and worship by examining how both official church teaching and contemporary theology depict the presence of the Holy Spirit; in so doing, they concentrate on the Spirit's relationship to the "pilgrimage of faith." First, Lennan and Pineda-Madrid provide an overview of the Second Vatican Council's approach to the Spirit, how the Council's teaching underscored the centrality of the Spirit for the church's unity and mission. Second, they bring the discussion of the Spirit into the present, with an analysis of two contemporary theologians, Víctor Codina and Elizabeth Johnson, who challenge the ecclesial community to a deeper trust in the Spirit.

The second part of the book—"Tracing the Movement of the Holy Spirit"—explores some of the ways the Christian tradition throughout its history has thought about and reflected on the experience of the Holy Spirit at work in our lives, the church, and the world. The chapters recognize that the activity of the Spirit not only precedes human efforts to describe it, but also exceeds the limits of all efforts to give an accounting of the Holy Spirit, who "indwells" humanity and the whole of God's creation. They show that faith in the Spirit is always a response to God's movement, that God is the one who initiates relationship with us. They show, too, that the authenticity of faith is linked inextricably with acceptance of God's Holy Spirit as being always and everywhere beyond the control of human beings.

The opening chapters in this second section engage with biblical portrayals of the Holy Spirit. First, Andrew Davis addresses directly the elusive concept that is "spirit" in the Old Testament. His investigation explores the myriad usages of the Hebrew word *ruaḥ,* a word that he describes as being "multivalent," as susceptible to a range of interpretations that reflect the elusiveness proper to "spirit." Nonetheless, Davis shows that the various uses share an emphasis on the life-giving presence of God, an emphasis that foreshadows what the New Testament conveys about the Holy Spirit. In the following chapter, Angela Kim Harkins reviews aspects of the New Testament's portrayal of the Spirit. In doing so, she draws on what the earliest Christians learned from the traditions of Judaism in order to highlight three effects of the Spirit that captured the attention of the first Christians. Taken together, those effects, all of which relate to creativity, recognize that the Spirit was far more than the source of a vague religious "feeling"; in fact, the Spirit was already seen as integral to the interpretation of Scripture and the practice of virtue.

The next three chapters in this second part share an interest in the historical traditions of Christian spirituality. First, Francine Cardman, concentrating on the postapostolic period of Christianity—the centuries that followed the formation of the first Christian communities—examines various controversies about the identity of the Spirit. She demonstrates that the struggles to clarify Christian faith in the Spirit were simultaneously struggles to clarify the implications that reception of the Spirit had for the life of the Christian communities. Second, Catherine Mooney analyzes the spirituality of the Middle Ages, exploring characterizations of the Spirit offered by major figures of that period. Mooney illustrates how theologies and devotional practices concerning the Holy Spirit both reflected social attitudes of the time and influenced those attitudes. Third, André Brouillette brings the review of spirituality into the later medieval or early modern period. As with Cardman and Mooney, Brouillette concentrates on particular figures—Ignatius of Loyola and Teresa of Avila—highlighting their interpretation of how the presence of the Spirit might be discerned and what dynamics may be operative in responses to the Spirit.

Since the Christian tradition considers not only what awareness of the Holy Spirit's movements might mean and how to name the experience of the Spirit, but also how to respond to the Spirit, how to live as people enflamed by the Spirit, the book's final part—"Embracing the Holy Spirit"—focuses on committed responses to the Spirit.

Here, O. Ernesto Valiente presents the life of Oscar Romero, the El Salvadoran archbishop martyred in 1980, as a life marked by the transformation that follows from being open to the movement of the Holy Spirit. Valiente charts the shift in Romero from being a cautious and traditional priest to being a champion of the poor and oppressed. He argues that it was the love that Romero knew in his life, the love of Christ in the Spirit, that enabled him to become a prophet and eventually a martyr.

The next two chapters explore spiritual charisms, gifts of the Holy Spirit, that require careful discernment. First, Margaret Guider studies the role and function of religious orders and ecclesial movements in the world church of our own time. She offers understanding of, on the one hand, our hope for a harmony among various charisms, and, on the other hand, the tensions and unreconciled divisions that take their toll on people of faith. She provides questions to discern what it means to embrace a spiritual charism and live it out in an authentic fashion. Second, Hosffman Ospino underscores the rapid rise of the Catholic Charismatic Renewal movement within the United States' Hispanic community, calling it the largest and most influential ecclesial movement. He delineates the ways this movement offers possibilities for the development of Hispanic Catholic leaders and for the renewal of parish life.

The final three chapters highlight the relationship between discernment and response to the Spirit. Theresa O'Keefe demonstrates that the period of adolescent development initiates a unique space for spiritual growth and transformation; that space is characterized by an adolescent's heightened self-consciousness. That self-awareness, which can lead a young person to greater acknowledgment of others, as well as of themselves, while also opening the possibility for self-giving relationships characteristic of the transition toward adulthood, can be interpreted in light of the Holy Spirit's movement in the life of the adolescent.

Andrea Vicini's chapter is a reflection on the role that our emotions play in our discernment of the movement of the Holy Spirit. Emotions are often challenging to experience and acknowledge, and for too long, they have been viewed as suspect when it comes to life in the Spirit. Recognizing this history, Vicini suggests instead that emotions illuminated by the Holy Spirit can guide our desire to live an ethical life, and they can help lead us toward transformation and conversion.

In the concluding chapter, Melissa Kelley directs our attention to the enlivening work of the Holy Spirit particularly during times of disruption, loss, or crisis that leave their mark on our lives, individually as well as socially. These disruptive life experiences create a space for us to make new meaning with our lives, that is, to remake the story of our lives in a way that wrestles with and eventually offers an account of the disruption. Kelley helps us behold the Holy Spirit's unceasing support for us, support that can sustain us especially during tumultuous times in our lives.

As giver of life, the Holy Spirit beckons us to pay attention to the spaces opened by the twists and turns of life—joyous, painful, and all the rest. *The Holy Spirit* encourages us to become more aware of the ways the Spirit inhabits those spaces, sitting with us as we wrestle with whatever troubles us, healing what needs healing, and all the while feeding our zeal, our fire, for Christ's mission in the world. The hope of the authors is that their work will help readers to appreciate anew the rich presence of the Spirit in their lives, and respond ever more ardently.

Pentecost, 2017

PART 1

EXPERIENCING
THE HOLY SPIRIT

1

The Spirit and the Nearness of God

Colleen M. Griffith

Theologians who seek to capture the immanent-transcendent Spirit in words are like children at play, blowing beautiful bubbles into the air and then chasing after them to hold on to them. The bubbles never yield to the children's attempts to grasp and possess them. In the theological rendition of the game, the Spirit doesn't either. Likened in Scripture to both "wind" and "breath," the Spirit of God necessarily resists human attempts to exhaust its multifaceted contours or control its movements.

The Apostle Paul sensed all of this. For him, the Spirit was something to be lived in and not manipulated. It was an experiential reality, an effective gift, whose reception was demonstrable. The Spirit was the self-communication of God, and as such, it was neither capturable, nor something that could be pinned down in human language. Paul describes the Spirit wisely, using multiple referents that reflect different points of emphasis. Thus, he speaks of the Spirit as one who leads (Rom 8:14), quickens (Rom 8:11), and reveals even the depths of God (1 Cor 2:10). He writes about the Spirit as the activator of gifts (1 Cor 12:4–11), the one who "bear[s] witness with our spirit that we are children of God" (Rom 8:16), and the one through whom "God's love has been poured into our hearts" (Rom 5:5). For Paul, it is the Spirit that "helps us in our weakness" and "intercedes with sighs too deep for words" (Rom 8:26). And the fruit of this Spirit is concrete and palpable: "love, joy, peace, patience, kindness, generosity, faithfulness, gentleness, and self-control" (Gal 5:22–23).

This chapter explores one rich and evocative sense of the Spirit of God attested to by Paul, namely the "indwelling Spirit." Inspired by 1 Corinthians 6:19, in which Paul asks, "Do you not know that your body is a temple of the Holy Spirit within you, which you have from God, and that you are not your own?" our focus is on the Spirit of God dwelling within personal bodies and the communal body. We consider activities of the indwelling Spirit as these prove suggestive for "life in the Spirit." Throughout, the metaphor "temples of the Holy Spirit" stands as a tender referent that underscores the intimate closeness of God.

ON THE INDWELLING SPIRIT

Often in Christian history, the Spirit has been rendered impersonally and elusively. Perhaps this reflects concern that the immanence of God might detract from God's transcendence. Yet the living one, who remains other than and distinct from the world, pervades it to "mysteriously empower creation from within."[1] It is an astonishing thing that God has chosen to live in and with us in the kind of intimate relational proximity that has given rise to the language of "indwelling."

Impersonal and elusive renderings of the Spirit may also be the result of a worry that an "indwelling Spirit" will give way to a "'God in a bottle' kind of individualism."[2] Yet the living God, who draws closer to us than we can imagine, reveals a much bigger vision than the one animating this fear. The Spirit of God breathes, beckons, loves, and prays from an expansive place of abiding within whole communities and their members, and within the entire created order as well, inspiring a sense of kinship throughout, for the sake of a common good that portends a coming reign. Such a vision is neither overly anthropomorphic nor privatistic and individualistic.

Throughout history, the indwelling Spirit has been revered and feared, loved and held suspect. Surely it has never been grasped in its full depths, and cannot be. Yet beholding the indwelling Spirit anew, even for a short while, offers people a deep reason for hope, and a basis for joy. For the Spirit keeps on revealing "the unspeakable closeness of God."[3]

Experiences of God's nearness are presented with regularity in Scripture. Anne Claar Thomasson-Rosingh notes, "From the creation story in the Hebrew bible, where God breathes the Spirit into the first human (Gen 2:7), to the story of Pentecost in Acts where the disciples are filled with the Holy Spirit (Acts 2:4), Scripture carries the idea of the Spirit living in people."[4] The people of Israel sensed the living God present with them. The priest-prophet Ezekiel, proclaiming a restoration when the people were experiencing crisis, communicated God's strong intent to abide with God's covenanted people: "I...will set my sanctuary among them forevermore. My dwelling place shall be with them; and I will be their God, and they shall be my people" (Ezek 37:26–27). Centuries later, the Johannine community, writing from their experience of life in Christ, presents Jesus in the Farewell Discourse as saying, "Those who love me will keep my word, and my Father will love them, and we will come to them and make our home with them" (John 14:23). In the Johannine tradition, words like *dwell*, *remain*, and *abide* hold lasting meaning; these words continue to communicate powerfully today, revealing dynamics of life in Christ through the Spirit. The indwelling one, then and now, signals God's nearness. This indwelling Spirit has a *localized* and *tangible* dimension, one that may be explored best through a sense of place.

DWELLING PLACES OF THE SPIRIT

One central dwelling place of the Spirit is the human itself. "Do you not know that your body is a temple of the Holy Spirit within you, which you have from God?" In 1 Corinthians 6:19, Paul underscores the Spirit dwelling within individual persons and the community. While the place of the Spirit's dwelling spills much wider than the human estate, Paul highlights particularly the *placedness* of the Spirit in the embodied members of the Christian community, stressing the significance of this placedness for human *bodies* and the communal *Body of Christ*.

Influenced by his Jewish heritage, Paul uses temple imagery when showing how God dwells among God's people. According to Paul, what was true for the physical temple of Jerusalem is now true for the Christian community and for the bodies of individual believers. The bodies of persons in community and the Spirit are joined as a temple of God, as the ultimate place of worship. The Spirit dwells within the community in a material way, and in persons, in their bodily selves. Does one of these "bodies," individual or communal, serve more truly than the other as the temple to which Paul refers? Paul himself refuses to focus on only one or the other.

Beyond Individual/Communal Distinctions

The social aspects of early Christianity receive strong emphasis in contemporary biblical scholarship. N. T. Wright provides a good reminder: "The gospel created not a bunch of individual Christians, but a community."[5] Thus, the "body" referred to as the temple of the Holy Spirit in 1 Corinthians 6:19, is construed often as the communal Body, the church. In a markedly similar passage, 1 Corinthians 3:16, Paul does accent the community as a temple of the abiding Spirit, and he regularly calls upon the community as community to remember who they are in Christ and in the Spirit.

First Corinthians 6:19 is thick with meaning, however, and there is more than one sense of "body" intended here. A sense of the Spirit dwelling in the physical bodies of individual members of the Christian community is apparent in this passage as well. Individual bodily persons, as incarnate subjects, make up the communal Body of Christ. And in that Body of Christ, individual bodies are not dispensable parts of the whole; each is an irreplaceable creation gifted and graced by the Spirit's presence for the sake of the community. The "body" as the "temple" to which Paul refers in 1 Corinthians 6:19 is therefore both individual and communal, physical and social.

Implications for the Living Bodies of Persons

Moving beyond "an individual/communal divide,"[6] Paul intends strong relationships between embodied Christians and the communal/ecclesial body. Because embodied selves collectively comprise the Body of Christ, what happens in one bodily realm in fact affects the other. The work of the Spirit vivifying individual bodies binds them to others, uniting them in the experience of Christian community.

By likening personal and communal bodies to a temple, Paul points in the direction of a bodily ethic. He reminds members of the Church at Corinth that as "temples of the Holy Spirit," they are to "glorify God" in and through their bodies, and again, that they are "not their own," but "belong to God." In the church at Corinth, some community members were involved in problematic relationships and lifestyles. Paul responded to this report by accenting the need for a body ethic in the living of community. Incongruent actions in the body were simply not in keeping with being a temple of the Spirit's dwelling. Individual persons and communities were to act as embodied persons in ways that glorified God. The mandate "glorify God in your body" served to guide persons' incarnate modes of being in the world.

Paul's likening the body to a temple of the Spirit reflects his strong valuation of the human body. The Spirit dwells in the full person, but it is the materiality of the person, the body, that receives explicit mention from Paul. "Matter matters" for Paul, as Franklin Harkins underscores in his chapter in this volume. Paul invites Christians to reclaim the physicality of their Christian spirituality and to consider the bodiliness of their faith.

Mindful that the body is the dimension of self in which people often feel most vulnerable, raw, untidy, limited, and finite, Paul's description is especially evocative. Perhaps experiences of embodied vulnerability and incompleteness are precisely where the Spirit meets us. The Pauline notion of the body as temple turns us positively toward our own bodies, and to what bodied selves indwelled by the Spirit are able to manifest that is profoundly relational, holy, intimate, and true. Contemporary Christians glean much from Paul's sense of the integration of the physical and the divine. In the divine-human encounter, the Spirit enters the corporeal realm. The human body becomes a place where God's presence can dwell, and the Spirit remains active in and through the embodied lives of believers.

Significance for the Communal Body

Paul's communal/ecclesial sense of the body as temple of the Spirit carries implications as well. Bernard Cooke observes that "it is essential to draw attention to the communal dimension of the Spirit's powerful embrace. Though it does touch each individual with creative regard for his or her distinctiveness, the outreaching of God that is the Spirit embraces the humans in their relationships to one another, that is, as a community."[7] The Spirit grounds ecclesial community and builds it up. Yves Congar observes, "The close bond between the Holy Spirit and the life of the Church has always been not only experienced, but also affirmed throughout the centuries."[8] One significant way that the ecclesial body is nurtured is through the Spirit's bestowal of charisms on behalf of the community, gifts offered for the good of the whole and for the mission that members of the community share together.

The great pastoral bishop of the fourth century, Basil of Caesarea, considered Christian life to be nourished greatly by such gifts. Basil writes, "All the members complete the Body of Christ in the unity of the Spirit, each member assisting the others with aid provided by the unique gifts it has received."[9] Basil's teaching on the Spirit rose from his vision for the communal/ecclesial nature of Christian life. He understood the sanctifying Spirit, referred to by him often as the "breath of God," to be the mediator of communion (*koinonia*), which brought persons to empathic regard for one another.

The mandate "glorify God in your body" assumes significance for communal/ecclesial bodies as well as individual bodies. Failure on the part of communities to value the communion mediated by the Spirit, lack of empathic regard in community life, abuses of power, and unwill-ingness to bring forth the gifts of community members are all sins against the Spirit and the communal body of God's indwelling. Insofar as mem-bers of the community refuse the call to be temples of the Holy Spirit, the communal body limps. The coupling of the temple metaphor with the mandate to glorify God in the body proves instructive when thinking about individual and communal/ecclesial life.

In the closeness of the indwelling Spirit, and in the presence of one another, persons come to know their interrelatedness in God, and can discern initiatives of the Spirit. Promptings of the Spirit are numerous. They occur in thoughts, movements, and as Andrea Vicini, SJ, high-lights later in this book, in the realm of bodily felt sense and human emotions. Because of God's grace, humans are able to sense the activities of the Spirit and to respond to them in freedom. The Spirit both *vivifies* persons and communities in the present, and *draws* them toward God's promised future of eschatological consummation. These actions of the Spirit have an "effect on human imagining,"[10] causing persons to hope mightily, envisioning what can come to be because of the inbreaking of God, and to act in accord with this hope, in keeping with the Spirit's lead.

ACTIVITIES OF THE INDWELLING SPIRIT

The *vivifying activity* of the indwelling Spirit is a "creative blessing,"[11] making new what stands in need of re-creation in order to live. This blessing is bestowed on all and is not dependent upon human efforts. The Spirit, as the personal presence of God and not some impersonal influence, animates and empowers, awakening persons bodily within, in their uniqueness. The fourteenth century Flemish mystic Jan van Ruusbroec (1293–1381) observes that God's Spirit "moves and impels each one in a particular way."[12] Accompanying creatures in love, the Spirit vivifies through a steady and faithful companioning of each, and does so without reserve. Ruusbroec, in his treatise *The Sparkling Stone* claims, "The living Spring of the Holy Spirit is so rich that it can never be drained dry."[13] The *vivifying activity* of the Spirit, universally bestowed and particularly manifested, endures as an integral dimension of God's givenness.

In his book *Breath of Life: A Theology of the Creator Spirit*, contemporary theologian Denis Edwards describes the vivifying Spirit as the "midwife of a new creation."[14] The metaphor is evocative, as midwives enliven those they accompany through their knowledgeable presence in times of vulnerability, moving in areas that are deep and intimate. Midwives are present in natural ways, seeing ahead of the birth giver. Engaged and involved, a midwife is also lovingly "other." She is not the one in labor or the one fatigued by the process of birthing. She is the one present to, for, and with the one in labor.[15] The involvement of the birth giver in delivering new life is never bypassed; it is focal and cherished. In these ways, the Spirit is like a midwife.

Midwives bring birth givers to new levels of self-awareness and to clearer understanding of transitional moments. Midwives intercede for birth givers as well. As a midwife, the Spirit both teaches and reminds (John 14:26). And the Spirit "groans for us, interceding on our behalf, with prayerful groaning that God's work in us might be brought to completion."[16] Because human beings are invited to participate in the birthing of God's mercy and justice in the world, the metaphor "midwife," as a description of the Spirit, communicates something profoundly orienting for our living.

Like every metaphor, however, this one has strengths and limits. "Midwife" is a helpful way of thinking about the Spirit when laboring toward "new birthings," but other aspects of the vivifying Spirit's activity do not find expression in it. The Spirit aids us in bringing what is nascent to maturity with its truth intact, but that vivifying Spirit also wakens what is fast asleep in us, and loosens what has become inflexible. It stirs what has hardened, coaxes what has stopped moving, and yes, even pulls life from death. No metaphor adequately captures all of this. The German polymath Hildegard of Bingen (1098–1179) used the Latin word *viriditas*, a noun that means "greenness," to point toward the multiple vivifying effects of the Spirit. Inspired by Hildegard's lead and utilizing her language, Elizabeth Johnson praises the vivifying Spirit as "a guide in the fog, a balm for wounds; a shining serenity; an overflowing fountain that spreads to all sides. She is life, movement, color, radiance, restorative stillness in the din. Her power makes all withered sticks and souls green again with the juice of life."[17] Through the Spirit's vivifying activity, creatures that wobble find their legs and that which is dying opens into a new possibility of life.

God's vivifying Spirit relates to human beings in their existential present. In its many manifestations, the vivifying Spirit reflects God's commitment to the flourishing of creatures in their finite, embodied lives now. The Spirit of God, however, acts also with a telos in view. The Spirit draws human beings to eschatological consummation, toward the promised goal and offer, that of God being all in all. This action, described by David Kelsey, highlights "the advent of the fulfillment of an open-ended promise by God to all that is not God."[18] In our human context, we experience the eschatological draw of the Spirit as a beckoning, an invitation to embrace "the more in the real"[19] and to do so with hope.

As the Spirit draws the human toward eschatological fulfillment, the promise of the reign of God moves closer to its realization. The Spirit beckons toward a time that is not yet our time, and an end for which we have been created but have not yet become. This draw of the Spirit, "God's eschatological blessing,"[20] is already an inbreaking of the end-time. The Spirit draws bodily human beings toward eschatological fulfillment, and in the Spirit's beckoning, God's promise is already at work toward that fulfillment.

The Spirit's eschatological draw is a gift bestowed that both shapes our imaginations and inspires hope-filled actions in the world. The Spirit draws us, as a flawed people in morally ambiguous contexts, inviting conversion. Thus, the eschatologically oriented activity of the Spirit presumes a transformation that begins in this life. The Spirit's beckoning, experienced in body and received in freedom, makes participation in the eschatological mission of God possible.

LIFE IN THE SPIRIT

Walking in accord with the Spirit (Gal 5:16) presumes a developing consciousness of the vivifying actions and eschatological draw of the triune God at work through the Spirit. The vivifying and eschatological activities of the Spirit point to "immanence" and "transcendence" in such a way that these are never mutually exclusive, but rather inextricably tied.[21] The Spirit of God in Christ, experienced bodily by us as *both* an "environing context" and something "intimately interior"[22] to us, is truly among and within us, and we are surrounded by it.

Life in this "circumambient Spirit"[23] unfolds in a this-worldly, historical context. It is inseparable from incarnate agency in the world that bespeaks reign of God values, as found in the life of Jesus. In Luke's Gospel, Jesus is reading in the synagogue, having been handed a scroll of the Prophet Isaiah, and he identifies himself with a telling passage:

> The Spirit of the Lord is upon me,
>   because he has anointed me
>   to bring glad news to the poor.

He has sent me to proclaim release to the captives
 and recovery of sight to the blind,
  to let the oppressed go free,
 to proclaim the year of the Lord's favor. (Luke 4:18–19)[24]

A true mark of the Spirit's indwelling becomes the carrying out of works of justice, for the building up of a community that is an effective sign of God's reign in the world.

Life in the Spirit unfolds in alignment with the truth of Christ. In each new situation of our lives, the draw of the Spirit is a tug toward what is most reflective of that truth. We are educated in our bodies, in the depths of marrow bone by the indwelling Spirit of Truth, the one given as a lasting gift to guide us in the ways of Jesus.

"COME, HOLY SPIRIT"

It is a familiar invocation. "Come, Holy Spirit," we cry, seeking new life for jaded hearts in the concrete circumstances of individual and communal lives. "Come," we sigh, longing for God to be poured out like refreshing rain (Isa 44:3) in arid-filled areas of our living and our world. We beseech the Spirit, who has opted to indwell bodies and the world, and yet is constrained by neither, the Spirit who accompanies and is active, but freely so, who is unyielding to human manipulation or domestication. We invoke the Spirit, not because the Spirit isn't already here ahead of us, but because there is much within us and around us that is not yet of God. We cry out, as the indwelling Spirit cries out within us, "Come, Holy Spirit!" Our gait feels wobbly, but the echo in the invocation invites rediscovery of the Spirit's closeness, which itself is the basis for joy.

2

The Holy Spirit
Makes Us Divine

Brian Dunkle, SJ

Although the authors of this volume hope to speak to a contemporary audience, our reflection on the identity of the Holy Spirit has an ancient pedigree. Since the time of Jesus, Christians have contemplated the specific place of the Holy Spirit in the blessed Trinity and in the life of the church. Today, however, describing the role of the Spirit seems more elusive than other types of theological speculation. In part, the difficulty stems from the Spirit's very title. Unlike the terms *Father* and *Son*, which are familiar to us from daily use, the word *Spirit* can seem vague and obscure, calling to mind something eerie that appears only to the peculiar and eccentric. Indeed, sometimes Scripture uses the term in just this fashion. As Jesus states in the Gospel of John, those born of the Spirit are like the wind, which "blows where it chooses…but you do not know where it comes from or where it goes" (John 3:8). The confusion contributes to a certain bafflement before the dynamics of the "spiritual" life. Given the vague status of the Spirit in our imaginations, many of us can focus our spirituality on something more concrete, especially on Jesus Christ, the Son, who offers a clear and reliable moral guide.

By contrast, theologians in the early centuries of the church devoted extensive attention to the role of the persons of the Trinity in daily life. Their concern centered on Scripture and salvation: What does the Bible tell us about God's plan for our creation and our destiny? One of many responses understood the Holy Spirit as playing a special role in a dynamic called "deification": the Spirit bestowed holiness and thereby infused godliness in us, making us "gods" by grace. The language sounds striking today (as it did to many in the early church), but I suggest that this basic dynamic, as found in patristic sources from Irenaeus (ca. 130–ca. 202) to Augustine (354–430), shows how even today the Holy Spirit, active in our prayer, service, and sacraments, enables our participation in the divine life of the Trinity, especially by leading us to look beyond the limited prospects for godliness that our culture supplies.

DEIFICATION IN THE EARLY CHURCH

When attempting to synthesize the many voices of the early church, one must be careful not to exaggerate their harmony. In the centuries after Jesus founded his community of disciples, we discover a broad variety of views and teachings in the surviving works that reflect and respond to a range of challenges and contexts; the story of early Christianity is anything but neat. Still, when the fathers of the church—as the principal theologians and spiritual writers of the church's early centuries are known—reflect on human salvation, they often identify the purpose of the incarnation of the Son of God in Jesus with the salvation and perfection of humanity. Jesus is God, come to heal us and to bring us to new life.

At the same time, when today we hear the term *salvation*, we generally think of "rescue," as in "helping us out of a mess." On this understanding, God saves us by forgiving our sins or allowing us to live at peace. In the early church, however, the idea of salvation as discovered in Scripture was more expansive. Salvation typically took on a cosmic dimension, implying the transformation and elevation of the entire universe.

Several images communicated the nature of this salvation. Some theologians spoke primarily of the victory of the cross over the devil, who held dominion over the universe after the sin of Adam and Eve.[1] Others emphasized the forgiveness of sins that was offered through the church and the sacraments.[2] At the heart of most of these accounts, however, was the importance of the incarnation. Because God was made one of us, we can be made one with God through participation and adoption. We then receive distinctive gifts and blessings through our union with Christ's saving work.

This account of the salvation is based on New Testament teachings. We find hints of it in the letters of St. Paul, who identifies the destiny of humanity as communion with God. Paul writes to the Corinthians about this exchange: "For you know the generous act of our Lord Jesus Christ, that though he was rich, yet for your sakes he became poor, so that by his poverty you might become rich" (2 Cor 8:9). The baptismal formula of Matthew 28:19–20, which links the rite of initiation to the "name" of the Trinity, provides the basis for the link between the sacraments and life in the Father, Son, and Holy Spirit. Yet these biblical references are quite often obscure and open to a range of interpretations. What exactly does Paul mean by "rich," and how does baptism in a "name" affect our very identity?

The first extensive theological exploration of the theme of deification appears in the writings of Irenaeus, a bishop who lived in southern France near the end of the second century. Irenaeus was the first to employ a clear "formula of exchange" in explaining this dynamic: "God became what we are in order to make us what he is himself."[3] Later thinkers, especially St. Athanasius of Alexandria (ca. 296–373), developed this idea—"For the Son of God became human so that we might become God"—and began to speak of the process as "deification" (*theopoiêsis* or *theôsis*).[4] To the present day, that term characterizes the view of salvation that dominates in the East, especially among Orthodox Christians, while many in the West have little sense of the central role it plays in theology and daily life. Perhaps under the enduring influence of the Reformation debates on justification, Western Christians tend to see God's primary encounter with humanity in terms of the offer of mercy and forgiveness.

THE TRINITY IN DEIFICATION

In the context of developing their thoughts on deification, many theologians were likewise reflecting on the distinctive activities of the Holy Trinity in whose name Christians are baptized: Father, Son, and Holy Spirit. As we've seen, the dynamic of deification centers on the saving action of the Son in taking on human nature as Jesus to share God's divine nature with humanity. But that outline might suggest that the formula of exchange involves only two parties: God the Father transcendent, and God the Son, one of us. By this account, the Holy Spirit seems like a detached observer: whereas the Son is sharing the work of the Creator with creation, the Holy Spirit has no role to play.

The New Testament, however, makes clear that the Spirit is intimately involved in bringing about this union; in the First Epistle of John, for instance, we learn that we remain in God "because he has given us of his Spirit" (1 John 4:13). Drawing on the scriptural witness, authors in the early centuries grew in the conviction that the Holy Spirit had a specific area of responsibility in the *economy*, the term that the early church used to describe the actions of God in relation to humanity (and, by extension, to creation itself). In the writings of Origen, a third-century theologian from Alexandria in Egypt who was one of the pre-eminent thinkers of the early Christian era, we find the suggestion that Father, Son, and Holy Spirit had distinctive roles in creating and restoring the cosmos to the divine life.[5] Origen occasionally maintains that the Father is primarily involved with creation, with bringing forth and sustaining what is from what is not. Within this order of creation, the Son, as Logos, has special governance of rational or "logical" creatures (the wordplay doesn't work so well in English, where the term *logical* implies quasi-mathematical deductions). Thus, the Word of God shares with creation God's own sensibility, giving order to the world and allowing rational beings in the world to examine and understand the divine plan. A central consequence of the Son's incarnation, therefore, is that the ways of God are no longer hidden from humanity: the truth of the universe is not some secret teaching but rather a person, Jesus Christ.

In this version of Origen's account of the economy, the Holy Spirit has a special responsibility for sharing God's holiness with chosen holy people, that is, the saints. Origen sometimes suggests that the Spirit "inspires" souls and thereby enables them to grow in virtue, especially in faith, hope, and love, and thereby to move closer to God.[6] Through the action of the Spirit, the church, distinct from any purely human institution, is made holy and built up into a community sharing the divine love.

As much as Origen's framework appealed to later Christian thinkers, the strict hierarchy had troubling implications; sometimes Origen makes it sound as though Father, Son, and Spirit are three separate beings, arranged in descending order from "true God" (the Father) to "created agent of the divinity." So, he writes,

> The God and Father, who holds the universe together, is superior to every being that exists, for he imparts to each one from his own existence that which each one is; the Son, being less than the Father, is superior to rational creatures alone (for he is second to the Father); the Holy Spirit is still less, and dwells within the saints alone.[7]

By this account, the Spirit is third in rank behind the Father and the Son, standing apart from the act of creation and present only in holy deeds. Certainly, Origen often qualifies the language of the passage to claim that all human beings are potentially saints and thereby open to the Spirit's action; yet such a "subordinationism" would imply that the Spirit is not true God but functions rather as a mediator between the divine and the human orders. Although Origen's general account of the role the Spirit plays in divinization influenced almost all subsequent thinkers of the early church, his sometimes strict taxonomy would conflict with later Christian convictions about the coequality of the three Persons of the Trinity.

THE HOLY SPIRIT IN DEIFICATION

Thus, in a fascinating twist, the fathers of the fourth century drew on Origen's paradigm to counter the apparent subordinationism in Origen, to demonstrate that the Holy Spirit was true God. They argued that if deification really happens, the Holy Spirit cannot be anything less than true God. If the Spirit gives to the holy the gift of divinity, the Holy Spirit must be truly divine; as the old dictum goes, "You cannot give what you do not have." Against rival groups in the fourth century who thought that the Spirit was some kind of angelic force that functioned as an intermediary between Creator and creation, orthodox thinkers developed the argument that the Holy Spirit is essential to the process of making humanity divine and therefore must be true God.[8] Like Jesus, the Son of God, who can accomplish the exchange between Creator and creation because he both is Creator and has a created human nature, so the Holy Spirit can elevate us to new life because the Spirit is the Creator of all life. To be sure, these same authors affirmed that the Holy Spirit accounted for other features central to the Christian faith: the truth of Scripture relies on the Spirit's "inspiration" of the prophets and the apostles, while the unity of the church stemmed from Spirit's role as unifier. But in the fourth century, the Spirit's work in deification became a special focus for theologians.

But what does this enactment of deification mean, both for God and for humanity? For God, at least, it implies the true unity of the Trinity: Father, Son, and Holy Spirit are one because the three are united in bestowing divine life. This basic theological doctrine was the major concern of fourth-century orthodox thinkers who hoped to articulate the church's belief in one God, active in the world. Their consensus continues to inform all trinitarian reflection today.

At the same time, the Holy Spirit as "god-maker" has profound implications in the life of the faith, both in the ancient and in the contemporary church. While Melissa Kelley's article in this volume shows how the Holy Spirit can help us "make meaning" after experiences of loss, the ancient sources show how the Holy Spirit gives not only discrete help, as in support along life's journey or forgiveness from sins, but also real participation in God's life. Certainly, deification does not collapse all distinctions between humanity and God: early theologians were careful to distinguish Christ's divinity, which was his by nature, from our derivative divinity, which comes through grace. Nevertheless, these sources attest to a remarkably exalted vision of human destiny.

The primary manifestation of this divine life is the gift most characteristic of Christ's life: immortality. Christ rose to show that he is immortal, and so we, too, can have confidence that through baptism we possess the immortality, the true life, bestowed on us by the Spirit. The assurance that our earthly existence is a mere foretaste of the true divine life given to us by the Spirit fosters hope and courage against the ravages of death.

At the same time, the process of deification and the reception of immortality are not, by this account, an automatic advance in status; we don't become all-good, all-powerful, and all-knowing when we're washed in baptism. Deification is rather an arduous, even painful, pilgrimage. The presence of the Holy Spirit is marked first by repentance, by shedding tears in sorrow for sin and by abandoning merely earthly ends—material gains, selfish lust, personal advancement. The "godlike" are then identified by their pursuit of the divine growth in charity, hope, and faith, as well as in other virtues, such as courage to face hostility and to endure suffering. These virtues are hardly easy or passive. The Holy Spirit does not elevate us by treating us like lifeless puppets; rather, the Spirit works precisely by making us more capable of embracing hard choices, of preaching difficult truths, and of struggling against tough odds. Thus, we recognize the heroes of our faith, saints both living and dead, not simply because they abandoned themselves to God in one passive gesture but because they allowed God to work through them as they became active and communal "instruments" of the Trinity.[9] On the one hand, as God's instruments, we live out the divine life by actualizing our specifically human capacities in their most authentic fashion—since we are spiritual, for instance, the Holy Spirit's action in us makes it easier for us to pray, to meditate, and to overcome the many concerns that threaten to distract us from God's love; on the other hand, since we are social creatures, the action of the Spirit fosters our communion and promotes the union of our ecclesial life. Paradoxically, deification makes us more, not less, human.

In the early church, we find that this transformative aspect of deification shows its effects in us in surprising ways. For ancient Christians, the consensus that the Holy Spirit was true God and was active in our own growth in holiness had profound implications for the life of faith. Christians, they believed, were no longer bound by the enslaving limits of humanity and society. The action of divinization broke through to raise them up.

The patristic belief in the deifying work of the Spirit helps account for the sometimes bizarre shows of holiness so impressive to early Christians. Asceticism, in particular, was very often esteemed as part of deification and life in the Spirit: those who embraced a life of sexual renunciation, like the fourth-century St. Macrina, the sister of St. Basil of Caesarea and St. Gregory of Nyssa, and those who devoted themselves to prayer and fasting, like St. Anthony of Egypt, were seen as living a somehow divine existence. While later historians sometimes view such lifestyles as masochistic and negative, as focused exclusively on sacrifice rather than on the joyful celebration of God's love, we should recall that these gifts were considered awesome boons in the early church, located in the totalizing culture of the Roman Empire. The life of virginity, while demanding, freed women from societal norms that expected them to accept some subjugation in marriage, which was often arranged for political expediency rather than for heartfelt love; in this context, the virginal life was a life of freedom.[10] Likewise, for potential monks, a life in the "wilderness" gave hope for an escape and a refuge to those who faced sometimes suffocating demands from society. Thus, the Spirit could penetrate the otherwise seamless dominion that the Roman Empire and the various ancient cultures held over Christians' prospects. By making Christians divine, God could rupture the limited meaning imposed upon them by their world.

Moreover, Christian deification was available to everyone. Here we note that those who were typically identified as "divine" in the ancient empire were the powerful and elite. Indeed, the language of deification had a parallel life in the political realm, where the emperor was generally recognized as a "god," initially only after his death, but in later centuries, even during his lifetime. At the same time, for ancient philosophers, divinity was often available exclusively to the educated nobility: ever since Plato suggested that philosophical contemplation required a life freed from menial labor, many linked self-transcendence with the deification of those who sought wisdom in a privileged setting. For ancient educated people of the Mediterranean, becoming godlike required resources and leisure.

By contrast, Christianity affirmed that social status had no relation to God's gifts, that both a young girl, like Ambrose's sister St. Marcellina, and an old man, like St. Anthony, could be brought into union with God through the action of the Spirit. Thus, again, we see how the presence of divine action can mark an inbreaking that delivers us from our limited horizons.

Indeed, deification occurred most directly not in sophisticated, philosophical contemplation, but in the gift of the sacraments. Even as some sources speak of personal participation in the divine through prayer and asceticism, we find many more reflecting on the implications of the Spirit's divinity for our life as church in the liturgy. Thus, baptism in the divine name, something given to us by the church, begins our path to divinity. Next, the completion of our initiation in the Eucharist marks a physical participation in God, a dynamic that John Baldovin describes later in this book as the work of the Holy Spirit in consecrating the gifts and transforming believers. As St. Ambrose of Milan writes, "Because our Lord Jesus Christ partakes of divinity and of the body, so you, who receive his flesh, participate in his divine substance through that nourishment."[11] Addressing a group of neophytes, that is, newly baptized members of the Christian community, Ambrose makes clear that the gift of deification is available to all who strive for the Lord as they further abandon sin. It is not a gift limited to a few "divine" elites.

Deification in the church was never considered a completed process that came with baptism or even with a life of exemplary virtue. Rather, Christians receive a mere foretaste of participation in the divine in this life, when generosity (a trait of the divine) comes more naturally, when loving prayer seems almost effortless. Deification thus points to the fullness of the Holy Spirit that we will know only with the eschaton, when God's plan for redemption is complete.

DEIFICATION, THE SPIRIT, AND SPIRITUALITY TODAY

In the contemporary world, an awareness of the deifying action of the Holy Spirit can help us better understand the Christian spiritual life. We often speak of "spirituality" with little attention to the word *spirit* at its heart. According to Wikipedia, *spirituality* refers, in general, to "the deepest values and meanings by which people live." In common speech, then, spiritual people are those who are self-reflective and conscientious, who aim to look beyond the day-to-day in search of higher values.

While this definition overlaps with a Christian understanding of the Spirit's action, it does not capture the heart of the dynamic that I have explored. A Christian spirituality, at least one informed by the patristic sources, finds its impetus not exclusively in my personal reflections but rather in dialogue with God's revealed action in the world. If the humanization of the Word really does have cosmic consequences, I must ask what those consequences are for the church and me. How are we to imagine deification in the Spirit today?

In response, we must first acknowledge that certain divine gifts have perennial relevance. Despite astonishing advances in medicine and pharmaceuticals, we still face death, the ultimate failure at dominating life. The gift of the Spirit, bestowed through baptism, offers the ultimate remedy to that failure: God gives us a share in immortality, in a life that goes beyond merely "being alive" to constitute vitality in its most profound sense, characterized by a joy in created being and a peace in the victory of Christ.

We might think, too, of the cultural expectations that the Spirit can shatter in our time just as in the Roman Empire. Our culture supplies our own "gods," models for our aspiration and imitation. While we do not offer these gods worship in any formal sense, we do treat them as idols, offering them deferential treatment and honored positions. Moreover, we still witness a drive to be "divine." Futurist and inventor Ray Kurzweil sums up a trend in contemporary thought that expresses deification in a technological key: "Evolution creates structures and patterns that over time are more complicated, more knowledgeable, more creative, more capable of expressing higher sentiments, like being loving....It's moving in the direction of qualities that God is described as having without limit."[12] For Kurzweil, God is characterized by power and creativity; we acquire God's qualities through ever more sophisticated technology. Is it by chance that our best female singers are named *divas*, that is, "goddesses," just as the Roman emperor was called *divus*, or "god"?

It is worth noting that both contemporary deifications are implicitly elitist. Stardom is limited to the very few and (often) the very well connected. Computers and circuits may well elevate our natural capacities, as they already have done, but, just as those most likely to be "divine" in the ancient world were the powerful, so those with access to such technological "elevation" will be the rich and the privileged. And just as the ancients were perennially frustrated in their desire for godlike immortality, so the modern deifiers will always fail to offer true "god-making" to their customers.

CONCLUSION

Christianity offers an authentic alternative to these methods of self-deification. Through the action of the Holy Spirit poured out through the sacraments, the divine life may be shared by all, from the infant to the elderly, from the poor and forgotten to the rich and elite, women and men. Moreover, deification is not some individual pursuit but rather a communal offering that is made within the life of the church, shared especially through service to the suffering.

As a church, our participation in God's life does not require technologies that aim at self-sufficiency but rather humble reception and subsequent growth in the Spirit. Just as in the church's early history, so also today the Holy Spirit can enable our growth in the virtues, especially our faith, our hope, and our love, beyond any limits that society would impose on them, to become heroic and even divine expressions of God's action in the world.

3

Matter Matters

Saintly Relics and the Holy Spirit

Franklin T. Harkins

In the early morning hours of Wednesday, March 7, 1274, having received the eucharistic body of Christ, Thomas Aquinas, in the forty-ninth year of his life, died at the Cistercian abbey of Fossanova.[1] The early biographer William of Tocco relates that shortly after Thomas's death, John of Ferentino, subprior of Fossanova, was cured of blindness after prostrating himself on the corpse of the deceased Dominican, "placing his own face on his face," and praying to God that—by Thomas's merits—his sight might be restored.[2] Because other miracles began to occur shortly thereafter, the Cistercians at Fossanova feared that the wonder-working remains of Thomas, to which they had exclusive access, would be stolen by his Dominican confreres or others. Consequently, they exhumed the corpse from its resting place, cut off the head, and hid it in a corner of the chapel. They reasoned that even if Thomas's body were taken from them, his head and its supernatural power would be theirs.[3]

By the time of Thomas's death, the medieval practice of relic theft had enjoyed a long history.[4] Nearly four decades earlier, in 1236, the head of the deceased Elizabeth of Thuringia was similarly separated from her body during the solemn translation of her remains. Afterward, it was carefully prepared for enshrinement and veneration by faithful pilgrims. In his "Sermon on the Translation of Blessed Elizabeth," Caesarius of Heisterbach explains concerning the saint's detached head, "To ensure that the sight of it would not strike horror into onlookers, the brothers separated the flesh, with the skin and hair, from the skull, with a little knife."[5] Emperor Frederick II then placed on Elizabeth's skull a golden crown with precious gems, a visible sign of the saint's transition from death and decay to the glory of eternal life through Christ and the Holy Spirit.[6]

Such details of postmortem dismemberment—even with an edifying end in view—strike us as gruesome and ghastly, flying in the face of our view of the proper respect to be given to those who have died, particularly those holy men and women in whom the Spirit of God is believed to have dwelt especially. By contrast, the Rite of Committal in the contemporary Roman Catholic liturgy seems to reflect more properly our own understanding of deceased Christian bodies, their fitting treatment, and their places of final rest:

> Lord Jesus Christ, by your own three days in the tomb, you hallowed the graves of all who believe in you and so made the grave a sign of hope that promises resurrection even as it claims our mortal bodies. Grant that our sister may sleep here in peace until you wake her to glory, for you are the resurrection and the life.[7]

Whereas such pastoral words may reflect a view of the human body that is diametrically opposed to the one that encouraged the holy mutilation of the bodies of Thomas Aquinas, Elizabeth of Thuringia, and other saints throughout the Middle Ages, the distance between the two is actually shorter than first glance suggests.

Both, after all, clearly express the conviction—bred in the bones of Catholic theology, liturgy, and faith—that matter matters, particularly the matter of which human bodies are constituted. And human matter matters preeminently because God the Son assumed a human nature in order to redeem human nature and make humans partakers of his own eternal, divine life through the gift of the Holy Spirit. In St. Paul's words to the Corinthians, "And God raised the Lord and will also raise us by his power. Do you not know that your bodies are members of Christ?...Or do you not know that your body is a temple of the Holy Spirit within you, which you have from God?" (1 Cor 6:14–19). In the first chapter, Colleen Griffith explored some theological facets of this rich scriptural image of

25

the body as a temple of the Holy Spirit. Here, we examine the medieval cult of the saints and their relics through the lens of this Pauline teaching to illustrate how powerfully, according to Catholic understanding, the Holy Spirit works in and through matter to inspire the life of faith.

In the *Cambridge Companion to Christian Doctrine*, Geoffrey Wainwright opens his article on the Holy Spirit by affirming, "God as such is spirit, holy in himself and transcending matter of which he is the Creator."[8] Whereas Christianity clearly teaches that God, *in se*, is spirit and, as such, surpasses material reality, it also affirms that this same transcendent, divine spirit accommodates—for soteriological purposes—to our material mode of existence. The second person of the Trinity condescended, we believe, to assume a true human nature and to die to redeem us, and he still stoops to feed us with his very body and blood in the Eucharist. And now that the incarnate Word has suffered, died, risen again, and ascended to the Father, the third person of the Godhead, the Holy Spirit, indwells and inspires our rational souls and our material bodies, sanctifying and strengthening us to bear witness to the good news of Christ. Indeed, at least since its second-century encounter with Gnosticism, Catholic Christianity has affirmed in various ways and countless contexts that matter matters for the life of faith of its adherents, both communally and individually.

In the Apostles' Creed, when the Church professes its belief in the "communion of the saints" (*communio sanctorum*), it recognizes two closely related meanings, namely the communion in holy things (*sancta*) among holy people (*sancti*). In expounding this twofold meaning of *communio sanctorum*, the *Catechism of the Catholic Church* highlights the Eucharist as that preeminent "holy thing" in and through which we commune more profoundly with the divine Spirit and with one another for the sake of the Church's mission and ministry: "The faithful (*sancti*) are fed by Christ's holy body and blood (*sancta*) to grow in the communion of the Holy Spirit (*koinonia*) and to communicate it to the world" (no. 948).[9] Such feeding, growing, and communicating are possible, of course, both because, as John Baldovin will explain in the next chapter, the sanctifying work of the Holy Spirit stands at the heart of the eucharistic conversion and because the body and blood of Christ are the very body and blood of God. Cyril of Alexandria famously explains in his *Third Letter to Nestorius*,

> This we receive not as ordinary flesh, heaven forbid, nor as that of a man who has been made holy and joined to the Word by union of honour, or who had a divine indwelling, but as truly the life-giving and real flesh of the Word. For being life by nature as God, when he became one with his own flesh, he made it also to be life-giving.[10]

Early medieval Catholicism was a highly mediated religion in which both Christ and the saints—and their respective bodies—played a role that was, quite literally, crucial (i.e., related to the *crux*, the cross of Christ, and its redemptive power). Indeed, like Christ's eucharistic body, the saints and their relics were understood and venerated as "channels through which God's grace was distributed."[11] In the ninth-century West, the Eucharist was considered one relic among others, though it held a certain pride of place because it was believed to be the body of Christ himself. The Eucharist was often placed together with saintly relics in local churches, either in altar stones, exposed on the altar, or elsewhere.[12] Incidentally, the ancient and medieval practice of placing relics of martyrs or other saints under a fixed altar is preserved in the Catholic Church to this day.[13] In 816, the English Council of Chelsea promulgated these instructions for the dedication of a church:

> Whenever a church is built, it should be consecrated by the bishop of that particular diocese. It should be blessed and sprinkled with water by him. Afterwards the Eucharist that is consecrated by the bishop during the same service should be put into a small box *with other relics* and reserved in the same church. But if he is unable to insert other relics, nevertheless this one can be efficacious in the highest degree because it is the body and blood of our Lord Jesus Christ.[14]

Here, the phrase "with other relics" indicates a basic identity presumed by the bishops at Chelsea between Christ's sacramental body and the bodily remains of Christ's saints. In the Middle Ages, relics re-presented what John Dillenberger has called "the full function of the saint, in which a part was equivalent to the whole," and in a similar way, the Eucharist made the Lord and his salvific power present to the community of faith. Indeed, Dillenberger affirms, "Even transubstantiation could be understood in this sense. Too crudely put but in line with this way of thinking, in the Mass the priest makes a relic."[15]

In contrast to this early medieval understanding of Christ's sacramental body as one relic among other holy remains, throughout the High and Late Middle Ages the Eucharist came to occupy a unique place in the church, in terms of both the conditions of its spatial reservation and the devotion it demanded.[16] On this latter point, the Council of Trent, in its *Decree on the Most Holy Sacrament of the Eucharist* (promulgated on October 11, 1551), taught that "all Christians…should reverently express for this most holy sacrament the worship of adoration (*latriae cultum*) which is due to the true God."[17]

Over against criticisms of the medieval cult of the saints leveled by Martin Luther and other reformers—who, in their understanding of Jesus as the sole mediator between God and humanity, sought a complete dissociation of the Head from his holy members (a spiritual dismembering, as it were)[18]—Trent reminded bishops of their pastoral obligation to communicate the indispensable interrelation between Christ and the saints in and for the life of Catholic faith. Having encouraged bishops to instruct the faithful to invoke the saints in order to obtain blessings from God through his Son, our Lord Jesus Christ, "who is the only Redeemer and Savior," the council fathers continue,

> [And they should teach] that the holy bodies of the saints and martyrs and others who live with Christ, whose bodies were living members of Christ and a temple of the Holy Spirit, going to be raised by him to eternal life and glorified, should be venerated by the faithful, through which [veneration] many blessings are given to humans by God.[19]

It is precisely because the saints lived with Christ so virtuously, through the indwelling of the Holy Spirit, during their earthly pilgrimages that their bodies, which will be raised to eternal and incorruptible life with him, serve as means whereby divine blessings, through Christ, come to the faithful who are still *in via*, as a promise of their own future resurrection.

Three centuries before Trent, Thomas Aquinas provided a similar theological rationale for the veneration of holy relics:

> But it is obvious that we ought to venerate the saints of God as members of Christ, children and friends of God, and our intercessors. And so we ought to venerate whichever of their relics with an honor befitting their memory, and especially their bodies, which were a temple of the Holy Spirit and organs of the Holy Spirit living and working in them and are going to be configured to the body of Christ through the glory of the resurrection.[20]

To the objection that it seems foolish to venerate a dead body that is incapable of sensing, Thomas replies that we reverence an insensible body not in and of itself, but rather "on account of the soul that was united to it, which now enjoys God, and on account of God, whose servants they [i.e., the saint's body and soul] were."[21]

At the heart of both of these injunctions to venerate saintly relics— and of the theology of relics more generally—is a twofold conviction: (1) holy men and women, in body and in soul, are members of Christ in this life and will be glorified and thus perfectly configured to Christ's own body in the next life through the resurrection; and (2) this membership in and configuration to Christ requires the indwelling of the Holy Spirit such that saintly bodies become the very temples of the Divine Spirit and the organs of its action. Let us briefly consider each of these components of the cult of relics, particularly regarding the Christian life of faith.

First, medieval Christians understood the bodies of saints to manifest and convey in an extraordinary way the saving power of the incarnate Word, to whom the saints were, and were being, configured. Because of the promise that the resurrected Christ will transform the lowly bodies of the faithful and conform them to his own glorious body (see Phil 3:21), it was believed that the mortal remains of the saints could not experience the corruption to which ordinary bodies would necessarily succumb. That saintly bodies did not decompose, but rather remained as supple as they had been in life, served as a sign of their own election and as a foretaste of the resurrected glory that all of God's chosen finally will enjoy.[22] One prominent example comes from Durham, England, where in 995 the city itself and in 1093 a magnificent Norman cathedral were founded on the miracle—repeatedly confirmed throughout the Middle Ages—of the incorrupt body of St. Cuthbert, the seventh-century monk and bishop of Lindisfarne.[23] In his *Libellus* on the miracles of St. Cuthbert, the twelfth-century monk and historian Reginald of Durham attests not only that the saint's body remained incorrupt and flexible at the joints, but also that the saint was believed to breathe in some inexplicable way (which breathing was necessary, of course, for his limbs to remain supple). Further suggesting the permeable boundary between death and life that St. Cuthbert enjoyed, Reginald reports that Alfred, son of Westou, who served as the guardian of the saint's body in the eleventh century, was believed to have trimmed Cuthbert's hair and nails and even to have conversed with him occasionally.[24] On this porous space between death and life in saintly bodies, understood as an anticipation of the resurrection, Charles Freeman writes,

> Christ's own Resurrection had shown that a dead body could triumph over death and reappear in an apparently living state, and this left an ambivalence over whether there was an absolute barrier between life and death in the bodies of saints. The Resurrection was not given the unique status it has among Christians today (when an absolute barrier between life and death has been confirmed by science), and believers were much readier to accept that a body, especially one of a saint, could enjoy a form of life after death just as Jesus had.[25]

Relatedly, the bodies of deceased saints were often believed to give off a pleasing smell, the "odor of sanctity," in contrast to the ordinary stench of decay.[26]

These traditions of the saints as existing between bodily death and resurrected life served, and continue to serve, as powerful reminders that through their material remains the Holy Spirit is, in the words of Geoffrey

Wainwright, "the guarantor of the eschatological prospect."[27] This conviction that God, through the Holy Spirit, does and will enliven the mortal bodies of the holy deceased is beautifully captured in one of the concluding prayers of the interment rite of Turku, Finland (1522), which is traceable to the seventh-century Gelasian Sacramentary of Rome:

> We faithfully entreat God, *to whom all things are alive*, that this
> body of our dear one, buried by us in infirmity, may rise to his
> saints and faithful ones, with whom he may be worthy fully
> to enjoy indescribable glory and eternal happiness, our Lord
> Jesus Christ granting, who lives and reigns with the Father
> and the Holy Spirit, God, through all ages of ages. Amen.[28]

Second, as the words of Aquinas quoted earlier make clear, the bodies of the saints are temples and organs of the Holy Spirit, and the faithful are to honor their remains on account of the rational soul that once inhabited these relics, "which [soul] now enjoys God, and on account of God."[29] These last two phrases are the vital ones. It is not the case, of course, that Catholics—whether medieval or postmodern—venerate the corporeal remains of every person; to do so would collapse the very distinction between saints and the rest of humankind. Rather, although the remains of every human are treated with reverence (e.g., every deceased body is incensed as part of the funeral liturgy), only those relics that were once inhabited by a rational soul possessing properly reordered human love—of God, of neighbor, and of self—are recognized as worthy of special veneration. Such ordinate human affection is characterized, in Augustinian terms, by loving God as an end (i.e., with *frui*, the love of enjoyment) and loving all other things as means (i.e., with *uti*, the love of use) by which to arrive at the ultimate enjoyment of God. On account of original sin, which our first parents committed by free choice but that subsequent humans necessarily inherit, human nature now needs a physician, namely Christ himself, to apply the medicine of grace in order to reorder our disordered loving.[30] For Augustine and the medieval Western theology that he influenced so decisively, this grace was associated with the divine love of which St. Paul speaks in Romans 5:5: "God's love has been poured into our hearts through the Holy Spirit that has been given to us."[31] It is God's own perfect love, then, infused in the rational soul by the Holy Spirit, that heals human loving and enables those who make good use of this grace to begin to enjoy (*frui*) God even in this present life and to arrive at full fruition in the next. Thus, Aquinas's teaching that the faithful should venerate saintly relics "on account of God" highlights the indispensable role of the Holy Spirit in enabling and cultivating the life of faith and properly ordered love among God's holy people.

Our brief consideration of the medieval cult of the saints and their holy relics has sought to underscore how profoundly matter matters to the life of Catholic faith. Examples of the veneration, and even mutilation, of saintly relics in the Middle Ages as well as theological and conciliar reflection on the practice of veneration suggest how deeply held—and literally or materially understood—were the Pauline teachings that the bodies of saints are living members of Christ (Rom 12:5; 1 Cor 6:15; 8:12; 12:12, 27; Eph 3:6) and temples of the Holy Spirit (1 Cor 6:19). Furthermore, accounts of deceased saints maintaining corporeal incorruption and flexibility, continuing to breathe somehow, conversing with the living, and exuding a fragrant odor exemplify the conviction that the corporeal remains of the saints continued, even in (putative) death, to be *living* members of Christ's Body by the power of the indwelling Spirit of God. Like the life-giving flesh of the living God that becomes present under the eucharistic species, the relics of holy men and women serve as means whereby divine benefits flow to the Christian faithful and the Holy Spirit continues to empower lives of extraordinary faith, love, and holiness. May we, in ways appropriate to our own context, come to a greater understanding and deeper experience of this truth— namely that the bodies of saints are members of Christ and temples of the Holy Spirit—as those devout medieval mutilators of St. Thomas and St. Elizabeth apparently did.

4

The Holy Spirit in the Eucharistic Prayers of the Roman Rite

John F. Baldovin, SJ

If you were to ask Catholics what the center of the Mass is, the majority would surely answer, "The words of Christ, 'This is my Body'…" or "the consecration." We have certainly been trained to think this way both by theology and by our liturgical practice. But that answer doesn't tell the whole story. The words of the Lord are framed within the Eucharistic Prayer (EP), which begins with the greeting of the priest, "The Lord be with you" and ends with the people's acclamation, "Amen." In fact, the church's official introduction to the Mass, *The General Instruction of the Roman Missal* (no. 78) calls the EP the "center and highpoint of the entire celebration."

One way of understanding this prayer is to see it as the articulation of the four actions that make up the entire celebration of the Eucharist proper: taking, blessing, breaking, giving. The Eucharist is made up of two parts: the Liturgy of the Word and the Liturgy of the Eucharist. In the first, we receive God's word, proclaim it, and ponder it. In the second, we respond to God's gracious initiative by doing what Jesus commanded us to do at the Last Supper in memory of him, namely take, bless, break, and give. Understood in this fashion, the EP is a kind of commentary on the second part of the liturgy. It is also a rich mine for theological reflection on the Eucharist since it represents the church's "rule of prayer." It is important to realize this "dialogue" and mutual influence between the church's rule of prayer (*lex orandi*) and its rule of faith (*lex credendi*). This is the reason why the expansion of the number of EPs in the post–Vatican II liturgical reform is so significant and why the choices made in the construction of new prayers need reflection, especially when it comes to our understanding of the consecration of the bread and wine.

A major element in the construction of the new eucharistic prayers has been the inclusion of an invocation of the Holy Spirit or *epiclesis*. The only EP that does not include an explicit epiclesis is EP I, known as the Roman Canon. The Roman Canon was the sole EP in use in the Roman Rite for at least fifteen hundred years. Recovering the epiclesis in our nine new EPs was due to historical research undertaken for more than a hundred years before Vatican II.[1] Suffice it to say, this scholarly endeavor began in the sixteenth and seventeenth centuries with an attempt to recover the EPs of the Christian East, and scholarship on the *anaphoras* (a Greek word that means "to raise up" or "to offer") and the epiclesis, in particular, blossomed in the twentieth century.[2] Of course, this historical research is a part of the general recovery of the theology of the Holy Spirit that will be considered in the next chapter.

Our concern, here, is twofold. First, I will consider the origin of petitionary prayer in the earliest eucharistic sources and then the adoption of a more formal and explicit invocation of the Holy Spirit in the classic eucharistic prayers of the Christian East, especially regarding how they relate to the notion of the consecration of the elements. Those Eastern prayers are known as anaphoras.

This historical section will help situate the development of the questions that are pertinent in today's theology of the Eucharistic Prayer, particularly the eucharistic consecration, since it was based on the study of the history of these prayers that we have been able to enrich our practice of eucharistic praying in the contemporary Catholic Church.

Second, I will discuss the place of the invocation of the Holy Spirit in the contemporary EPs of the Roman Rite with reference to the renewed prayers of other Christian churches. A reflection on the significance of this development will conclude the essay.

THE EPICLESIS IN THE EARLY EUCHARISTIC PRAYERS

There are no examples of an explicit invocation of the Holy Spirit over the gifts or over the community in the earliest Eucharistic texts. The role that the epiclesis plays in the Eucharistic Prayer, however, is foreshadowed in several early texts. One example (among a number) comes from the *Didache*, an early manual of church discipline that dates from the late first or early second century.[3] Two sets of prayers and some acclamations frame a meal in chapters 9 and 10 of the book. Each set of prayers includes three paragraphs. The first two are blessings or thanksgivings but the third is a petition. In both instances, the prayer is for the eschatological gathering of the church. The prayers in chapter 10 end with a set of what seem to be acclamations:

> May grace come and the world pass away.
> Hosanna to the God of David.
> If any is holy, let him come; if any is not let him repent.
> Maran atha. Amen.

The last of these acclamations is Aramaic for "O Lord, come" or "the Lord comes" (*maran atha*). This and the other are the earliest prayers to demonstrate some sort of request that the Lord *come* upon the celebration. Other early prayers, like a fragment of a eucharistic prayer from Egypt, known as the Strasbourg Papryus,[4] also show that eucharistic praying always combined some form of praise and thanksgiving with a petition, usually for the church.

In the fourth century, we begin to observe the development of an explicit petition for the Holy Spirit. Evidence can be found in three anaphoras: chapter 3 of the so-called *Apostolic Tradition*, the anaphora of Sarapion of Thmuis (Egypt), and the anaphora of Addai and Mari (East Syria).

Although parts of the anaphora of the *Apostolic Tradition* may well have been added to an earlier third-century text, we do have here an explicit petition for the Holy Spirit. This petition (now it can properly be called an epiclesis) is located after the thanksgiving, institution narrative, and anamnesis–oblation, the formula for remembering the passion, death, and resurrection of the Lord, and an offering of the gifts. The epiclesis reads thus:

> And we ask that you send your Holy Spirit upon the offering of your holy Church; that, gathering her into one, you would grant to all who receive these holy things (to receive) for the fullness of the Holy Spirit for the strengthening of faith in truth.[5]

Note that although the Holy Spirit is invoked upon the offering, nothing is said about transformation, but rather the purpose of this invocation is for holy communion.

Another fourth-century example is the anaphora of Sarapion of Thmuis, in Egypt. Once again, the invocation follows the institution narrative (although another petition to "fill this sacrifice with your power" followed immediately upon the "Holy, Holy, Holy"). This epiclesis asks that God's "holy Word" come upon the gifts to make them the "body of the Word" and the "blood of Truth" and that the gifts be a "medicine of life" for the partakers.[6] Here, we have a clear idea of asking God ("your Word") to do something: to transform the gifts into the body and blood of Christ. It is possible that this formula refers to a kind of undifferentiated idea of the Spirit prior to the definitive affirmation of the divinity of the Holy Spirit at the second ecumenical Council of Constantinople (381).

A third example may reach back into the third century. The anaphora of Addai and Mari is the primary Eucharistic Prayer of the Church of the East, a church that resulted from the split that followed the Council of Ephesus (431) and followed Nestorius, the condemned Patriarch of Constantinople. This prayer, like many of the early texts up to the fourth century, does not contain an institution narrative ("This is my Body," etc.). The prayer's epiclesis asks specifically for the hallowing of the gifts "for remission of debts, forgiveness of sins, and the great hope of the resurrection from the dead, and new life in the kingdom of heaven."[7] Of course, there are a few other effects of the Holy Spirit developed by writers in the early period, as noted in the second chapter on the Holy Spirit and divinization.

Space does not permit a thorough examination of the developed epiclesis in the classic eucharistic prayers like the anaphoras of Mark (Egypt), James (Jerusalem), Basil (in both its Egyptian and Byzantine forms), and John Chrysostom (Syria and Constantinople).[8] Suffice it to say that in these petitions we find two verbs that characterize the request for the Spirit and that demonstrate a development in the theology of consecration of the elements. The first is *anadeixein* (show forth); it represents a theology of typology, that is, the gifts are consecrated *because* they represent the offering of the church, which is the offering of Christ. The second is *poiein* (make); it represents a specific request to make something holy, to transform the gifts through the power of the Holy Spirit.[9] A similar development, without an explicit invocation of the Spirit, can be found in the change in Ambrose's (fourth-century Milan) quotation of the EP in his sermons to the newly baptized, *On the Sacraments*. Here, the change is from asking God to "make [*fac*] for us this offering approved, reasonable, *acceptable because it is the figure* of the body and blood of our Lord Jesus Christ, who…"[10] to the Roman Canon, the Roman Rite's only EP from the fourth century to the late twentieth, which asks God to "make this offering wholly blessed, approved, ratified, reasonable and acceptable, *that it may become to us* the body and blood of your beloved Son, Jesus Christ our Lord; who…"[11]

The Roman Canon is something of an outlier in the development of the tradition of the Eucharistic Prayer, for it has never had an explicit invocation of the Holy Spirit—either for consecration or for the effects of communion. It could be that the earliest form of the Roman Canon preceded the otherwise universal adoption of a Spirit-epiclesis.[12] The Roman Rite remained without an epiclesis, at least an explicit invocation of the Holy Spirit, for fifteen hundred years, until Vatican II. However, a petition or invocation of the Holy Spirit is universal (except for the Roman Canon) in the East at least from the end of the fourth century. This led medieval theologians in the East and the West to take two different approaches to the idea of the consecration of the bread and wine. The East, on the one hand, while not denying the importance of the words of Christ, emphasized the role of the Holy Spirit in consecrating the gifts. The West, on the other hand, whose prayer does not even mention the Holy Spirit except in the concluding doxology—"through him, with him…"—put all its money on the words of Christ as a formula of consecration. In the process, the idea of the whole EP as a prayer that articulated the action of the Eucharist (taking, blessing…) was lost.

THE EPICLESIS TODAY— SPLIT AND UNIFIED

The reform of the Eucharistic Prayer in the wake of Vatican II is itself a fascinating story. The Constitution on the Sacred Liturgy said nothing about adding any EPs to the Roman Rite, but considerable dissatisfaction with the Roman Canon had been expressed for some time. Some dissatisfaction arose from increasing knowledge of and appreciation for the prayers of the Christian East that we have just surveyed. Pope Paul VI decided that the Roman Canon would remain basically intact with few minor changes, and that instead several new EPs would be added to the Missal.[13] And so three prayers were added to the Roman Missal. To these, new prayers were added: two prayers for reconciliation, a prayer for various needs, plus three prayers for use at Masses with children, the latter of which are published separately from the Missal.

In particular, several early prayers served as resources for two of the new prayers: the anaphora of the *Apostolic Tradition* and an Egyptian (shorter) form of the anaphora of St. Basil. The latter, like the anaphora of St. John Chrysostom, the major Eucharistic Prayer of the Byzantine Rite, belongs to a family of EPs that have usually been called Antiochene or West Syrian. But these prayers had an epiclesis that followed the institution narrative. Given the insistence that the request for consecration had to precede the institution narrative in order to be consistent with the Roman Canon and the traditional Roman Catholic theology that the consecration was accomplished by the words of Christ, a consecratory epiclesis was provided prior to the narrative. For example, "Sanctify these gifts by the outpouring of your Holy Spirit, that they may become the Body and Blood of your Son, whose command we fulfill when we celebrate these mysteries."

A second epiclesis, however, was inserted after the anamnesis-oblation that followed the narrative. In the same second Eucharistic

Prayer for Reconciliation, for example, the epiclesis goes like this: "Holy Father, we humbly beseech you to accept us also, together with your Son, and in this saving banquet graciously to endow us with his very Spirit, who takes away everything that estranges us from one another." In various ways, this second epiclesis asks for the fruits of the Eucharist and leads to specific intercessions. The result of putting one form of epiclesis before the institution narrative and another after it has been called the "split epiclesis." The following chart gives a visual comparison of the two basic structures.

Contemporary Roman Catholic Prayers	Antiochene/ West Syrian
Dialogue	Dialogue
Preface—variable	Preface—invariable
Sanctus	Sanctus
Post-sanctus	Post-sanctus
Epiclesis 1 (for consecration)	Institution Narrative
Institution Narrative	Anamnesis and Offering
Memorial Acclamation	**Epiclesis (for consecration and for the church)**
Anamnesis and Offering	
2nd Epiclesis (for the church)	Intercessions
Intercessions	Doxology/Amen
Doxology/Amen	

The fact that after Vatican II the Catholic Church adopted an explicit epiclesis of the Holy Spirit has opened the question of how the consecration of the elements occurs and when. It is clear that at least from the High Middle Ages onward the Western church regarded the words of Jesus (institution narrative) as a formula of consecration. In fact, there was a good deal of debate during the twelfth century regarding the exact moment of consecration. Did it occur immediately after the word over the bread? Only after the entire formula had been spoken over both elements? Or twice, once for each element?[14] Eventually, the theory that the consecration was complete after the word over the bread prevailed. This theory required "the theology of concomitance," namely that blood must be present in a living body, and that theory, in turn, supported the removal of the cup from the laity. St. Thomas Aquinas went so far as to claim that *only* the institution narrative was sufficient for the consecration and that if the priest omitted the rest of the Eucharistic Prayer, the Mass was still valid although the priest sinned mortally.[15] The Council of Florence (1439) stated explicitly that the consecration takes place *verborum virtute*—"*by the power of the words [of Christ].*"[16] Not a word about the role of the Holy Spirit. This attitude was so common in the Late Middle Ages that Martin Luther in his German Mass could reduce the EP to the institution narrative itself, and recommend that the bread and wine be distributed individually after each dominical word.[17]

The Eastern Christians, however, tended to consider the epiclesis, which followed the words of institution and prayer of offering as consecratory, enlivening the action by the work of the Holy Spirit. They do not necessarily deny the importance of the words of institution but they do insist that the epiclesis is needed for the completion of the action.[18] As we noted above, several early anaphoras, indeed all of these prayer texts that we can be sure originated before the fourth century, do not contain an institution narrative at all. It seems, in fact, the anaphora of Addai and Mari as well as the anaphora described by Cyril of Jerusalem in the late fourth century and possibly that described by Theodore of Mopsuestia (also late fourth century) all lack an institution narrative, while at the same time incorporating an epiclesis.[19] Moreover, as witnessed by John Chrysostom,[20] the Christian East favors the idea that the consecration of the elements was accomplished for all by Christ at the Last Supper and is effected by the church's representation of that event in the Eucharist.

The post–Vatican II liturgy skirts the question of when the consecration occurs by "splitting" the epiclesis with a plea for consecration of the gifts preceding the institution narrative and a plea for the effects of the Eucharist on the communicants and the Church following it. As John McKenna notes, this solution exacerbates the long-standing obsession of the Roman Rite with a formula of consecration. It diminishes the impact of our need for the Holy Spirit by making the request for consecration a kind of introduction to the "real thing."[21] It also damages the important connection between the consecration of the gifts and the effects of that congregation on the church and the communicants: "Humbly we pray that, partaking of the Body and Blood of Christ, we may be gathered into one by the Holy Spirit" (EP II), "grant that we who are nourished by the Body and Blood of your Son and filled with his Holy Spirit may become one body, one spirit in Christ" (EP III).[22]

The contemporary eucharistic liturgies of other churches generally place a unified epiclesis after the institution. A good example is found in the prayers of the United Methodists: "Pour out your Holy Spirit on us gathered here, and on these gifts of bread and wine, that we may be for the world the body of Christ, redeemed by his blood."[23] Although there might be a benefit in having several structures for the Eucharistic Prayer, that is with both unified and split epiclesis, it seems to me that the unified postinstitution narrative epiclesis better expresses the point of the Eucharist as a whole, which is as much about our transformation as it is about the transformation of the gifts. This is the case because the connection between the two is much clearer in a unified epiclesis.

CONCLUSION: THE SIGNIFICANCE OF THE RECOVERY

The liturgical recovery of the Holy Spirit via the epiclesis is part of the bigger story that has seen a renewed appreciation of the Spirit among Catholics in the wake of Vatican II. The inclusion of a petition for the Holy Spirit in the new prayers of the Roman Rite after Vatican II has encouraged the church to "breathe with two lungs," the churches of the East and of the West, to use the phrase made popular by Pope John Paul II. The benefits of the development are not merely ecumenical but also theological. As Yves Congar, the Dominican theologian, pointed out, the Eastern tradition of eucharistic praying has been much more trinitarian as opposed to the Western, which has tended to confine itself to a christological focus that does not acknowledge the crucial role of the Holy Spirit in all the Church's activity.[24] The trinitarian approach enables a fuller appreciation of salvation history and the ongoing role of the Holy Spirit in making the church into the Body of Christ.

In the same vein, Congar also noted that the pre–Vatican II Roman liturgy tended to emphasize the historical roots of the Eucharist in Christ's institution, whereas the epiclesis in the Eastern liturgies points us forward to the eschatological fulfillment of all in Christ.[25] Such an eschatological emphasis is essential for Christians today so as to appreciate how the Eucharist makes demands of us to be the Body of Christ for the world as so well expressed in the Methodist prayer quoted above: "that we may be for the world the body of Christ, redeemed by his blood."

Finally, the recovery of the epiclesis can help us break free from what I called above our "obsession" with the institution narrative as a kind of "magic moment." Many theologians today would insist that the entire prayer is consecratory and that the debates between East and West over a moment of consecration are misguided. Those debates surely are misguided and sterile, for they prevent us from appreciating the richness of our traditions of praying.

The *Catechism of the Catholic Church* makes a bow in the direction of not confining the consecration to a single formula by saying, "The Church Fathers strongly affirmed the faith of the Church in the efficacy of the Word of Christ and of the action of the Holy Spirit to bring about this conversion" (no. 1375). Virtually the same affirmation was made in the landmark ecumenical consensus document, *Baptism, Eucharist and Ministry* of the Faith and Order Commission of the World Council of Churches: "It is in virtue of the living word of Christ and by the power of the Holy Spirit that the bread and wine become the sacramental signs of Christ's body and blood."[26] Such an appreciation further helps us to see how the Eucharistic Prayer is part of the whole of the sacramental action from presentation of the gifts through communion and thus to clarify the role of the ordained minister as one who represents Christ in the context of the Church's action and not independent of it.[27]

As we have seen in the foregoing, the inclusion of the epiclesis and other references to the Holy Spirit in the post–Vatican Roman Rite eucharistic prayers represent an important advance in eucharistic theology and hopefully in eucharistic piety as well. But the implications of this development are not only sacramental but also ecumenical and ecclesio-logical. More significantly, we can hope that the renewed liturgical appreciation of the Holy Spirit will deepen our faith in the necessity of the Holy Spirit's assistance not only in sacramental worship but in the rest of our lives as well.

5

The Holy Spirit and
the Pilgrimage of Faith

Richard Lennan & Nancy Pineda-Madrid

Shortly after his election in 2013, Pope Francis presented his vision for the church, a vision that came in the form of The Joy of the Gospel, *Evangelii Gaudium*. That document expresses Pope Francis's passion for a missionary church, a church that embodies God's mercy in response to the pain of the world, and so rejects the temptation to be inward looking, aloof, or judgmental. For Pope Francis, the church's capacity to be merciful is connected intimately with its trust in God's Holy Spirit, who prompts the community of faith to embrace the freedom of God and to renounce "the attempt to plan and control everything to the last detail" (no. 280).[1] To grow as a merciful community, therefore, the church must allow the Spirit to "enlighten, guide and direct us, leading us wherever [the Spirit] wills" (no. 280).

The link that Pope Francis highlights between the Spirit and the church is one that has become more prominent in Catholic thought over the last fifty years. That contemporary prominence contrasts sharply to the situation that prevailed for much of the second millennium, during which the Spirit was not central to the Catholic imagination, as will be discussed more fully in this chapter. The Second Vatican Council was the immediate catalyst for ending the long neglect of the Spirit. The contribution of Vatican II to an expanded awareness of the Spirit's presence and activity is summarized neatly in an encyclical by Pope John Paul II: "In a certain sense, the Council has made the Spirit newly 'present' in our difficult age" (*Dominum et Vivificantem* 26).[2]

The Council did not develop a comprehensive pneumatology for the church, but it helped Catholics to become more aware of the role that the Spirit plays in the church and in the life of faith. In so doing, Vatican II retrieved for contemporary Catholics the rich body of wisdom contained in the Bible, the liturgy and theology of the early church, and the insights of Orthodox Christians.[3] Effectively, the Council's teaching encouraged members of the church to embrace their vocation to live the gospel in the world, a vocation proper to the church as a community of Spirit-filled disciples. That communal focus shaped how Vatican II understood even the church's structures, which the Council depicted in relation to the Spirit and to the mission of the whole ecclesial community. As we will note, the emphasis on shared, Spirit-directed discipleship provided the basis for the embrace of ecumenism with other Christians, openness to non-Christian religions, and the promotion of constructive engagement with the wider world, the world in which the Spirit is alive and active.

First, we will review Vatican II's teaching on the Spirit, focusing on the church as a Spirit-led, pilgrim community called to mission. Second, from that foundation, we will examine how two contemporary theologians, Víctor Codina, SJ, and Elizabeth A. Johnson, CSJ, have developed the Council's thought for the present day, identifying further aspects of the Spirit's role within the community of faith and beyond. This chapter underscores the ways both the church's official teaching and the writings of theologians bring the Spirit into relief as the one who sustains the church and all of God's creation in the present, while also leading them into their future fulfillment in Jesus Christ.

THE HOLY SPIRIT IN
THE TEACHING OF VATICAN II

Writing in 1964, Pope Paul VI, who was elected pope during the Council, highlighted the link between openness to the Spirit and the church's faithfulness to Christ: "The Church is, as we know, enlightened and guided by the Holy Spirit, Who is still ready, if we implore [the Spirit] and listen to [the Spirit] to fulfill without fail the promise of

Christ" (*Ecclesiam Suam* 26).[4] That description reminded members of the church that their ancestors in faith turned repeatedly to the Spirit as they sought, often amid tensions and even open conflict (cf. Acts 15:1–5; Gal 2:11–14), to clarify their mission in the context of new circumstances and new questions. The goal of their discernment was always to arrive at what "has seemed good to the Holy Spirit and to us" (Acts 15:28).

The documents of Vatican II echo the New Testament in depicting the Spirit as engaged with the daily life of the church to promote authentic discipleship. The Council portrayed the activity of the Spirit as integral to the Christian community, enabling that body to manifest in history the life-giving mercy and reconciliation of God, the gifts of God's self-giving made present in the life, death, and resurrection of Jesus Christ. Consistent with that vision, the Council presented the church in relation to God as Trinity.

The Constitution on the Church, *Lumen Gentium* (LG), the Council's principal exploration of the identity and purpose of the Christian community, underscores the abiding presence of the Spirit. In designating the church as both "the people of God" and "sacrament," Vatican II showcased the link between the Christian community and the Spirit, who "dwells in the church and in the hearts of the faithful, as in a temple" (LG 4).[5] As we shall see, the Council stressed that this intimate bond between the Spirit and the church exists not for the private enjoyment of members of the community, but to form the church as a community of disciples committed to live the good news of Jesus Christ in the events of the everyday world (LG 9).[6]

Since it concentrated on the Spirit dwelling in the church, Vatican II understood the church to be a people called to holiness, a people whose members "by regeneration and the anointing of the Holy Spirit, are consecrated to be a spiritual house and a holy priesthood" (LG 10). In addition, the Council taught that the Spirit "guides the church in the way of all truth and, uniting it in fellowship and ministry, bestows on it different hierarchic and charismatic gifts, and in this way directs and adorns it with his fruits" (LG 4). The focus on the Spirit as teacher and guide of the church communicated clearly the Council's conviction that the church is not only a body able to develop and grow, but one that must develop and grow. Vatican II expressed that conviction succinctly by describing the Christian community as a "pilgrim" (LG 48).

As a pilgrim, the church is led by the Spirit toward the fullness of life in Christ; along the way, it is the Spirit who prompts growth in faith, hope, and love. The Spirit "moves the heart and converts it to God," thereby enabling God's revelation to be "more and more deeply understood" (*Dei Verbum* 5).[7] The Council identified Scripture, the word of God, and the Eucharist as the primary means by which the Spirit nourishes the church for its growth.[8] In addition, the Council was clear that pilgrimage does not suggest aimless wandering. In fact, the Council's Pastoral Constitution on the Church in the Modern World, *Gaudium et Spes* (GS), specifies unambiguously the church's purpose: "Animated and drawn together in his Spirit we press onwards on our journey towards the consummation of history which fully corresponds to the plan of his love: 'to unite all things in him, things in heaven and things on earth' (Eph 1:10)" (no. 45).[9]

The church's pilgrimage, its relationship to Christ and the Spirit, provided the framework for the Council's analysis of the church as a missionary community. Thus, the Decree on the Church's Missionary Activity, *Ad Gentes Divinitus* (AG), argues that "the church on earth is by its very nature missionary since, according to the plan of the Father, it has its origin in the mission of the Son and the Holy Spirit" (no. 2). In Christ, the church exists "to lead [people] to the faith, freedom, and peace of Christ" (AG 5), while through the Spirit, the church "must walk the road Christ himself walked, a way of poverty and obedience, of service and self-sacrifice" (AG 5).

Although Vatican II was explicit in its presentation of the church's unique, Spirit-initiated, and Spirit-guided mission, it was equally forthright in its acknowledgment that the Spirit's presence in the world was neither controlled by the church nor dependent on the initiative of the church. Rather than divide the world into light and darkness, into spheres where God's Spirit was and was not present, Vatican II taught that all "men and women are continually being aroused by the Spirit of God" (GS 41). Similarly, the Council affirmed that within civil society, "the holy Spirit offers to all the possibility of being made partners, in a way known to God, in the paschal mystery" (GS 22). Relying on biblical texts such as Acts 10:44–47 and 11:15, the Council stated that "[the Spirit] at times visibly anticipates apostolic action, just as in various ways [the Spirit] unceasingly accompanies and directs it" (AG 4). Vatican II, therefore, echoed the New Testament, where the Spirit was at times active among the Gentiles prior to the proclamation of the gospel, as noted earlier.

Notwithstanding its emphasis on the world as a venue for God's self-communication in the Spirit, the Council acknowledged that the Spirit's voice was not the only one that could be heard in the modern world. Even amid the contemporary cacophony of opinions and world-views, however, the Spirit aided the church "to listen to and distinguish the many voices of our time and to interpret them in the light of God's word in order that the revealed truth may be more deeply penetrated, better understood, and more suitably presented" (GS 44).

The Council's presentation of the church as a Body called to mission in the world emphasized that only a united church could properly reflect the God incarnate in Jesus Christ. For that reason, Vatican II stressed the Spirit's role as the source of the church's unity in faith (LG 9). The Council recognized also that the unity flowing from the Spirit was not reducible to uniformity. Rather, echoing St. Paul's understanding of the variety of gifts in the one Body of Christ (Rom 12:4–8; 1 Cor 12:1–31), the Council depicted the church as a Body blessed with the range of the Spirit's gifts (LG 7). For that reason, the Council's approach to both the inner life of the Catholic Church and to ecumenical relations held unity in creative tension with diversity.

To appreciate the Council's approach to the church's unity and diversity, it can be helpful to review Vatican II's teaching on the relationship between the church's bishops and the other members of the one community of faith. The Council did not provide a thoroughgoing analysis of that relationship, but it is evident that the bishops at Vatican II proceeded from the conviction that the Spirit cannot be at war with itself: the church's leaders and its members share the one Spirit, and so are called to unity in faith and mission. More specifically, the Council taught that "the whole body of the faithful," whose faith is "aroused and sustained by the Spirit of truth," "cannot be mistaken in belief" (LG 12). This strong endorsement of the Spirit at work in the faith of the whole church exists alongside an equally strong affirmation that the church's bishops are guided by "the light of the holy Spirit" in their role as authoritative teachers in the church (LG 25).

As we know from the history of the church since Vatican II, the relationship between the bishops and the members of the church at large is not always a smooth one. Clearly, only if all members are convinced that the Spirit nurtures a church that is one, holy, catholic, and apostolic, with all the complexities and interrelationships those qualities imply, can the church as a whole do justice to what begins at Pentecost. In affirming that the Spirit is, simultaneously, at work in both the community of all the baptized and those who exercise episcopal authority within that community, the Council challenged the church to opt for neither polarization and the triumph of factionalism nor what Karl Rahner designates as "stagnation and the peace of the graveyard."[10] A pilgrim church, therefore, must be willing to live with the tension that accompanies the Spirit's "both…and" way of acting: that the Holy Spirit both "allots to each one individually just as the Spirit chooses" (1 Cor 12:11) and is, simultaneously, the source of the "one body" of Christ (1 Cor 12:13).

Beyond its focus on the Catholic Church, Vatican II also addressed the Spirit's role in serving the unity and diversity within the communion of the Christian churches. Here too, the Council drew on the implications of the church's existence as a pilgrim. In the centuries that followed the Reformation, Catholics had viewed other Christians with a deep and pervasive suspicion, but Vatican II adopted as a priority the need for better relationships between the divided Christian churches, stressing that "there increases from day to day a movement, fostered by grace of the Spirit, for the restoration of unity among all Christians" (*Unitatis Redintegratio* 1).[11] In promoting "dialogue" between the churches, the Council urged Catholics to remember "that anything wrought by the grace of the Holy Spirit in the hearts of our separated brothers and sisters can contribute to our own edification" (no. 4). Catholics, therefore, could be a source of enrichment for other Christians, but could also be enriched by the ways in which other Christians had appropriated the gifts of the Spirit. In short, the whole pilgrim church could continue to grow into a more authentic reflection of Christ through the Holy Spirit.

Karl Rahner claimed that the Holy Spirit acted as "the element of dynamic unrest if not of revolutionary upheaval" in the church.[12]

Vatican II provides ample support for Rahner's contention. The "dynamic unrest" of the Spirit is evident in the Council's own history and way of operating. In addition, its documents bequeathed to the church not a blueprint that details minutely how the church ought to act in every circumstance, but a vision for a community of disciples attentive to the Spirit's movement in the world at large and among the pilgrim people of God. In the decades since the Council, the Christian community has sought to embody, and develop, that vision. The following sections will illustrate how two contemporary theologians, Víctor Codina, SJ, and Elizabeth A. Johnson, CSJ, have responded to the Council's hopes for a Spirit-filled community serving the mission of Christ in the modern world.

VÍCTOR CODINA, SJ

As is true for every theologian, the contributions of Víctor Codina, SJ, show the imprint of his life journey. Several factors coalesced to shape Codina's theology of the Holy Spirit. Codina was born in Barcelona, Cataluña, Spain in 1931 and grew up in a religiously devout Catholic family. During his early life, the city of Barcelona, along with the rest of Spain, suffered a bloody civil war (1936–39) that ended when General Francisco Franco seized power, transforming Spain into an autocratic, repressive state, strongly inclined toward fascism. Franco remained dictator of Spain until his death in 1975, after which Spain returned to a democracy. Franco left his mark on the church by forging a national Catholicism aimed at reinforcing his autocratic political rule. In response to these forces, Codina, from early on, would advance a theological vision that implicitly critiqued and rejected Francoist Spain and the form of Catholicism it built up.[13]

Second, at the age of seventeen, Codina entered the Jesuits and was educated on a strict diet of neo-Scholastic theology, which lacked an openness to engagement with the world and its ever-new questions. Looking for something more, he became part of a group critical of the direction of the Catholic Church in Spain. Ordained in 1961, he left Spain to become a student of Karl Rahner at the University of Innsbruck. From 1963 to 1965, he worked on his doctorate at the Gregorian

University in Rome, imbibing the heady ferment of the Second Vatican Council meeting a few blocks away. His dissertation, and ensuing research, demonstrated his serious study of Eastern Orthodox theology and spirituality.[14] This study, as well as the pneumatology of Yves Congar, left its effect on his theological work. Codina's imagination was further stirred three years later, when in 1968 the Latin American bishops developed a bold, new response to Vatican II at their conference meeting in Medellín, Colombia. Throughout this time, Codina developed a regard for the pilgrim church.

Finally, in 1982, after teaching in Barcelona for many years, Codina moved to Bolivia, where he has lived, taught, and worked ever since. From his more than thirty years in Bolivia, he has developed great esteem for its indigenous peoples and their rituals, symbols, and images. These not only resonated with his earlier study of Eastern Orthodox theology but also contributed to the originality of his theological work.

Codina has published more than ten books and numerous articles addressing pneumatology, ecclesiology, Eucharist, the sacraments, Christology, religious life, and liberation theology, with his overarching interest being the intersection of the Holy Spirit and the church. Unfortunately, his work, most of it published in Spanish, is not well known outside of the Spanish literate world, and especially not in the English-speaking world.

Codina, above all else, calls our attention to how a faith community receives ecclesial teaching and makes that teaching its own. The Holy Spirit is integral to this process, which he affirms was abundantly evident at Medellín. At this episcopal conference, the bishops sought a response to Vatican II that would take seriously the continent's great majority of poor persons, whose poverty remained entrenched in unjust economic structures so endemic to Latin America. For Codina, the Medellín Conference Documents can only be understood as an original reception and creative rereading of the Vatican II documents. Indeed, Medellín as well as Vatican II must be regarded as pneumatological events; that is, as honest responses to the active promptings of the Holy Spirit.[15] Even so, he observes, the church has not been able to take advantage of the opening to the Spirit introduced by Vatican II and Medellín. In large measure, this is due to the preceding centuries of limited work on the Holy Spirit.

Codina notes, as do many other theologians, that the second millennium saw a widespread and increasing erosion of theological attention to the Holy Spirit in the West. The roots of this decline can be traced to the rise of modernity with its suspicion of tradition and its privileging of rationalism. During this decline, believers continued to respond to the action of the Spirit through their devotions, their liturgical practices, their honoring of the mystics, and so forth. While these practices certainly express the significance of the Holy Spirit in the life of faith, theological thinking about the Holy Spirit was quite limited. Consequently, theology of the Holy Spirit was restricted to speculative thought about the Trinity, reducing the appreciation of the Spirit's role in everyday Christian life.

Although the church's magisterium and most priests appealed to the Holy Spirit to bless the hierarchical, priestly structure of the church and to accentuate the superiority of the priestly form of life above that of the laity, there was little discussion related to the "people of God" and the Holy Spirit. As a result, appreciation of the richness of the Holy Spirit narrowed. The pneumatological vitality so evident in the early church was substantially reduced to the purview of the magisterium, which appeared as the agent of the gifts of the Holy Spirit and as the source of all authority regarding the Holy Spirit. Writing in 2008, Codina claimed that although Vatican II transformed Catholic thinking on the Holy Spirit, there nevertheless remains a tendency on the part of those in authority in the church to associate the Spirit's action exclusively with maintenance of the church's structures.[16]

Medellín, therefore, has the capacity to transform our ecclesial imagination, asserts Codina, because it turns our attention to "reception," which Codina defines as "the process of a vital assimilation, by the body of the church, of truths and rules issued by higher authorities....It is not simple obedience, but a liturgical and vital 'amen' by which the community makes its own an ecclesial teaching."[17] This may include how a community takes on specific rules of the church, or the way a community celebrates liturgy and the sacraments, or the like. By paying attention to "reception," he contends, the church will deepen its consciousness of the Spirit's robust presence in the world today. Reception necessitates a vigorous theology of the Holy Spirit and an acute awareness of the church as pilgrim. This understanding of the praxis of reception was widely assumed, if not articulated, during the first millennium of the church. However, as mentioned earlier, it disappeared over the subsequent centuries with grievous consequences. The grievous consequences, according to Codina, include the rupture and divide between the clergy and laity, between the Eastern and Latin Churches, between the churches of the Reformation and the Church of Rome, and the rupture within the Catholic Church between the church and the modern world.

What would be the most life-giving theological approach in response to these divisions? For Codina, it would need to be an approach that foregrounds the significance of the Holy Spirit, especially when describing *how* we are church and our practice of being church. Without a robust regard for the role of the Holy Spirit, the church becomes weak. The Holy Spirit and Jesus Christ must both be understood as integral to the ongoing life of the church. Echoing Congar, Codina writes, "The early Church was deeply conscious of its connection to the Holy Spirit. The Church is born of the Spirit, is sanctified through the Spirit and lives by the Spirit of Jesus. From its origin, the Church has the experience of its double principle structure: the Christological and the Pneumatological."[18] Because of the Spirit's active presence in the world, there is a communion of saints, the forgiveness of sin, our bodily resurrection, and the possibility of eternal life. Indeed, as Codina makes clear, much is at stake for us in our affirmation of the Holy Spirit's divinity and centrality.

A corollary of the Spirit's central role in the church is that the Spirit makes possible the reception, and thus inculturation, of the faith in diverse local churches. For Codina, the Spirit is the "origin of pluralism and of communion in the same faith, [and thus is the same] Spirit that gives the sense of faith to the faithful and enables the faithful to remain steadfast in the truth even in the midst of ideological torments."[19] Moreover, while Latin American liberation theology has regularly engaged in a rigorous analysis of socioeconomic and political problems, there exists today a new emergent cultural paradigm.

Prompted by the Spirit, this new cultural paradigm, in the words of Codina, challenges us to "also have present women, the indigenous and African Americans, religions, the land, religious rituals and fiesta."[20]

Implicit here is the conviction that the Spirit speaks through voices and realities that each represent different experiences of marginalization. This conviction echoes constantly throughout his work. What this speaking means is that today we must turn our attention to new theological subjects and new themes, even as we continue to insist that the "criterion of discernment to correctly understand this new paradigm of culture will always be the poor and the life of the poor."[21] The Holy Spirit has always spoken in novel and unexpected ways, and for Codina, this Latin American emergent cultural paradigm is a contemporary example, one congruent with the Spirit at Pentecost *and with the people of God on pilgrimage*.

Moreover, the church needs to think theologically from the perspective of poor persons, he claims, not only "with their desire for justice and freedom from poverty," but also "with their cultures and utopian aspirations, with their religiosity."[22] As a response to the Holy Spirit, Medellín exemplified an attempt to think theologically with poor persons from this much broader perspective. Medellín, in its original re-creation of Vatican II, endures as a rich example of "reception" and a new Pentecost.

ELIZABETH A. JOHNSON, CSJ

Elizabeth A. Johnson's life journey began in 1941 in Brooklyn, New York, where she grew up in an Irish Catholic family. She was the first born of seven children in a home that "included beloved cats and dogs." Her interest in theology began in 1959, when, as an undergraduate at Brentwood College, she was captivated by "the question of suffering in the context of God's relationship to the world," and by "the clarity and precision of Aquinas' thought" as well as "the cosmic sweep of his vision." As a young adult, she was drawn to religious life, becoming a member of the Sisters of Saint Joseph (Brentwood, Long Island, New York). These years saw the transformation of the church through the visionary work of Vatican II, as well as the emergence of the women's movement, the civil rights movement, and the antiwar movement of the 1960s and '70s. Johnson came of age during a watershed in United States' history that transformed the imagination of the nation and, especially among the young, sparked a drive on many fronts to forge a better world. Inspired by Vatican II, the overwhelming majority of United States' communities of women religious, including the Sisters of St. Joseph, transformed their leadership structures, making them more discerning, egalitarian, and transparent.[23]

By 1971, Johnson had earned an MA at Manhattan College and spent several years teaching religion and science in Catholic high schools. In 1981, Johnson became the first woman to earn a doctorate in theology at the Catholic University of America (CUA), the only university in the United States founded and sponsored by the United States' Catholic bishops. Moreover, she was among the first women allowed to acquire a doctorate in theology from a United States Catholic university, where it was common practice to admit only priests or seminarians into doctoral programs in theology to the systematic exclusion of all women. Reflecting on her doctoral studies at CUA, Johnson remarked, "I never had a woman professor, I never read one woman author. There were none to be had. It was a totally male education." She wrote her dissertation on the Christology of Wolfhart Pannenberg, a German Protestant theologian, and went on to serve as a professor of theology at CUA for the next ten years. Her early thinking was influenced by pioneers like Elisabeth Schüssler Fiorenza and Sandra M. Schneiders, as well as by the witness of the four American women, three of whom were women religious, killed by death squads in El Salvador in 1980. Today, she is Distinguished Professor of Theology at Fordham University (New York City, the Bronx) where she has taught since 1991.[24]

She has published ten books and numerous articles, which together demonstrate her steadfast and broadly focused commitment to justice and the dismantling of oppression in all its forms, with an attention to gender and the social sin of sexism. Her contributions engage the doctrine of God, religious language for God, creation, the Holy Spirit, the Communion of Saints, Mariology, ecumenism, and interreligious dialogue.

What Johnson so wonderfully brings to our attention is an uncanny perspective on three voices, too often rendered silent in mainstream theology, namely, the Holy Spirit, women, and the natural world. An affinity, at least symbolically, exists among these three.[25] She invites us to consider such an affinity.

Johnson sets the stage for her discussion of the Holy Spirit by focusing on the triune God, particularly the triune relationality within God. She reminds her readers that the faithful came to know "the one God through the Word's becoming flesh and the Spirit's enlivening [of the] community," thereby reflecting God's relationality. Mindful of the church's less developed presentation of the Spirit, she observes,

> I have found this trinitarian framework to be of utmost importance. It secures the fact that language about the Spirit is not about some lesser being or weaker intermediary, but is referring without dilution to the incomprehensible holy mystery of God's own personal being. The Giver of life is not a diminutive or insubstantial godling, a shadowy or face-less third hypostasis, but truly God who is "adored and glori-fied" along with the Father and the Son, as the creedal symbol of faith confesses.[26]

Further, as truly God, the Spirit unceasingly "creates, empowers, and fills the whole world with life."

The Spirit is the God who comes already, always, and everywhere, calling humanity and the whole of creation to ever more life. It is the Spirit who compels energetic love itself, encouraging all creatures to take the next step to life and love in abundance. The Spirit meets us precisely where we are, a point developed well in the first chapter, drawing us more deeply into relation with ourselves, with the triune God, with others, and with the whole of creation, expanding our capacity to receive as well as give love. As the Spirit draws us into relation, the Spirit prompts the pilgrim church to be about the mission of Christ.

Keenly aware that the Holy Spirit is identified as the *third* person of the triune God, Johnson questions the consequence of this ordering of the divine persons, and the commonplace perception that the Spirit occupies a subordinate role in relation to the first and second persons of the Trinity, the Father and Son respectively. In *She Who Is*, Johnson places and engages the Holy Spirit first in her constructive work on the Trinity, and so before the Father and Son.[27] Using this atypical ordering, she "claims an agency for the Spirit that disturbs the conventional patriarchal

Trinitarian structure."[28] This strategy operates not only to transform the theological value of women's experience, but functions to transform our theological regard for the natural world. Throughout *Ask the Beasts*, Johnson strongly underscores the agency of the Holy Spirit. She clarifies how the Spirit constantly initiates and never ceases to sustain, to heal, and to redeem the whole of creation.

By placing the Holy Spirit first in her ordering of the trinitarian persons, Johnson exposes the flaw in attempts to balance gender within the Godhead by identifying the Spirit as female—in such attempts, divinity stands represented in both male (Father and Son) and female (Spirit) terms. Johnson, however, contends that this strategy leads believers to perceive women as secondary, and to think of the Holy Spirit as tertiary. In addition, theology's longstanding neglect of the Holy Spirit (rendering the Spirit vague and amorphous) coupled with the way theology has overlooked the experiences of women, means that identifying the Spirit as female does not solve the problem of finding gender balance in our naming of God but deepens it. This result further exacerbates neglect of the Holy Spirit and the overlooked theological significance of women's experience.[29]

Johnson also shows that neglect of the Spirit contributes to the lack of attention paid to the religious value of the natural world; as Johnson writes, these "seem to go hand in hand." Nonetheless, the religious value of the natural world is becoming a more pressing concern for theologians as evidence of global warming and environmental deterioration increase. Furthermore, Pope Francis, with *Laudato Si'*, calls us to care for our common home.[30] So, Johnson asks, how is the Spirit of God present in the whole of the natural world including the ends of the cosmos? Since the primary mission of the Spirit is to be "the Giver of life," the affirmation of "divine love at the center of the evolutionary world" necessitates attending to the Spirit's action in the world. This necessity is a daring assertion on her part. By attending to the Spirit, we "discover that love of the natural world is an intrinsic part of faith in God."[31] And, in making this discovery, we see that our faith makes demands of us in terms of our relation to the natural world.

In recognizing the Spirit as subject and agent, as first to meet human beings and all creatures where we are, Johnson foregrounds the active presence of God in the concrete events of history, inviting us to see that "the spark of life is kept flaring by the Holy Spirit, Giver of life, the vivifier who dwells within all things empowering their advance."[32] Since the natural world is a principal locus for encountering the Holy Spirit, when we damage or waste the earth, we sin against the creativity of God, insists Johnson.[33] To receive fully the invitation that the Spirit extends to us, we need to consider how we deepen our capacity for responsible stewardship of the earth and of its creative, life-sustaining force in our lives. Indeed, who we are as a pilgrim church must include the evolutionary world.

Drawing on Karl Rahner, Johnson underscores that "in evolution the activity of divine presence must be thought of as something so *interior* to the creature that it enables the creature to 'achieve a really *active* self-transcendence.'" The Creator God does not act as the finite or immediate cause of some new reality, with human beings and other finite creatures being passive recipients. Rather, quoting Rahner, Johnson affirms that God is "'the living, permanent, transcendent ground of the self-movement of the world itself.' Hence, 'under the dynamism of divine being and under the continuous divine creative power, the material stuff of nature evolves in the integrity of its own processes.'" The self-transcending capacity that is inherent in human beings, other creatures, and the various species on planet earth affirms God's creation such that "the material of the world itself has the God-given inner ability to become ever more."[34] This self-transcending capacity applies to animals and other species because of their capacity to evolve and adapt to their environment over time.

Johnson, therefore, resists the idea of a divine ruler who holds supernatural control over all that occurs on earth in a fashion that interrupts the integrity of natural causes. She takes seriously the theological challenge of respecting the enormous creative impulse of both God the Creator and of creation itself.

Far from being in competition with the laws acting around us, including natural selection, the hand of the God of love empowers the cosmos as it evolves these very laws and their emergent effects. The world develops in an economy of divine superabundance, gifted with its own freedom in and through which the Creator Spirit's gracious purpose is accomplished.[35]

With Vatican II, the church reawakened to being a pilgrim people on a journey of faith. This turning point in the church's self-understanding compelled our gaze to the Holy Spirit. Building on the renewed appreciation of the Holy Spirit in the teaching of the Second Vatican Council, both Codina and Johnson summon their readers to consider what might be learned of the Holy Spirit from below, from the everyday Christian life experiences of those whose voices are typically marginalized. In addition to the diverse human groups, the natural world must be included here. If such a strategy is employed, might this lead to a new consciousness of the Spirit, one analogous to that of the early church and one encouraging the growth of an even more vigorous, life-giving church community? Indeed, such a consciousness is already evident in many sectors of the church today, as these two theologians, and many other essays in this book, make amply evident. Codina and Johnson, however, dare an even more audacious beholding of the Spirit, one that invites our openness to the superabundant creativity of God expressed in surprising ways.

PART 2

Tracing the Movement of the Holy Spirit

6

Spirit,
Wind, or Breath

Reflections on the Old Testament

Andrew R. Davis

Anyone who has learned a second language knows what a challenge it can be to produce a translation that is both faithful to the original language and consistent with the grammar and style of the translated language. This challenge is certainly familiar to translators and interpreters of the Bible, since they must render its ancient Hebrew, Aramaic, and Greek into modern languages. The difficulty is especially acute when dealing with words that carry theological significance. One such Hebrew word is *ruah*, which denotes "spirit" but also "wind" and "breath."

Divided into two parts, this chapter first provides an overview of *ruah* in the Old Testament and explores how the study of a biblical concept can inform Christian theology. This overview will be by no means comprehensive, since there isn't enough room to cover all the (almost four hundred) instances of the word.[1] Rather, we focus on its use as a term for "spirit," and show that this meaning applies to vertical (divine–human) as well as horizontal (human–human) relationships. The chapter then examines the multivalence of *ruah* by looking at two passages— Genesis 1:2 and Ezekiel 37:1–14—in which the word's meaning is ambiguous and offers a valuable framework for thinking about the work of the Holy Spirit in contemporary communities of faith.

RUAH AS THE SPIRIT OF GOD

One of the most important meanings of biblical *ruah*, especially from a theological perspective, is its denotation of the spirit of God. The ancient Israelites understood God as the source of an animating spirit that enlivened all creation. One of the best illustrations of this belief comes at the end of Psalm 104. After praising the glory and majesty of Yahweh's creation, the Psalmist reflects on all creatures' dependence on Yahweh for their sustenance:

> These all look to you
>> to give them their food in due season;
> when you give to them, they gather it up;
>> when you open your hand, they are filled with good
>>> things.
> When you hide your face, they are dismayed;
>> when you take away their breath [*ruah*], they die
>> and return to their dust.
> When you send forth your spirit [*ruah*], they are created;
>> and you renew the face of the ground. (vv. 27–30)

This reflection on divine providence includes the physical and the spiritual needs that God has the power to satisfy. The double use of the word *ruah* indicates that human life depends on Yahweh sharing his divine spirit. Without it we return to dust (*'apar*), but with it we are created (*bara'*) and the earth (*'adama*) also is renewed. There are strong echoes here of the Creation stories in Genesis 1—3, which likewise feature God's *ruah* in creation (*bara'*; 1:1–2), and human breath as a divine gift that transforms the dust (*'apar*) of the earth (*'adama*) into a living being (2:7). Thus, what makes humans alive is their participation in the divine *ruah*, which God graciously shares with us, and this *ruah* is not given exclusively to humans but involves all creation.

The strength of this belief in God's spirit as essential for human life can be further demonstrated by an intriguing and poignant passage from the Book of Job, where Job swears to speak truthfully:

As God lives, who has taken away my right,
    and the Almighty, who has made my soul bitter,
as long as my breath is in me
    and the spirit [*ruah*] of God is in my nostrils,
my lips will not speak falsehood,
    and my tongue will not utter deceit. (27:2–4)

Job's oath, like all sworn promises in antiquity, invokes a deity who would guarantee its fulfillment, but in Job's case the divine guarantor of his oath is the same God "who has taken away my right" and "made my soul bitter" (v. 2). Yet after he names God as the source of his suffering, Job describes God as the source of his life; the parallelism between "my breath" and "the spirit [*ruah*] of God is in my nostrils" (v. 3) indicates that the two are equivalent (cf. Ps 51:10–12 [12–14]). These verses show just how deep-rooted in the biblical worldview was the belief that the breath of human life derives from and depends on God's *ruah*. Despite his profound estrangement from God and his doubts about divine justice, Job does not question that God's *ruah* remains the source of his existence. Job serves as a reminder that even when we feel separated from God, the divine spirit remains within us, animating us and binding us to God's own life.

The gift of the divine spirit did not just enliven humans but also empowered them for divinely appointed tasks. The best biblical examples of this aspect of divine *ruah* come from the Book of Judges, in which Yahweh raises up leaders from among the people to deal with occasional crises. These "judges" are more military than judicial, and their leadership begins when "the spirit [*ruah*] of Yahweh" comes upon them, enabling them to deliver Israel from its enemies (Judg 3:10; 11:29, 32). Sometimes this formula is embellished, as with Gideon, whom the *ruah* "clothed" (6:34, ESV) and Samson on whom the *ruah* "rushed" (14:6, 19; 15:14). This kind of charismatic leadership continues with Israel's first kings, Saul (1 Sam 10:6, 10; 11:6) and David (1 Sam 16:13), but ultimately gives way to the dynastic succession of monarchy. Some of these charismatic leaders are unlikely heroes (Judg 6:15; 11:1–2; 1 Sam 9:21), but their shortcomings only underscore the power of God's *ruah* to carry out his divine will through modest human agents.

The divine spirit's empowerment of human agents can also be seen in biblical prophecy. An interesting feature of this use of *ruaḥ* is its transmission from one prophet to another. So far, we have focused on the vertical movement of *ruaḥ* from God to humans, but the examples of Moses and Elijah show that God's gift of the divine spirit is one that can be shared horizontally between humans. Moses's successor Joshua is identified as one "full of the spirit [*ruaḥ*] of wisdom, because Moses had laid his hands on him" (Deut 34:9; cf. Num 27 :18, 23). Similarly, when Elijah passes his prophetic mantle to Elisha, Elisha asks him for a double portion of his *ruaḥ* (2 Kgs 2:9). After Elijah ascends to heaven a few verses later, Elisha's companions recognize that Elijah's *ruaḥ* indeed rests on Elisha (v. 15).

Perhaps the most remarkable account of the transference of the divine spirit in prophetic leadership occurs in Numbers 11:16–30, when Yahweh tells Moses to gather seventy elders to share the burden of his leadership. Yahweh says he will take some of the spirit (*ruaḥ*) that is in Moses and put it in the seventy (v. 17). When that happens a few verses later, the spirit inspires the seventy to speak and act like prophets (v. 25). This *ruaḥ* is not limited to those seventy elders, however, but inspires prophetic action in two others who had remained in the camp (v. 26). When Joshua resents their behavior, Moses rejoins, "Would that all Yahweh's people were prophets, and that Yahweh would put his spirit [*ruaḥ*] on them!" (v. 29, translation altered). This passage shows not only the divine source of prophetic *ruaḥ* but also Yahweh's desire for this spirit to be shared generously among the people.

This review of *ruaḥ* as divine spirit in the Old Testament has shown two important aspects of its meaning. First and foremost, God's *ruaḥ* is the source of human life, the divine spirit that animates all creatures and connects us to God. This spiritual affinity is so fundamental that it binds us to God even when God seems remote or, in the example from Job, cruel. But *ruaḥ* is more than the foundation of human life; it is an active force in the world that enables humans to carry out the divine will. Often the spirit is associated with leadership but not always in ways we might expect. Indeed, biblical examples of this dynamic *ruaḥ* show a preference for human agents who lack status or innate ability to lead.

The biblical representation of *ruah* as a vital force that enables human life and empowers leaders within communities of faith bears a strong resemblance to Christian beliefs about the Holy Spirit. In the Nicene Creed, we proclaim the Holy Spirit to be "the giver of life who proceeds from the Father and the Son," an emphasis that is consistent with the Old Testament depiction of God's *ruah*. Both identify the spirit as a life-giving power that originates with God who shares it with creation. Moreover, Christian tradition has likewise drawn attention to the role of the Spirit in Christ's ministry and our discipleship. Jesus himself makes this connection to *ruah* when he identifies himself the one anointed by the spirit of God to proclaim good news to the poor (Luke 4:18–21; cf. Acts 10:38). Jesus's statement is a quote from Isaiah 61:1–2 in which the prophet identifies the spirit (*ruah*) of Yahweh as the source and means of his mission. This mission extends to Christians who are anointed by the same spirit and thus share in its divinity, as discussed earlier by Brian Dunkle.[2] My goal in drawing these points of comparison between biblical *ruah* and the Holy Spirit of Christian faith is not to conflate the two or suggest that the latter can be read in the former. Rather, I hope to show how the biblical concept of *ruah* anticipates key features of the Holy Spirit and to suggest that Christian reflection on one can be enriched by study of the other.[3]

RUAH AND ITS MULTIVALENCE

As noted at the beginning of this chapter, "(divine) spirit" is just one meaning of the Hebrew word *ruah*. While the preceding discussion of this meaning and its two principal characteristics find strong support in the Old Testament, we should be mindful that other instances of the word are more ambiguous. Indeed, the semantic range of *ruah* can make it difficult to render in English because sometimes its three basics meanings—wind, breath, spirit—overlap in one occurrence of the word, and the translator must decide which of the three English words makes the best sense. Let us now examine two biblical passages—Genesis 1:2 and Ezekiel 37:1–14—where we find this kind of overlap. These more ambiguous occurrences yield a different kind of theological significance. Unlike the previous section, whose survey of biblical passages allowed us to identify key characteristics of *ruaḥ*, this section will not lead to conclusive statements. Rather, I hope to show that the ambiguities of *ruaḥ* mirror a difficulty common to communities of faith, namely, the challenge of discerning how the spirit is moving in their midst. The discernment required of translators when they encounter an uncertain usage may shed light on how others can "translate the spirit" into the life and work of their communities.

A famous example comes from the very beginning of the Old Testament, indeed the second verse of the Bible. After describing the earth as a formless void and the darkness covering the abyss, Genesis 1:2 reports that "the *ruaḥ* of God swept over the waters" (au. trans.). Interpreters are divided on how to read this instance of *ruaḥ*. Most English translations, including the New American Bible Revised Edition (NABRE), the New Revised Standard Version (NRSV), and the New Jewish Publication Society *Tanakh*, render this *ruaḥ* "wind." The translation makes sense. For one thing, it is easy to imagine a powerful wind gusting over the primordial deep, and just because the *ruaḥ* is "of God" does not mean the word must denote the divine spirit. We have plenty of examples of plain old wind blowing forth from Yahweh (Exod 10:13, 19; 14:21; Isa 11:15). Scholars will also point out that Creation in Genesis 1 is really the result of the divine word, not spirit, so we should not read too much into the *ruaḥ*. In fact, many regard this wind as itself part of the "formless void" that gets transformed through creation. This view explains why some translations, including the NABRE, render the phrase "a mighty wind" rather than "a wind from God." For these translators, "from God" doesn't really mean God but something god-like in its force.

While these readings are understandable, the translation of "wind," especially "mighty wind," fails to capture key nuances of Hebrew *ruaḥ*. Elsewhere in the Old Testament, the word is associated with God's creative activity (and that of humans [see Exod 31:3; 35:31]).[4] We noted above Psalm 104:30, which not only identifies *ruaḥ* as the instrument of creation and renewal, but even echoes other vocabulary from Genesis 1. To this example could be added Psalm 33:6, which declares that "by Yahweh's word the heavens were made; by the *ruaḥ* of his mouth all their host" (au. trans.). Besides connecting *ruaḥ* with Yahweh's creation of the heavens, this passage shows that the attempt to make a sharp distinction between God's *ruah* and God's word is misguided. Nevertheless, this verse adds a new wrinkle since the *ruah* from Yahweh's mouth suggests breath as an attractive translation. In fact, this is how modern English translations render the word. Thus, we are left with three instances of *ruah*, which all describe God's creative activity, but each shades to a different aspect of *ruah*, resulting in three different translations: wind (Gen 1:2), spirit (Ps 104:30), and breath (Ps 33:6). Of course, Hebrew speakers have no need to choose, since the single word *ruah* encompasses all these nuances, but English translators are left with a dilemma that is not easily resolved.[5]

Another well-known and challenging use of *ruah* occurs in Ezekiel's vision of the dry bones (Ezek 37:1–14), where the word occurs ten times but with at least four different nuances:

[1] The hand of the LORD came upon me, and he brought me out by the spirit [*ruah*] of the LORD and set me down in the middle of a valley; it was full of bones. [2] He led me all around them; there were very many lying in the valley, and they were very dry. [3] He said to me, "Mortal, can these bones live?" I answered, "O Lord GOD, you know." [4] Then he said to me, "Prophesy to these bones, and say to them: O dry bones, hear the word of the LORD. [5] Thus says the Lord GOD to these bones: I will cause breath [*ruah*] to enter you, and you shall live. [6] I will lay sinews on you, and will cause flesh to come upon you, and cover you with skin, and put breath [*ruah*] in you, and you shall live; and you shall know that I am the LORD."

[7] So I prophesied as I had been commanded; and as I prophesied, suddenly there was a noise, a rattling, and the bones came together, bone to its bone. [8] I looked, and there were sinews on them, and flesh had come upon them, and skin had covered them; but there was no breath [*ruah*] in them. [9] Then he said to me, "Prophesy to the breath [*ruah*], prophesy, mortal, and say to the breath [*ruah*]: Thus says the Lord GOD: Come from the four winds [*ruhot*], O breath, and breathe [*ruah*] upon these slain, that they may live." [10] I prophesied as he commanded me, and the breath [*ruah*] came into them, and they lived, and stood on their feet, a vast multitude.

[11] Then he said to me, "Mortal, these bones are the whole house of Israel. They say, 'Our bones are dried up, and our hope is lost; we are cut off completely.' [12] Therefore prophesy, and say to them, Thus says the Lord GOD: I am going to open your graves, and bring you up from your graves, O my people; and I will bring you back to the land of Israel. [13] And you shall know that I am the LORD, when I open your graves, and bring you up from your graves, O my people. [14] I will put my spirit [*ruaḥ*] within you, and you shall live, and I will place you on your own soil; then you shall know that I, the LORD, have spoken and will act," says the LORD.

The first occurrence of *ruaḥ* is the divine spirit that brings Ezekiel to the valley (v. 1), but most instances of the word denote the breath that will animate the rearticulated bones (vv. 5–6, 8, 10). In verse 9, we read that this breath (*ruaḥ*) will come from the four winds (*ruḥot*), and in verse 14, we find *ruaḥ* not just reviving the people but empowering them to return to their homeland. Most intriguing of all in this passage is Yahweh's command to Ezekiel in verse 9 that he should prophesy *to* the *ruaḥ*, telling it to come forth from the four winds and breathe into the bones. The prophet relays this divine command to the *ruaḥ*, leaving the impression that the breath is somehow separate from Yahweh,[6] even though it is the same Hebrew word from the "spirit of Yahweh" in verse 1. This passage from Ezekiel, especially verse 9, demonstrates the remarkable elasticity of Hebrew *ruaḥ*.

Except for verse 14, translators have generally agreed on how to render the different uses of *ruaḥ*—"spirit" in verse 1, "breath" in verses 5, 6, 8, 9, and 10, and "winds" in verse 9. Some translate *ruaḥ* in verse 14 as "breath" (JPS) and others as "spirit" (NRSV, NABRE). "Spirit" is preferable because of the verse's echoes of verse 1, which include the repetition of the verb "to rest" (Heb. *nwḥ*) and the only two explicit mentions of the divine *ruaḥ* ("spirit of Yahweh" and "my spirit"). The latter connection is important because it shows that the various uses of *ruaḥ* in this passage are framed by clear references to the divine spirit. However else the word is used in the passage, *ruaḥ* has its beginning and ending with God.

This framing device leads me to a larger point about the various uses of *ruaḥ* in Ezekiel 37:1–14. Although translators are compelled to render the word three different ways and commentators are keen to distinguish the nuance of each usage, we should not fail to appreciate the capacity of the Hebrew language and worldview to hold all these meanings together. Biblical *ruaḥ* is first and ultimately a divine reality, but it is also one that is available to all of creation. Ezekiel's vision of the dry bones depicts that availability as both a feature of the created order (wind) and a gift from God (breath) that comes through the mediation of the prophet. This passage encapsulates the wide-ranging presence of *ruaḥ* as it moves between the divine sphere and the earthly sphere, and the prophet even envisions *ruaḥ* in verse 9 as an independent agent. The three English words required to convey this movement obscure the conceptual unity that is possible in Hebrew. The *ruaḥ* of God is the same *ruaḥ* that moves in and through creation, bringing new life and empowering humans to carry out God's plan of salvation.

How does this multivalence speak to the church today? For one thing, the Hebrew concept of *ruaḥ* opens us to a broader experience of the Holy Spirit. The tendency in the Old Testament to conflate the divine spirit with simple wind or breath implies that the spirit of God was not extrinsic from these earthly realities; they were signified by the same Hebrew word. This range of meaning invites us to adopt a similar openness to the presence of the Holy Spirit, such that the Spirit need not be separate from our mundane experiences. If the divine spirit can pervade something as commonplace and personal as our very breath, then what limit could we place on its manifestation? Such breadth is consistent with the Christian view of the Holy Spirit, which, as Richard Lennan has shown, is no less infinite than God's love revealed in Jesus Christ: "Since the purpose of the Spirit is to make present the love of God revealed in Jesus Christ, the love that…is unlimited in scope and extension, the presence of the Spirit cannot be restricted to one place or one form."[7] Faith in the "everyday" manifestation of the Spirit is a feature of the Catholic Charismatic Movement, as discussed in chapter 13, which calls attention to the gifts of the Holy Spirit that are expressed in the day-to-day practice of faith.

The unlimited scope of the divine spirit leads to a second point of comparison between Hebrew *ruaḥ* and the Christian understanding of the Holy Spirit, namely, the need for discernment of spirits. Just because every instance of *ruah* in the Old Testament could signify the divine spirit does not mean that every instance should be translated this way. Other translations are possible and often preferable. This ambiguity requires the translator to examine the context of each usage: to identify how *ruah* fits into the syntax of its verse and surrounding verses, to compare its translation in other versions of the Bible, such as the Septuagint, the Targums, and the Vulgate, and to weigh alternative meanings.

In this way, the translator's task is similar to the discernment of spirits in Christian prayer. People of faith, too, must distinguish between "how the Spirit moves" and "how the wind blows." In chapter 10, André Brouillette cautions against discernment that is too subjective (simply equating one's thoughts with the Spirit) or too objective (treating the Spirit simply as an external reality). He recommends Scripture, Tradition, and communities of faith as "ecclesial referents" that can ground individual discernment in the larger work of the Holy Spirit. Situating an individual experience of the Holy Spirit within the larger context of its presence in the church and the world is not unlike the Hebrew translator's analysis of *ruah*. Both tasks recognize that the presence of God's spirit cannot be separated from its context. Our understanding of God's *ruah* in the Old Testament requires a fuller knowledge of the Scriptures, just as our discernment of the Holy Spirit requires a fuller knowledge of the Spirit's work in Christian tradition and communities.

The Old Testament has much to offer Christian reflection on the spirit of God. Our survey of the Hebrew *ruah* highlighted the divine spirit as the source of all life, the force that binds creation to God's own life, and the power that enables humans to carry out divinely appointed tasks. After exploring this divine aspect of *ruah*, we examined the multivalence of the word that offers an important lesson about discernment. The elasticity of Hebrew *ruah* opens us to a broader experience of the Holy Spirit and requires a process of discernment that is analogous to the discernment of spirits in Christian prayer. Hebrew translation and Christian discernment involve similar challenges and call for the same kind of attentiveness. This challenge is not unique to Hebrew *ruah*, but its denotation of the divine spirit makes it an especially rich example of this correspondence.

7

The Holy Spirit and the New Testament in Light of Second Temple Judaism

Angela Kim Harkins

Our discussion of the Holy Spirit in the New Testament is informed by the different functions of the Spirit in Second Temple Judaism (519 BCE–70 CE), an era that followed Israel's return from the Babylonian exile.[1] The vibrant Second Temple period gave rise to what later became Christianity and Judaism. Biblical scholars of the nineteenth and early twentieth centuries scarcely paid attention to the Second Temple period, largely due to their quest for the historical origins of ancient Israel. Today, however, the study of the Second Temple period has emerged as a distinct field and a most suitable context for understanding the New Testament.

How we think about the past is profoundly shaped by our experiences in the present age. Two major events of the twentieth century have transformed our understanding of the New Testament: the Holocaust and the discovery of the Dead Sea Scrolls in 1947. The horrors of the Holocaust and the discoveries of those ancient writings by Jewish groups near the time of Jesus have forced scholars to reimagine the diverse expressions of Judaism during the time of Jesus. Consequently, there has been a transformation in how Christians think about themselves vis-à-vis the religious other. This broader appreciation for the diverse forms of Judaism prior to and contemporaneous with the New Testament period is an important characteristic of biblical scholarship in the last two generations.

Many disciplines in the humanities have felt the impact of the events of the First and Second World Wars, and biblical studies is no exception. The horrors of the Holocaust shined a spotlight on Christian understandings of Judaism, both past and present, leading many scholars to a more serious study of the Jewish identity of Jesus and his apostles. However, a word of caution: our aim to highlight points of continuity between ancient Jewish and Christian understandings of the Spirit is not to draw the conclusion that what we know as the Christian doctrine of the Holy Spirit was presented clearly in diverse forms of Judaism during this time. Instead, we seek to situate the understanding of the Spirit in the New Testament within its larger Jewish context. In doing so, we hope to encourage a greater awareness of and sensitivity to the relationship that Christians have with Judaism today.

The discovery of the Dead Sea Scrolls is rightly called the most important manuscript discovery of the modern period. It has not only opened a window to different forms of Judaism in the late Second Temple period (second c. BCE to early first c. CE); it has also transformed how scholars think about the earliest Christian groups. Rather than imagining Christianity as a single sudden rupture with Second Temple Judaism, often characterized negatively as a heavily legalistic and ritualized faith, the relationship between these diverse groups was more complicated and is better conveyed by the language of continuity and change. This broader appreciation for the diverse forms of Judaism prior to and con-temporaneous with the earliest Christians is a distinctive feature of the scholarship that emerged in the second half of the twentieth century.[2]

These fundamental changes in how scholars think about the biblical period serve as the backdrop for our discussion of early Christian understandings of the Holy Spirit. The Spirit not only played a key role in otherworldly ecstatic experiences, it was also instrumental in the acquisition of revelatory knowledge and the cultivation of virtues. In contrast to modern assumptions about experiences of the Spirit as immaterial and private, encounters with the Spirit in Second Temple Judaism and the New Testament effected this-worldly transformations and experiences. These transformative encounters were constitutive of how individuals understood themselves and how they came to be understood within their communities.

THE EARLIEST CHRISTIAN
UNDERSTANDINGS OF THE SPIRIT

Meredith McGuire opens her discussion of spirituality stating, "Many of us were brought up thinking that the spiritual realm is completely apart from the mundane material realm—perhaps even opposed to it....To the contrary, spirituality fully involves people's material bodies, not just their minds or spirits."[3] This point highlights one of the major assumptions that modern readers likely bring to this topic of the Spirit. As has been rightly noted in earlier chapters, the Spirit was experienced through the body and physical matter. Ancient understandings of spirit (*pneuma*) did not see it as disembodied and lacking in materiality. Within the broader Hellenistic world, *pneuma* was conceptualized as an airy substance that had a material quality but not density. David Litwa explains,

> Scholars and exegetes are more and more coming to the conclusion that it [*pneuma*] did not mean immaterial "spirit." It is more suitably translated by "breath" or "wind." Among ancient philosophers and medical professionals, it was thought of as a corporeal substance, though not a solid, earthly substance like earth and water. It was much more like air. Air, however, was thought to be naturally cold and misty, whereas pneuma was hot, fiery, fine, and subtle. Many Stoics described pneuma as a mixture of air and fire, and identified it with the substance of aether, or the fiery air that existed in the upper reaches of the universe.[4]

The material quality of the Spirit is also presumed in Paul's discussion in 1 Corinthians 15, in which he speaks about the pneumatic body.[5] The ancient understanding of the Spirit retains aspects of presence or materiality even though it is experienced in a variety of ways. Notably, experiences of *pneuma* were tied to transformations of the believer and changes in status that had consequences in this world. Experiences of the Spirit in the New Testament were not understood to be strictly interior, immaterial, or private.

Discussions of the Spirit in the New Testament may readily call to mind the ecstatic and vibrant understanding of the Spirit that is exemplified by the Book of Revelation, in which the Spirit transports John into heavenly scenes and reveals prophetic visions (Rev 1:10; 4:2). It is this efficacious power of the Spirit that allows for otherworldly journeys and the vision of the Son of Man, all of which are described in vivid detail (Rev 1:13–16; 4:2—5:14). So too, in the Book of Acts, Stephen is said to be filled with the Holy Spirit when he sees the glory of God in the heavens with Jesus at the right hand of God (Acts 7:55–56), a vision that follows his lengthy and impassioned speech recounting the history of Israel's transgressions. Yet, unlike Stephen's vision, John is not a silent observer of otherworldly events in the Book of Revelation; his transport into the heavens allows him to interact fully with the heavenly figures. These examples of prophetic ecstasy are not unlike the Spirit-induced state that enabled Ezekiel to see the visions recorded in that book (e.g., Ezek 2:2).

Scholars have long recognized the need to situate the earliest Christian understandings of the Spirit and its effects within a broader context, but what was noted in this relationship was the break between Christianity and Judaism.[6] Rather than highlighting ecstasy as the quintessential hallmark of the Spirit in early Christianity, we do well to broaden our scope to take in the multiplicity of functions that the Spirit had in the late Second Temple period, including intellectual activity (e.g., the writing and interpretation of Scripture) and the cultivation of virtues. In other words, visionary transport and otherworldly encounters illustrated in the Book of Revelation are but one of several interrelated experiences of the Spirit that early Christianity shared with other earlier and contemporaneous forms of Judaism.[7]

In what follows, we will briefly examine these three different types of pneumatic experience as they appear in the New Testament and contextualize them within the contemporary Jewish writings of the Second Temple period: (1) ecstatic experiences (e.g., prophecy, visions, and tongues), (2) the production and interpretation of sacred texts, and (3) the cultivation of virtues. These distinctions are useful for providing structure to our discussion; however, bear in mind that such categories are artificially imposed, since the experiences to which they refer are profoundly interrelated.

Ecstatic Experiences of the Spirit

The Holy Spirit is associated in the New Testament with key events that fall under the category of ecstatic experiences: prophecy, visions, and tongues. In the classic presentation of the Spirit in Acts 2, the disciples are gathered together during the Festival of Weeks (Heb. *Shevuot*), a feast that commemorated the first fruits of wheat. This pilgrimage festival is the only one that is not precisely calculated in the Hebrew Scriptures because its dating is tied inextricably to Passover. *Shevuot* was calculated by counting seven weeks after the waving of the *omer*, a ritual in which a bundle of the grains that had been harvested was offered ceremonially to the Lord. This occurred on the day after the Passover Sabbath or, for Greek-speaking Jews, fifty days (*pentecoste*) after Passover. While it is not explicitly identified as such in the Book of Exodus, *Shevuot* commemorates Israel's entry into covenant relationship with God in the wilderness at Mount Sinai.[8] For our discussion, it is notable that the festival of *Shevuot* was associated with the ingathering of members during the Second Temple period. Early Jewish traditions preserved in the Book of Jubilees also identify this feast with the making of the covenant and as the occasion for the subsequent renewal of the covenant (e.g., Jub 6:17–22). It is thought that the communities of the Dead Sea Scrolls also celebrated this festival as a renewal of the covenant and ingathering of new members.[9] In a similar way, the author of Acts associates the festival with the bringing in of new members; the experience of a strong rushing wind, fire, and the gift of tongues marks this event of transformation:

> When the day of Pentecost had come, they were all together in one place. And suddenly from heaven there came a sound like the rush of a violent wind, and it filled the entire house where they were sitting. Divided tongues, as of fire, appeared among them, and a tongue rested on each of them. All of them were filled with the Holy Spirit and began to speak in other languages, as the Spirit gave them ability. (Acts 2:1–4)

This passage reports a vivid bodily or this-worldly manifestation of the Spirit (for example, the gift of tongues). Like the Gospel of Luke,

Acts emphasizes forgiveness of sins (2:38) and promises "the gift of the Holy Spirit." The chapter ends with the report that three thousand individuals were baptized that day and that many more continued to be added day by day. The optimistic and programmatic account of the beginnings of Christianity in Acts 2 highlights the gift of tongues as the sure manifestation of the Spirit in this world.

While the language of the Spirit and the spiritual is often assumed to refer to private or interior experiences today, for the author of Acts, the Spirit and its manifestations are clearly concrete and physical. The effects of the Spirit are perceptible by those around who recognize the foreign languages that are being spoken. It is worth noting that this positive account of the gift of tongues in Acts differs from the situation described in Corinth in which Paul sees the gift of tongues as a threat to the unity of the community. According to Paul, tongues were "speech that is not intelligible" and a "speaking into the air" (1 Cor 14:8–9).[10] Instead, Paul urges the Corinthians to prophesy and to pray for the power to interpret so that the community as a whole may be built up. Despite the ambiguity over *glossolalia*, the gift of tongues, in the earliest Christian context (e.g., Acts 2 and 1 Cor 14), that gift exemplifies well the kind of ecstatic experience that was more commonly had in the Greco-Roman cultures of the late Second Temple period rather than that found in ancient Israelite prophecy.[11]

The Spirit's Role in the Production and Interpretation of Scripture

The ecstasy known from prophetic experiences of the Spirit is not unlike the role the Spirit plays in the production of Scripture and in the understanding of these texts, both of which were crucial during the time of the New Testament. The spiritual dimension of the process of interpretation is suggested by Paul when he exhorts the Corinthians to pray for the power to interpret prophecy rightly (1 Cor 14:4–5). Another clear reference to the instrumental role of the Spirit in the process of interpretation occurs in 2 Peter: "First of all you must understand this, that no prophecy of scripture is a matter of one's own interpretation, because no prophecy ever came by human will, but men and women moved by the Holy Spirit spoke from God" (1:20–21). The first century of the common era marks a time when the canon of Jewish Scriptures was still in formation and when the New Testament was being produced. What can it mean to be moved by the Holy Spirit in the process of the production of Scripture and its proper interpretation?

According to the first-century Hellenistic Jewish philosopher Philo of Alexandria, the Spirit assists in endowing understanding upon those who come to God "with mind unhampered and naked" (*On Giants* 53).[12] Philo, whose writings were preserved by Christians but not by later forms of Judaism, speaks here about the production of Scripture and the teaching and interpretation of texts as interrelated spirit-driven phenomena.[13] Philo gives us a way of imagining how intellectual and spiritual experiences were thought to converge in a moment of insight when he recounts the acquisition of knowledge as an ecstatic spiritual experience (*On the Migration of Abraham*, §34–35). Elsewhere in book 3 of *On the Special Laws*, Philo describes his own experience of studying Scripture, specifically allegorical interpretations of Scripture, as a kind of phenomenal ascent (§1–6). Similarly, Moses's ascent to Mount Sinai (Exod 24:2) becomes the occasion for Philo to discuss the transformative power that the Spirit exerts on the mind during its intellectual movement toward God (*Questions and Answers on Exodus* 2.29).[14] According to Volker Rabens, these and other experiences of *pneuma* in Philo speak to the "entire religious-ethical" transformation of the individual.[15] Such transformation is also presumed by early Christian writers who wrote about the Spirit's instrumental role in the reading and understanding of Scripture.

According to the author of the Book of Acts, Peter is "filled with the Holy Spirit" before he gives a bold defense of himself to the Jewish authorities in Jerusalem (4:8). Through this brief speech in which he cites a passage from Psalms 118:22, we read that Peter and his companions, otherwise uneducated men, made themselves known as the companions of Jesus. This particular psalm is one that is cited by Jesus in each of the Synoptic Gospels.[16] On the one hand, Peter's bold speech can be understood as a reenactment of a teaching that he learned from Jesus himself; on the other hand, it is also possible to say that it was the Spirit that transformed Peter's teaching into an experience of Christ's presence.

Another example of the Spirit's role in the teaching and interpretation of sacred texts is the story of Philip's encounter with the Ethiopian eunuch in the Book of Acts. This story of the eunuch's conversion is the second of four conversion stories presented in Acts: (1) the conversion of the Samaritans in Acts 8:1–25; (2) the Ethiopian eunuch in 8:26–40; (3) Saul of Tarsus in 9:1–19; and (4) Cornelius the centurion in 10:1–48. In each of these, the Spirit plays a critical role in the events that take place. While at first the "angel of the Lord" instructs Philip to go to the road to Gaza (8:26), later it is the Spirit who urges Philip to go directly to the chariot that is carrying the Ethiopian eunuch (8:29). In these scenes, the Spirit plays an instrumental role not only in bringing Philip to the eunuch, but also in his exegesis of the Isaian passage. These events, along with Philip's compelling testimony about the Gospel (8:35), eventually lead to the eunuch's baptism.

The Cultivation of Virtues

In addition to the extraordinary otherworldly manifestations of the Spirit in ecstatic states, the Spirit features too in the ethical behavior of the human person in this world. Paul combines features from both in his exhortation to the Philippians. There he writes that the Philippians can possess this quality of radiance and "shine like stars in the world" as "blameless and innocent, children of God" (Phil 2:14–15), if they succeed in putting aside their murmuring and arguing. Other passages in the New Testament closely identify the Spirit as God's abiding gift that dwells within and enables the virtuous life. The Johannine language of "abiding" or "remaining" suggests this image of the indwelling of the Spirit. In the opening testimony given by John the Baptist in the Gospel of John, the Spirit is said to "descend [on] and *remain*" in Jesus (John 1:33; emphasis added). This Spirit of truth (John 14:17; 15:26; 16:13) is the one who will come after Jesus and "remain" in the disciples (John 14:16–17). It is the indwelling of the Spirit that allows for virtuous activity such as bearing witness to the truth in the world (e.g., John 16:7–11).

These effects of the Spirit are similar to the ways in which virtuous dispositions and traits are described in Second Temple texts, such as the Book of Jubilees. Moses's opening prayer in that work asks God to "create for them a pure heart and a holy spirit," to which God responds, "I will create a holy spirit for them and will purify them in order that they may not turn away from me from that time forever. Their souls will adhere to me and to all my commandments" (Jub 1:21, 23–24). Such passages highlight that it is the Divine Spirit that animates ethical behavior. With a worldview presumed by this and other Second Temple texts, the author of 1 John uses similar language about different types of spirits to contrast the good spirits that dwell in individuals and those spirits that are in individuals who are not to be trusted (1 John 4:1, 5–6). Modern translations specify the *pneuma* of God in 1 John 4:2 in capital letters as the "Spirit of God," whereas the "spirit of the antichrist" (v. 3), the "spirit of truth," and the "spirit of error[/deceit]" (v. 6) are all put in lower case to signal the difference to readers in most modern translations of the Bible.[17] These are different kinds of spirits, illustrating how the indwelling of the Spirit was understood to be somehow similar to—albeit distinct from—the divine Spirit. As is suggested by Moses's prayer in the Book of Jubilees, the Spirit is instrumental in ethical behavior (cf. 1 John 2:28—3:10).

In his Letter to the Romans, Paul speaks broadly of how the Holy Spirit, as received from God, allows for the cultivation of virtues: "And not only that, but we also boast in our sufferings, knowing that suffering produces endurance, and endurance produces character, and character produces hope, and hope does not disappoint us, because God's love has been poured into our hearts through the Holy Spirit that has been given to us" (Rom 5:3–5). Elsewhere, Paul speaks of virtues as a manifestation of the Spirit and contrasts them with the vices that signify the works of the flesh (cf. Gal 5:16–26). Paul describes the fruits of the Spirit as "love, joy, peace, patience, kindness, generosity, faithfulness, gentleness, and self-control" (Gal 5:22–23). These virtues are well suited for the harmonious relations that Paul repeatedly urges in his letters, but especially so for the Galatians.

Finally, in a testimonial defense of his own authority, Paul's speaks of his own embodied virtues as evidence of the Holy Spirit:

> As servants of God we commend ourselves in every way: through great endurance, in afflictions, hardships, calamities, beatings, imprisonments, tumults, labors, watching, hunger; by

purity, knowledge, forbearance, kindness, the Holy Spirit, genuine love, truthful speech, and the power of God; with the weapons of righteousness for the right hand and for the left; in honor and dishonor, in ill repute and good repute. (2 Cor 6:4–8, translation altered)

Here the powerful effects of the Spirit in the form of virtues are presented in an evidentiary way. Given the circumstances of Paul's relationship with the Corinthians, the Spirit made manifest in Paul's virtuous capacities plays a crucial role in how he renegotiates his apostolic authority with that church. All of these passages discussed here speak about the transforming effects of the Spirit and how they are manifest in the virtuous life of the believer. Such understandings of the effects of the Spirit in the virtuous life have a long legacy in the Christian tradition.

CONCLUSION

While the fullness of the Christian doctrine of the Holy Spirit is not present in forms of Second Temple Judaism, there are notable points of continuity in how the Spirit was imagined as working in this world. The Spirit is said to act upon individuals in astonishingly unexpected and unpredictable ways. This means of access between this world and the otherworld demonstrates how individuals in the past understood themselves to be inextricably in relation with Christ and other beings who dwelled in the heavenly realms. The ecstatic experiences of prophecy, visions, and glossolalia are familiar ways in which we imagine the Spirit in the Christian life. Yet, in addition to these, we do well to remember how the Spirit plays a key role in the interrelated phenomena of the cultivation of wisdom and virtue. Together these experiences of the Spirit in the biblical period were constitutive of individual identities as "holy men and women," "prophets," "apostles," "believers," and "children of God." In brief, this survey of the diverse transformative effects of the Spirit in Second Temple Judaism and in the New Testament makes clear the notable point that this-worldly changes in identity and status were effects of the Spirit. The next chapter similarly highlights this significant role of the Spirit in the early church. These experiences of the Spirit in the New Testament period demonstrate how individuals in the past understood themselves to be in complex relationships with beings who were not of this world, pointing to the diverse and dynamic ways that self and identity were constructed within ongoing negotiations of power and status.

8

Three Sightings of the Holy Spirit in the Early Church

Francine Cardman

When the Apostle Paul arrived in Ephesus, he encountered "some disciples" and asked them if they had received the Holy Spirit when they became believers. They replied, "No, we have not even heard that there is a Holy Spirit." Since they had received only John's baptism of repentance, he baptized them "in the name of the Lord Jesus" and laid hands on them, whereupon the Holy Spirit came on them and they began to prophesy and speak in tongues (Acts 19:1–7). This small incident attests to the presence, absence, and potentially challenging role of the Holy Spirit in the lives of Christians then and now. It recalls John's promise of one who would baptize with the Holy Spirit and fire (Luke 3:16), as well as the tongues of fire and gifts of speech at Pentecost early in Luke's narrative (Acts 2:1–6). That formative moment is often regarded as the birth of the church, the beginning of the promised messianic age, in which God "will pour out [God's] spirit on all flesh; your sons and your daughters shall prophesy" (Joel 2:28). The newly baptized Ephesian followers of Jesus, caught up in the Spirit of prophecy, were a case in point.

Relating the spread of the gospel from Jerusalem "to the ends of the earth" (Acts 1:8), Luke casts his history of the church's beginnings as the embodied history of the Spirit in the world of the Roman Empire. Taking its lead from Luke's perspective, this chapter examines three "sightings" of the Spirit in the life of the early churches, events that led variously to recognition, resistance, and resolution among individuals, small groups, and emerging institutional leadership. The first is a second-century "charismatic renewal" movement known as the "New Prophecy," through which stricter codes of conduct were revealed to believers, and in which women prophets played a prominent role. The second focuses on martyrdom and apostasy in the third century, and the question of who was authorized by the Spirit to forgive serious sins. The third is the testimony of the "ordinary" gifts of the Spirit expressed in liturgy and prayer, which formed the experiential and theological basis for resolving the fourth-century controversy over the divinity of the Holy Spirit.[1]

THE NEW PROPHECY

The generations after the earliest churches continued to experience the Spirit's spontaneous manifestation in the gift of prophecy, as had been evident at Pentecost and among the Corinthians in Paul's time. Prophesying, speaking in tongues (glossolalia), and receiving visions, women and men invoked and acted on the Spirit's counsel. As churches grew in number and size during the second century, they could no longer rely on itinerant apostles, prophets, and teachers for guidance through their letters and occasional visits. More stable structures of ministry began to develop that, at least at the beginning, also embraced prophets who had chosen to settle in small, local churches. The long process of institutional development was uneven in its momentum and reach among churches in the cities and provinces of the Roman Empire. The offices of bishop, presbyter, and deacon did not take root widely or deeply until at least the mid-third century, while episcopal hierarchy consolidated later in the fourth.

The New Prophecy movement arose in Asia Minor (roughly southwestern Turkey today) at a time when social and political tensions in the region were heightened by the martyrdom of Polycarp, bishop of Smyrna, and others in that city (c. 155). In part, the movement may have grown out of tensions within the churches as prophecy and other spontaneous gifts seemed to recede in relation to evolving ministries and church order. Virtually no writings from disciples of the New Prophecy have survived; so much of what we know about it has had to be teased out from the writings of its opponents. Recent study of inscriptions and epitaphs has brought us closer to those who identified with the movement.

Montanus, Priscilla, and Maximilla began prophesying about 162. They proclaimed that the Spirit was speaking through them in the voice of the Father, Lord, Son, or Christ, revealing the new age of the Paraclete as promised in John's Gospel (John 14:15–17, 26). Their urgent message was the requirement of stricter spiritual discipline among Christians, the expectation of suffering and martyrdom, and the necessity of living *now* as citizens of the new Jerusalem promised in the Book of Revelation (Rev 21). The prophets emphasized fasting and sexual continence, and prohibited remarriage after a spouse's death. Those in the movement considered the renewed spirit of prophecy and its revelations to be the completion of Jesus's revelation, the perfecting of the church in a new age of the Spirit that would usher in the end. Opponents viewed the movement as disruptive innovation, false prophecy, and contrary to the revelation of Jesus and the Spirit as witnessed in the Scriptures. Both asked where the Spirit was to be found and followed.[2]

Among the striking aspects of the New Prophecy is the prominence of Priscilla and Maximilla. Assuming that Montanus was the real leader, opponents labeled the movement "Montanism," thereby demoting the women prophets to accessories. But their leadership was significant and their example not lost on women, who found the movement attractive as women's leadership was becoming marginalized in many church communities. The Spirit's authorization of women's voices and leadership through prophetic inspiration is a dynamic that reappears at times of change or marginalization of women in the church's history, as Catherine Mooney's essay shows. Later critics of the New Prophecy were particularly exercised by one of Priscilla's visions that may have been appealing to some women at the time, as it is for some today. She reports, "Appearing as a woman, Christ came to me in a bright robe and put wisdom in me, and revealed to me that this place is holy, and that it is here that Jerusalem will descend from heaven."[3]

The prophetic leadership of Priscilla and Maximilla, which followers regarded as authorized by the Spirit; the presence of women among the clergy established by Montanus for the churches of the New Prophecy; and the persistence of women prophets, deacons, presbyters, and bishops in the next generations of the movement were sources of irritation for bishops claiming to represent what is "catholic" in faith and practice—that is, both widespread and true—against what they regarded as Montanist sectarianism and error. In his *History of the Church*, Eusebius, bishop of Caesarea (c. 313–c. 340), quotes an early opponent who reported that Montanus had raised up two women, who had left their husbands and "whom he filled with the sham spirit, so that they chattered crazily, inopportunely, and wildly, like Montanus himself" (*History* 5.16).[4] That is, they prophesied in an ecstatic state, perhaps speaking in tongues, behavior that another critic charged was unheard of among prophets in Judaism or Christianity (*History* 5.17), despite the account of the Ephesian believers in Acts 19. "Holy bishops of the time" attempted to exorcise the evil spirits in Priscilla and Maximilla, but were kept away from the former and failed utterly with the latter. Maximilla reflects such opposition in an oracle: "I am driven as a wolf from the sheep. I am not a wolf; I am word, spirit, and power." Another early critic reported that groups of "catholics" had met in several parts of Asia around 179 and rejected the New Prophecy (*History* 5.16). But the movement continued nonetheless, empowered by the Spirit to whom both parties appealed and whose authority both claimed.

Near the end of the fourth century, the bishop Epiphanius of Salamis disapprovingly described something like a penitential ritual among later Montanists. In the service, seven virgins, dressed in white and bearing lamps, prophesied and led the congregation in lamentation over humankind's sins. Epiphanius also noted dismissively that "they have women bishops, presbyters, and the rest; they say that none of this makes any difference because 'there is no longer male and female; for all of you are one in Christ Jesus' (Gal 3:28)."[5]

Montanism as such perdured in Asia Minor into the sixth century, then began to fade away under the pressure of the emperor Justinian's new laws against heretics (c. 530) and the destruction of the shrine in Pepuza that contained the bones of the three original prophets (550).

MARTYRDOM AND THE SPIRIT

Even as the New Prophecy met with opposition in Asia Minor, its influence was felt in the West. Persecutions in Lyon (Gaul/southern

France) in 177 and Carthage (Roman Africa/Tunisia) in 202/203 evoked the movement's apocalyptic sensibilities, disciplined faithfulness, and receptiveness to visions. Half a century later, widespread imperial persecution provoked a crisis in Carthage over the spiritual credentials of martyrs and confessors and the ecclesial authority of bishops regarding the forgiveness of apostasy (250s). In both the earlier and the later persecutions, the power of the Holy Spirit was made manifest through the martyrs' witness, endurance, charismatic authority, and example. Yet not all were able to confess their faith under such duress. Was their failure forgivable, and on what authority? Could the Spirit that sanctified believers in baptism and empowered the martyrs' confession of faith also be the Spirit who forgives even the sin of apostasy?

Following the persecution in Lyon and nearby Vienne, Christians there sent a letter to churches in Asia Minor, from which many had emigrated, recounting the suffering and triumphs of the martyrs as a cosmic struggle in which Christ and the Spirit overcame the adversary (Satan) through their deeds. In Carthage, an unknown editor composed the *Passion (Martyrdom) of Perpetua and Felicity*, a narrative incorporating the personal accounts of two visionary martyrs, Perpetua and Saturus, and framed it as a demonstration of the Spirit's continuing activity in the church.[6]

Incidents in each city illuminate the baptismal and confessional dimensions of martyrdom and bear on forgiveness of sins. In Lyon, about ten of those arrested and interrogated had initially denied their faith. Expecting to be released, they were sentenced instead to die as common criminals. As confessors and deniers alike awaited their separate deaths, "The martyrs brought favour to those who bore no witness." The previously "stillborn" were reborn "through the martyrs" and "learned to confess Christ" (*Lyon*, 77). They died as martyrs (the root meaning of the term is "witness"), their apostasy washed away in a second baptism by blood. Learning to confess Christ through the martyr's example, they relied on what the Spirit gave them to speak at the time of trial (Mark 13:11). One of the deniers, Biblis, demonstrated this graphically by coming to her senses while on the rack, breaking the devil's grasp on her by confessing that she was a Christian (*Lyon*, 69, 71). Confession of faith, baptism (being born again), and forgiveness of sins are the work of the Spirit, whether by water or by blood.

In Carthage, there were no apostates among the catechumens who had been arrested and then baptized before they were imprisoned. The Spirit that empowered their confessions of faith—in baptism and during their trial—also spoke through Perpetua's prophetic visions while she was in prison. Having cried out spontaneously during group prayer the name of her brother Dinocrates, who had died at age seven, Perpetua began to pray for him. That night, she had a vision in which she saw him as the thirsty, dirty, wounded child who had died of a facial cancer; some days later she had another vision in which he had been transformed, now healed, washed, refreshed, and delivered from suffering (*Perpetua*, 8). Perpetua's visions of Dinocrates strongly suggest that her prayers for him affected his otherworldly baptism.

Perhaps they also had some subtle influence in the controversy fifty years later in Carthage about the Spirit's power to forgive serious sins after baptism, especially apostasy, and who was vested with the spiritual authority to extend that forgiveness. At the time of Perpetua's martyrdom, the churches in Carthage and Rome already permitted onetime forgiveness of murder and fornication. Tertullian, a brilliant, fierce, and prolific lay theologian in Carthage, described the practice approvingly in a small treatise *On Penitence* (c. 198–203). Under the influence of prophecy and the new, rigorous discipline revealed by the Spirit among some Carthaginian believers, however, Tertullian reversed himself and repudiated the forgiveness of apostasy, condemning at the same time flight during persecution, to which he had once also given his approval.[7] Tertullian's conflicting positions on forgiveness of sins and the discipline required of Christians facing persecution foreshadowed serious conflicts in North Africa and Rome in the mid-third century. The Holy Spirit's role in forming virtuous Christians, as noted in the previous chapter, is a key factor in Tertullian's reversals and the later controversy over forgiving apostasy.

The emperor Decius (249–51) attempted to shore up Roman civic religion and the imperial cult by issuing decrees requiring all people to sacrifice to the gods and obtain a certificate of compliance. The decrees fell most heavily on Christians; Jews seem to have been exempt. Large numbers of Christians capitulated. Once enforcement had ceased, many of the "lapsed" Christians sought to return to the church, creating a crisis about forgiveness of apostasy.

In Carthage, the crisis was particularly acute. Cyprian, the bishop, had taken shelter outside the city, overseeing the church through letters carried by presbyters who served as liaisons. Some Christians died as martyrs; others suffered harsh imprisonment. The latter were known as "confessors" for enduring the consequences of confessing their faith. They were regarded as filled with the Spirit, possessing the power to forgive sins. With Cyprian absent, some of the lapsed sought readmission to communion through "letters of peace" from the confessors. When the persecution ended, the North African bishops met and decided that the lapsed could be forgiven—but only by their bishops. They agreed to consider letters from the confessors, thus partially acknowledging their spiritual status, but firmly asserting episcopal authority as decisive. Similar decisions were taken in Rome. Underlying tensions, however, about the relationship of Spirit, office, and charismatic gifts remained unresolved.

Within a year, there were schisms in Rome and Carthage about forgiving apostasy. In Rome, conflict centered on whether apostasy could be forgiven at all. Was it the sin against the Holy Spirit that cannot be forgiven (Mark 3:28–30; cf. Matt 12:31–32; Luke 12:10)? In Carthage, the confessors and Cyprian clashed over the nature and sources of ecclesial authority and the power to reconcile the lapsed. Cyprian claimed the spiritual authority of office; the confessors claimed the spiritual authority of their witness and suffering, but also considered Cyprian seriously compromised by his absence during the persecution. Cyprian died a martyr in a subsequent spate of persecution, as did Stephen, the bishop of Rome (258). The fractures in theology, practice, and community were left unhealed, neuralgic points that would become inflamed again during the great persecution of Diocletian at the start of the next century, and continued into the early fifth century. Between the two persecutions, Christians enjoyed almost forty years of relative peace from imperial pressures.

THE DIVINITY OF THE HOLY SPIRIT

The fourth century marked a sea change in the life of the churches. After the trauma of Diocletian's persecution (303–11), Christians welcomed the emperor Constantine's formal toleration of Christianity (and all other religions) in 313. Constantine's reliance on the Christian God led him increasingly to favor the church in subsequent decades, but he was not baptized until he was on his deathbed in 337. Christianity's growing visibility and political influence were accompanied by the consolidation of episcopal hierarchy. At the same time, widespread theological controversy in the eastern part of the empire led to the development of trinitarian doctrine, which was confessed in the Nicene Creed and articulated in theological treatises over the course of the century.

This final "sighting" of the Spirit in the early church may, at first glance, appear to be quite different from the previous two. A second look, however, discloses similarities: it arises from and reflects the same complexities of the church's history and the embodiment of the Spirit in the world of the Roman Empire as do the others. It may lack the narrative drama evoked by the Montanists or the martyrs. But, I suggest, it brings us close to the ordinary experiences of the Spirit in the life of believers.

Of necessity, I leave aside here the controversies over the divinity of the Word incarnate in Jesus Christ that originated in a theological dispute in Alexandria (318) between the presbyter Arius (hence the label "Arian controversy") and his bishop, Alexander, then spread rapidly among laity and clergy in the East. Those disputes led to the Council of Nicaea and its Creed (325), which all but two bishops present approved and Constantine supported. Nevertheless, turmoil continued in the tumultuous decades that followed, until a more successful resolution took hold at the Council of Constantinople (381). In the mix of fierce theological conflict and politics (ecclesiastical and imperial), the Holy Spirit was a focus of attention from the 360s onward. Opponents and defenders of Nicaea struggled to interpret the crucial declaration of the Creed, that the Son/Word is "of the same nature (or being)" as the Father. Those rejecting the divinity and equality of the Word had no patience for speaking of the Holy Spirit's divinity when that question arose. Most of those supporting Nicaea took up the cause of the Spirit.

Recognition of the Holy Spirit's divinity coalesced especially around practices of Christian prayer, liturgy, and sacraments. These were lived experiences before they were the stuff of theological argument. Their trinitarian implications were drawn out, for the most part, only when lived questions demanded. To understand the fourth-century disputes about the divinity of the Holy Spirit, it is necessary to review briefly the liturgical life of Christians in the second and third centuries.

Early references to the baptismal rite report that new believers were baptized "in the name of the Father and of the Son and of the Holy Spirit" (Matt 28:19). They link immersion in the waters of baptism to the waters brooded over by the Spirit "in the beginning" (Gen 1:1–2). Instruction of candidates for baptism emphasized these ritual words, actions, and symbols, as well as the Spirit's role in forgiveness of past sins and rebirth to new life. Tertullian's treatise *On Baptism* (c. 198) is the earliest extended discussion of the elements of the baptismal rite and their significance: washing, anointing with oil (chrism, unction), and prayer, "the imposition of hands inviting and welcoming the Holy Spirit" (*On Baptism*, 8). Third- and fourth-century texts on liturgy and church order also record rites of exorcism that were part of preparation for baptism. There is a lively sense of the Holy Spirit's presence and power at work in each of these ritual actions.

The invocation of the Holy Spirit in the eucharistic prayers of the gathered community is discussed in more detail in chapter 4, so I will not focus on this important aspect of liturgy and the work of the Spirit. However, I will note that, as early as Justin's *First Apology* (c. 155), the presider gave praise and thanksgiving for the bread and wine "to the Father of the universe through the name of the Son and of the Holy Spirit" (1 *Apology*, 65). Justin also observed that, outside the liturgy, believers continued to give thanks for all they receive, blessing "the Maker of all things through his Son, Jesus Christ, and through the Holy Spirit" (1 *Apology*, 67).[8]

Emerging ordination rites in the third and fourth centuries centered on the prayer of all assembled that the Spirit descend on the one chosen and approved by all. In the ritual, the bishop voiced a formal prayer invoking the Spirit on behalf of all present, followed by laying hands on the one being ordained.[9] It is important to note that the act of laying on hands was older than Christian ordination rites and functioned in multiple contexts of prayer and blessing: baptism, exorcism, forgiveness of sins, and healing. In each case, it connoted and made present the power of the Spirit through the prayer of the believing community.

Praying, blessing, thanking; washing, anointing, laying on hands: all are verbal, visual, and bodily invocations and actions of the Holy Spirit. It is particularly in reference to these embodied experiences that theologians argued and the Council of Constantinople affirmed that the Holy Spirit is God. The creed approved at Nicaea ended with a half-sentence afterthought: "…and [we believe] in the Holy Spirit." The Creed of Constantinople, which today we call the Nicene Creed (because it affirmed and clarified Nicaea), expanded those few words into a full, third article of belief. Each statement in that final section affirms the work of the Spirit who gathers and unites (the church), forgives and sanctifies (baptism and the forgiveness of sins), and gives life and makes new (resurrection, eternal life). In these life-giving and sanctifying actions, as the recipient of prayer, and as the one who empowers prophecy, the work of the Holy Spirit is work that only God can do. Hence, the Spirit that proceeds from the Father (John 15:26) is God just as the Son begotten by the Father is God. What later councils would declare of their decisions can also be said of Constantinople in 381: "For it has seemed good to the Holy Spirit and to us" (cf. Acts 15:28).

Even the most prayerful decisions, however, can have unintended consequences, and the creedal confession of faith in the Holy Spirit's divinity was no exception. The Nicene Creed as put forth by the Council of Constantinople simply states that the Holy Spirit proceeds from the Father, period. Through an accident of history, the Creed as recited in the Western liturgy came to include a Latin addition, the word *filioque*, describing the Spirit's procession as "from the Father *and the Son*." It probably originated in sixth-century Spain, among anti-Arians, to bolster the Son's (Word's) divinity and equality with the Father by having the Spirit proceed from both. The addition made its way into the kingdom of Charlemagne (late eighth century) when he funded the production of liturgical books in which the Creed included the *filioque*. It reached Rome about 1000 and contributed to a schism between the churches of the West and East in 1054. A symbolic step was taken in 1965 toward resolving the schism when Pope Paul VI and Ecumenical Patriarch Athenagoras I met in Jerusalem and lifted the mutual excommunications of 1054. The *filioque* remains in the Western Creed today, however, a source of division still and a contested embodiment of the Spirit in history.

CONCLUSION

Each of the three sightings of the Spirit observed here could be thought of as asking and attempting to answer the question evoked by the story of Paul's encounter with the believers in Ephesus: *What Holy Spirit?* Each sighting can also be understood as reflecting and challenging the perceptions of persons and groups as to the whereabouts and activities of the Spirit as they recognize, name, and claim it, sometimes even as their exclusive possession. In each, we can observe the ways in which context shapes possibility and the Spirit eludes its limits. History is a messy affair, yet it is where we encounter and embody God's Holy Spirit. From that perspective, each of these historical sightings can also challenge us to reflect on the ways we recognize or refuse the Holy Spirit in the ongoing history of the church and the world in our day.

9

Medieval Writers

Women, Men, and the Holy Spirit

Catherine M. Mooney

Many people think of the twelfth through sixteenth centuries as the golden age of Christian spirituality because so many spiritual teachers and mystics emerged during this period and still inspire people today. Spirituality shares some of the same landscape as theology, but without being the same thing. Theology generally regards the study of God, and theologians often strive to articulate their insights in language that is both rational and organized. Spirituality has more amorphous boundaries and is less oriented toward a systematically analytical study of God. Spiritual texts convey insights about God, but are often more exhortatory, aiming to deepen the readers' experience of God. They include texts such as sermons, prayers, letters of advice, and accounts of personal encounters with God. It is more accurate to speak about spiritual*ities* rather than a single spirituality during these centuries because there is so much diversity among great spiritual teachers. This is certainly true regarding their understandings and experiences of the Holy Spirit.

In this chapter, I present a sample of their teachings, organizing them under three broad rubrics—monastic, mendicant, and mystical writers—each group representing a period in which they stood out. In the process, I will show that perspectives on the Holy Spirit are influenced not only by these varying religious identities and chronological periods, but also by the distinct social locations of men and of women. This can stimulate consideration today about how apparently theoretical spiritual ruminations regarding the Holy Spirit touch the very core of our existential lives.

MONASTIC WRITERS IN THE TWELFTH CENTURY

Monks and nuns devoted their time fully to the pursuit of God by fleeing society, enclosing themselves within monasteries, contemplating the Scriptures, and praying. Twelfth-century monastic spirituality had a corporate cast: as individuals bound for life to a community of like-minded seekers, they aimed to liberate themselves from an obsession with self to become part of a greater whole. Rather than analyze Scripture logically, they sought more to allow God's word to penetrate, inspire, and transform them. Monastic rumination on the Holy Spirit included less reasoning and more lyricism: it aimed to excite wonder and devotion. An optimistic confidence in an essential harmony joining God, human-ity, and the natural world is a hallmark of this period.[1] We see these qual-ities in two of the most influential monastic figures of this period, Bernard of Clairvaux (d. 1153) and Hildegard of Bingen (d. 1179). Both have been canonized as saints and proclaimed doctors of the church, indicat-ing that their spiritual teachings merit attention.

Bernard, one of the most prominent churchmen of his time, viewed with great suspicion the growing cadres of theologians who employed reason and logic to understand the things of God. If one word had to be chosen to characterize Bernard's spirituality, it would be love. God was, above all, love, and love is what bound the three persons of the Trinity into One. It is no coincidence that Bernard devoted many dozens of lengthy sermons to the Old Testament Song of Songs, an erotically charged poem celebrating the love between the bride and bridegroom, traditionally thought to signify the church and Christ, but in Bernard's sermons, often denoting as well the individual soul and Christ.

Following a well-established Christian theological tradition, love was the trait Bernard most particularly associated with the Holy Spirit. The Spirit infuses the bride with the interior virtues of faith, hope, and love that help the bride toward her salvation. Bernard recognizes the

Spirit's social dimension too, for like "perfumes sprinkled on the [bride's] breast," the Spirit pours exterior graces such as eloquence and the power to heal and to prophesy, gifts meant to be shared lavishly with one's neighbors, that is, one's fellow monks. Notably, Bernard cautioned that one first had to be filled interiorly with love before such gifts could brim over and be shared with others. His advice suited a monastic milieu where monks and nuns could, in relative solitude, cultivate the interior life, freer than people outside the monastery whose lives demanded constant interaction with many neighbors.[2]

Elaborating the Song of Song's best-known verse, "Let him kiss me with the kiss of his mouth" (Song 1:2, Latin Vulgate), Bernard calls the Holy Spirit "the kiss" of love that joins the lips of the Father and the Son. Christ the Bridegroom, in turn, gives that kiss, the Holy Spirit, to the bride, thereby drawing her into the erotic life of the Trinity. The bride represents both the church, as when Christ breathed the Holy Spirit on the apostles,[3] and the individual soul. Prioritizing love over academic knowledge, Bernard tells his listeners that they can know when they have been kissed by studying the "book" of their own experience. Finding there even the mere *thirst* for divine love is already a sign that one has tasted the kiss of the Spirit. With grace, ardor expands and, to the one who knocks, God will always open the door to greater intimacy.[4] The Spirit that is love is more than emotion for Bernard. Indeed, it opens the path to self-discovery, inspires one to charity, and imparts true knowledge.

Hildegard of Bingen (d. 1179) is one of the most multitalented figures of the twelfth century. Most known today as a visionary, Hildegard was similarly accomplished as a theologian, artist, musician, playwright, scientist, healer, preacher, politician, and religious founder. Like Bernard, this monastic nun wrote in allegories and metaphors rather than the discursive logic prevalent in medieval schools. Deeply trinitarian, she divides her best-known visionary work, *Scivias* ("Know the Ways of the Lord"), into three parts aligned with the three persons of the Trinity: creation (the Father), redemption (the Son), and sanctification (the Holy Spirit). One of her visions, the Trinity in Unity, is a flame: the Father being brilliant light shining on the faithful; the Son scarlet power in whose body divinity declares its wonders; and the Holy Spirit fiery heat "burning ardently in the minds of the faithful."[5]

Hildegard of Bingen:
Miniature from the
Rupertsberg Codex
of the *Scivias*

Hildegard was already in her forties when she launched the visionary career that would make her famous. She had experienced visions
since her childhood, but kept them mostly to herself, finding them
strange and doubting God would speak through such "a poor little
woman." But finally, God breaks through. One can discern the Spirit's
role in her enlightenment since she uses the Spirit-associated terms of
fire and heat to describe this momentous event:

> It happened that…when I was forty-two years and seven
> months old, Heaven was opened and a fiery light of exceed-
> ing brilliance came and permeated my whole brain, and
> inflamed my whole heart and my whole breast, not like a
> burning but like a warming flame, as the sun warms anything
> its rays touch. And immediately I knew the meaning of the
> exposition of the Scriptures.[6]

Hildegard had manuscript illuminations painted to depict her
visions. The image above, which she also oversaw, shows the fiery flames
entering her brain and inspiring her with divine knowledge, which her
avid monk secretary, Volmar, sought to hear and record. Indeed, like
other women of her time barred from formal study and preaching,
Hildegard could speak, write, and preach only by claiming that none of
her words were her own, but rather all came to her and through her
directly from God. Spirit-filled speech replaced her long years of silence.

Prelates, the powerful, and the poor sought her divine knowledge to settle both theological and this-worldly matters. A prior called her the "revered dwelling place of the Holy Spirit," while an abbot felt he was consulting the Holy Spirit itself when consulting Hildegard.[7]

Hildegard would have shared many of Bernard of Clairvaux's claims about the Spirit—indeed, the two were acquainted and he helped persuade a pope to allow her to write. But while Bernard's sermons often focus on the monk's personal growth, Hildegard's theological treatises highlight the grand themes of salvation history and the relationship between the divine and natural worlds. Drawing on the traditional theory of four elements—earth, fire, water, and air—Hildegard presents the Spirit as a suffusing presence vivifying the cosmos and individual soul. The Spirit warms, moistens, and "greens" humanity. Just as it breathed soul into the dry dust of Adam, so too through baptism and the waters of virtue the Spirit irrigates and rehydrates souls parched through sin.[8] Both monastics, however, optimistically portray a natural world shot through with supernatural realities, the divine dwelling within, and beckoning both soul and cosmos to spiritual salvation.

MENDICANT WRITERS IN THE THIRTEENTH CENTURY

In the thirteenth century, people became increasingly attuned to the growing disparities between the poor and rich in a society that continued to prosper, but without sharing the wealth equally among all people. While monastic life still flourished, many people sought out new forms of religious life that would allow them to be Christians "in the world," pursuing lives of devotion outside monastic enclosures, among and in service of their neighbors. A new attention to all things human in this period tended to de-emphasize a focus on the divine, powerful, and conquering Christ and emphasize instead the human, humble, and suffering Christ who walked with them as a brother. This intense reflection on the second person of the Trinity colors many formulations of the Holy Spirit.

Mendicants, most famously represented by the Franciscan and Dominican orders, were among the new religious groups arising at this time. In tune with their times, mendicants centered their spirituality on the poor, crucified Christ. Desirous of sharing their lot with him, they chose to live in poverty and, in fact, derived their very name, "mendicant," from the Latin term for begging (*mendicans*), a practice that enhanced their proximity to the poor Christ and aligned them also with the poor prevalent in medieval cities whom, along with others, they sought to serve. This new Christology influenced both Francis of Assisi, the founder of the Franciscans, and his celebrated follower Clare of Assisi to write about the Holy Spirit in very particular ways. In contrast to Bernard and Hildegard, Francis and Clare left no comprehensive treatments regarding the relationship of the divine and human worlds. Rather, we cull their views from texts such as rules and letters written for very specific purposes. Inhabiting a world more evidently rent by social tensions and each leading a religious community beset by controversies, they speak in less allegorical and more literal language to address specific problems.

Francis, perhaps the best-known and best-loved saint of all time, was so popular by the time of his death in 1226 that he was canonized within just two short years. He often invokes the Trinity and peppers his writings with references to the Father, Son, and Spirit. But his indisputable focus is on Christ, poor and humble, two virtues that in Francis's mind are inextricably bound together. He counseled his brothers to follow Christ's footprints, reminding them of Jesus Christ's words: "Sell everything you have and give it to the poor…and come follow me" and "take up [your] cross and follow me."[9] In a revealing move that seems to elide the Holy Spirit and Christ, Francis several times spoke of the "Spirit of the Lord," that is, the Spirit of Christ.[10] While Francis would have, of course, acknowledged that the persons of the Trinity were both three and one, he underlines the relationship of both God the Father, and God the Spirit, with Christ, the second person.

This association of the Spirit with Christ comes through again in a remarkably original statement about Christians' multifaceted relationships with God. Francis exhorts them to be "spouses, brothers and sisters, and mothers" of the Lord Jesus Christ. He elaborates, correlating each of these relationships with a person of the Trinity. First, we are spouses when "joined by the Holy Spirit to the Lord Jesus Christ." Here,

Francis uses the Latin term for "joined" (*conjungere*) that was often used in this period to speak of "conjugal" relations.[11] This recalls, in part, Bernard of Clairvaux's and others' notion of the Holy Spirit as love or a kiss, but Francis here keeps the focus more solidly on Christ. Second, we are brothers and sisters when we do the Father's will (see Matt 12:50). Although not explicitly stated here, doing the will of the Father, for Francis, always involved following the Son in poverty and humility. Finally, we are mothers of the Lord Jesus when we "carry Him in our heart and body through a divine love…and give birth to Him through a holy activity which must shine as an example before others." Francis thus associates our identity as spouse with the Holy Spirit, our identity as brother or sister with the Father, and our identity as mother with Christ, but all three of these relationships, as he underlines at the outset, relate us to the Lord Jesus Christ.[12]

Clare of Assisi (d. 1253), also canonized within two years of her death, was one of Francis's first followers. Documents suggest that before church authorities required her to live enclosed in a monastery (a regulation affecting many religious women), she may well have lived much like Francis's first male followers, living from the work of her hands and alms, tending to the sick and needy, and cultivating a spirituality focused on the poor, crucified Christ.[13] Her writings have preserved yet one more of Francis's unusual formulations regarding the Holy Spirit. In a clear departure from traditional expressions regarding an individual's relationship with the Holy Spirit, Francis claimed, wrote Clare, that she and her sisters had "espoused themselves to the Holy Spirit."[14] In other words, rather than stating that the Holy Spirit joined the women as spouses to Christ, Francis was claiming that the Holy Spirit itself was their spouse. The Marian overtones of this statement are unmistakable, especially since Francis elsewhere called Mary herself "Spouse of the Holy Spirit."[15] Francis frequently and more conventionally spoke of Christ as spouse, and in specific comments to Clare and her sisters, he makes clear that he expected them to live the "perfection of the holy Gospel," which for Francis always meant following Christ in poverty and humility. Perhaps even more so then does his unconventional conviction that the women were themselves spouses of the Spirit stand out.

But how did Clare herself think about her and her sisters' relationship with the Holy Spirit? An ardent admirer of Francis, Clare—even after many of Francis's followers began to stray from his command to live in radical poverty—remained within the tight circle of followers who continued to hew to his teachings. So, it is notable that while Clare quoted Francis's statement identifying the Holy Spirit as her and her sisters' spouse, she herself never speaks of the Spirit in these terms. In one of four letters to her close associate Agnes of Prague, Clare twice echoes Francis's triple formulation, calling Agnes spouse, mother, and sister of Jesus Christ.[16] Indeed, adhering to conventional spousal language, Clare reserves the term *spouse* for Jesus Christ alone.[17] She repeatedly spoke of herself as a follower of Christ, although tellingly, after her death, men who wrote about her escalated Francis's Marian remark about Clare by more insistently patterning her after Mary.[18]

Clare's Christ-centered spirituality accommodates the Spirit in brief phrases that are more suggestive than definitive. For example, Clare writes that the "Spirit of the Lord"—the same phrase used by Francis—called Agnes to a life of perfection. "Perfection" here indicates a life following Christ in poverty and humility.[19] Elsewhere, Clare, echoing Francis, admonishes her followers to desire to "have the Spirit of the Lord and Its holy activity."[20] But who or what is this Spirit—the Holy Spirit, the Holy Spirit in relationship to Christ, or simply the spirit of Christ himself? Since capitalization is a modern convention imposed on these medieval texts, it is hard to know. A similar ambiguity surrounds Clare's comment contrasting the "tongue of the flesh" with the "tongue of the Spirit" (or "spirit").[21] Indeed, only once does Clare seem surely to be speaking of the Holy Spirit. In an emotional farewell letter written just before her own death to her friend Agnes, Clare rejoices in "the joy of the Spirit" because Agnes has been espoused to Christ.[22] The little light shed in Clare's (admittedly rather brief) corpus nonetheless illuminates an important point about the Holy Spirit in this age: attraction to the human Christ who saves was so concentrated that it was difficult to speak of the Spirit without immediately adverting to Christ.

MYSTICAL WRITERS IN
THE FOURTEENTH CENTURY

The Holy Spirit's prominence among spiritual writers increased in the later Middle Ages. The reasons for this change are complex, but one dynamic merits mention. Once academic theology—the theology that the monk Bernard had so scorned—became ensconced and the predominant mode of theology in schools across Europe, it lost some of its early sheen. Learned clerics, earlier confident that their new logical methods might aptly explain many Christian truths, grew more skeptical about logic's reach as their own theological arguments sometimes foundered in apparent contradictions and dead ends. An aura of mystery surrounded more of Christianity's deepest truths.

Some curious gender fallout attended this development because officially recognized theologians were men; indeed, women were barred entirely from theological schools and universities. While religious men had many avenues for spiritual achievement open to them—whether they were priests, preachers, teachers, or saints, for example—religious women had very few. Women, considered by both men and women to be the moral and intellectual inferiors of men, attained significant spiritual authority almost only when they recognized themselves and were recognized by others as conduits through whom God and, more particularly, the Holy Spirit spoke. This was a two-edged sword: on the one hand, women were mere empty vessels through whom a greater authority spoke—their words were not their own; on the other hand, since they communicated God's words rather than mere human words, what they said trumped anything even the most educated cleric might say.

Certainly, too, the Spirit spoke through men, but significantly, the learning of great schoolmen such as Thomas Aquinas (d. 1274) began to be portrayed increasingly as a gift of the Holy Spirit. Not only theologians, but also laypeople began to pay more attention to the Holy Spirit, believing that the Spirit could directly influence all the baptized.[23] This assumption opened new doors to spiritual spaces formerly less accessible to laypeople, including women. Close studies of holy people during these centuries show categorically that holy women, much more than holy men, were likely to be recognized as visionaries, prophets, and recipients of divine messages.[24] The extraordinary case of prelates turning to a woman like Hildegard of Bingen in the twelfth century multiplied in this later period as learned men and others turned to inspired women to solve theological conundrums or obtain other sorts of divine information. Thus, we have the astonishing examples of the aristocratic nun Bridget of Sweden (d. 1373) and the simple lay Dominican woman Catherine of Siena (d. 1380) admonishing popes to return an exiled papal court to its seat at Rome. These and numerous other women, well known in their own day if less so in ours, gathered round themselves circles of devotees, including religious and laity of both sexes and clerics. In one intriguing case, the male and female followers of a holy woman came to believe, after her death, that she had been herself the very incarnation of the Holy Spirit.[25]

DISCERNMENT OF SPIRITS

But the more democratized spiritual leadership facilitated by the growing belief that God spoke through many types of people itself provoked other changes. First, the Holy Spirit's perceived activity during the late premodern period stimulated renewed interest in the discernment of spirits. Discriminating between the influences of good spirits (thought to be associated with God and the Spirit) and evil spirits (associated with Satan) traces its origins to earliest Christianity. But treatises on the art of spiritual discernment only really took off in the fourteenth century when scholars at the University of Paris, the most important theological school in Europe, responded to the upsurge in people claiming divine revelations. Crises such as the bubonic plague, famines, brutal wars, and a papal schism further prompted suspicions that diabolical spirits were at work.

Second, in some quarters, this enhanced scrutiny created a backlash against the less privileged in society, including women. Most influentially, the Parisian master Jean Gerson (d. 1429), in a series of manuals on discerning spirits, shored up male clerical prerogative by asserting a hierarchy of credibility: divine communications received by prelates, theologians, and others in high ecclesiastical positions were more likely to be from good spirits than those received by people lower down the hierarchy.

Women, in Gerson's view, were particularly susceptible to spiritual deception. In fact, he disputed the canonization of Bridget of Sweden and criticized both her and Catherine of Siena for proffering deluded advice to popes. Ironically, Gerson's learned skepticism regarding inspired people, especially women, backfired on him when, toward the end of his life, he defended Joan of Arc (d. 1431). Joan was soon thereafter condemned to death in a clerical trial that used Gerson's own rules for the discernment of spirits to reject the maiden's claims that the voices she heard were good rather than evil spirits.[26] Curiously, the Holy Spirit is hardly named during Joan's lengthy trial. Spirits, both good and evil, had seemingly taken on a life of their own.

Third and finally, the theological turmoil surrounding spirits was the soil for the witch craze that killed thousands of people, mostly women. More positively, however, it nurtured new approaches to discerning the action of the Spirit, as chapter 10 will discuss in relation to Ignatius of Loyola (d. 1556) and Teresa of Avila (d. 1582). In the heated sixteenth-century climate regarding good and evil spirits, these two guides, it is worth noting, each had to negotiate their own run-ins with an Inquisition still wary of interior spiritual experiences. While ever aware of the action of diverse spirits themselves, each guide subtly and positively joined the discernment of spirits with the confident belief that the Holy Spirit is always present urging the seeker toward love.

The men and women discussed in this chapter articulate strikingly distinctive conceptions of the Spirit. Kiss of intimate love; font of interior virtues; source of neighborly charity; voice of the silenced; vivifying force of the cosmos; spouse of the poor; divine inspiration mimicked by demons—although none of these images necessarily excludes the others, the Spirit clearly seems to shape-shift according to the varying human desires and needs of diverse chronological periods, religious identities, cultural contexts, and gender status. The wind blows where it will; one hears its sound, but does not always know where it comes from or where it goes. Thus, the evangelist John evokes a Spirit permeating the earthly environment yet evading full human grasp (John 3:8). So too, it seems, the monastic, mendicant, and mystical writers discussed in this chapter suggest an ever-elusive Spirit who, like the weather, is always changing and full of surprises.

10

Discerning the Action of God

André Brouillette, SJ

Discerning God's voice is an art more than a science. It entails a quest for a God who is in action, who cannot be seized, but certainly felt and heard. A radical choice of attentiveness to the discreet traces of the Spirit's passage must be made, and unfold over time. The tradition inherited from our holy predecessors, both through their lives and teachings, can guide the discerner along the way.

The Holy Spirit is hard to seize and depict. For that reason, the creedal statement of the Council of Nicaea (325) simply named the Spirit alongside the Father and the Son in one movement of adoration. The Council of Constantinople (381) delicately added some qualifications about the third person of the Trinity, as the one who is giver of life and has spoken through the prophets. Medieval liturgical hymns, expressions of the faith of the church in prayer, developed the understanding of the Spirit as Creator, the one who fills the earth and hearts, the giver of gifts, of light, and of truth. The Spirit is impelled to come: *Veni Creator Spiritus*, *Veni Sancte Spiritus*, conveying the belief that the Spirit is God in movement.

However, the Holy Spirit has not generated the same literary or artistic creativity that the second person of the Trinity has. The Son is the unique *icon* of God, God's face and image, and the very Word of God. The Spirit is by nature neither. Consequently, the difficulty of depicting and voicing the action of the Spirit is rooted in her nature. But the Son is not the only active person of the Trinity; the Spirit constitutes the very means of the continued presence of God to human beings. Since the action of God in the world is channeled in the Spirit, it is the language of the Spirit that should be deciphered by human beings to detect the divine action in the world.

In this chapter, we will attempt to unravel and illustrate the language of the Spirit in human life. How can the action of God be deciphered by discerning the promptings of the Spirit? The teachings of two great Spanish saints of the sixteenth century, Teresa of Avila (1515–82) and Ignatius Loyola (1491–1556), contribute much to the endeavor. Following a brief presentation of both saints, we will see how Ignatius's emphasis on interiority, on tracing God's presence in one's life, illuminates the language of God. Then, the dynamics of the movement of the Spirit will be sketched in a threefold way, following a framework based on Teresa's writings. Finally, the chapter, drawing also on insights from the twentieth-century theologian Yves Congar (1904–95), will highlight some criteria and agents for discernment.

TERESA OF AVILA AND IGNATIUS LOYOLA

Ignatius Loyola and Teresa of Avila were contemporary Spanish mystics. They were even canonized together in 1622, alongside Francis Xavier. Although they never met, Teresa knew about Ignatius, even mentioning him among holy founders of religious orders.[1] Teresa also had extensive contacts with members of the young Society of Jesus. Most famously, she had spiritual conversations with St. Francis Borgia, who was to become a spiritual author and successor of Ignatius. Teresa also took advantage of the foundation of the Jesuit college of St. Giles in Avila; some Jesuits became her trusted spiritual advisors. Over the years, Teresa and the Society collaborated closely in a variety of apostolic enterprises. The Ignatian influence on Teresa is crystal clear.

Teresa was a prolific author, and many of her writings are autobiographical, starting with the book of her *Life*. Even the *Interior Castle*, though organized systematically, and not chronologically, offers a thinly veiled account of Teresa's own spiritual journey, especially in the highest mansions. As such, Teresa's writings present an extensive and invaluable narrative of her original experience in the Spirit. Teresa also wrote didactically to support the spiritual growth of her sisters, especially with her

Way of Perfection, but her teaching is marked primarily by the testimony of her experience, her own and that of others she encountered. Her witness has spoken to countless generations, and she is still read widely today. Here, we will not draw on the didactical teaching of Teresa on prayer and spiritual life, but on the testimonial wealth of her embodied experience of being Spirit filled.

The writings of Teresa stand in stark contrast with those of Ignatius Loyola. Although Ignatius dictated to a Jesuit companion some spiritual reminiscences about the important years of maturation of his vocation and left spiritual notes covering a few months of his life, his contribution is not primarily one of direct testimony. His magnum opus is the *Spiritual Exercises*, whose enduring value is uncontested as a Christian guide to discernment. The *Spiritual Exercises* are divided into four "weeks" or steps. At first, the retreatant is led to confront his or her sinfulness, but also God's mercy. The second week emphasizes the discipleship of Jesus and one's personal vocation and mission in the footsteps of Christ. The third week is centered on the passion of Christ, which was the result of his carrying out his mission; it constitutes a reality check for anyone who wishes to follow him. The fourth and final week highlights the resurrection of Jesus and the sending forth of the disciples. At the heart of the pedagogy of the *Spiritual Exercises* lies the discernment of the Spirit that the retreatant is called to master progressively.

We will highlight some features of that spiritual pedagogy in this chapter, as Ignatius will provide us with a fruitful framework to envision the action of the Spirit in our life. Teresa's theology of the Holy Spirit, as seen through the narration of her spiritual journey, will illustrate and dialogue with the Ignatian insights with which she herself was familiar. Considering the enduring value of the theological insights of both Teresa and Ignatius, as well as their originality and their complementarities, they are helpful dialogue partners in our quest for discerning the action of God.

THE LANGUAGE OF GOD

At the beginning of his *Spiritual Exercises*, Ignatius states unequivocally that the person giving the exercises ought to let the "Creator and

Lord communicate himself directly to the faithful soul."[2] The role of the spiritual director is thus not to speak God's word—not even through the words of the Bible—but to lead the retreatant to hear how God is speaking to her or him. What is assumed here is that God has a language in which God communicates directly with human beings. Teresa even alludes to the language that the Spirit "seems to speak."[3] As is illustrated by the images and metaphors of fire, wind, or dove used to describe the action of the Holy Spirit, God speaks beyond the word, and God's language is not merely discursive. The "language" of the Spirit differs from that of the word, but is totally aligned with it.

Hence, the presence of the Spirit in one's life is not typically captured by words, but by the traces of the Spirit's passage. The nondiscursive language of the Spirit pertains to the affective realm; we are eminently *touched* by the Spirit. Saint Paul locates the recognition of the presence of the Spirit in the fruits of her presence: love, joy, peace, patience, kindness, generosity, faithfulness, gentleness, and self-control (Gal 5:22–23). These effects are not intrinsically divine; they can come also from external elements, or from oneself. The recognition that it was indeed the Holy Spirit who gave a feeling or inspired words or actions can sometimes be achieved in retrospect: we can judge a tree by its fruits, as the saying goes. Like the disciples on the road to Emmaus whose eyes were blind to the presence of the Lord at their side, we often realize God's presence a posteriori, by reflection on what we have already experienced. Looking at the fruits brought unexpectedly by a gesture, an encounter, a word, or a life choice, one can fathom how even something which appeared at the time small, insignificant, or frail can be recognized as inspired by the Spirit. However, to distinguish the *source* of ideas, words, potential actions, feelings, or desires in *real time* is not easy to achieve, since in the maelstrom of our mind and heart, many different desires, affects, memories, grudges, and information collide that can overpower God's whisper.

With this challenge in mind, Ignatius developed a grammar of the language of the Spirit. The two basic signs of that grammar are consolation and desolation.[4] Consolation, on the one hand, is akin to Paul's fruits of the Spirit: inner peace, joy, and love. While experiencing consolation, the individual feels closeness with God, expressed as faith and trust. That closeness with God can also be experienced in the form of tears while praying or thinking about Christ's passion; thus consolation cannot simply be equated with a feeling of happiness or contentment. Desolation, on the other hand, entails sadness, dryness, a feeling of estrangement from God, lack of faith, hope, and charity. During an Ignatian retreat, the retreatant is placed in ideal conditions to recognize and then monitor the inner movements affecting him or her. As when learning a new language, the individual has first to grasp the landscape of that language, its sounds, referents, scope, and general music. By being attentive to the inner movements of consolation and desolation, one becomes more sensitive to noticing with greater acuity the traces of the Spirit in him- or herself.

When the ground is established, the issue of the "speakers" arises: Who has a voice in one's inner life? Are all inner promptings and movements, especially positive ones, signs of the Spirit? Using the anthropology of his time, Ignatius distinguishes three main speakers. The first is *oneself*! We are the main agents of our inner lives, thoughts, and so on. Unlike contemporary psychology, Ignatius's attention is mostly focused on the elements that are not coming from us, the discernment of "spirits."[5] The second speaker is the "*good spirit*," which is God in the Holy Spirit. Ignatius is prudent in his use of the vocabulary of the Holy Spirit,[6] referring often to divine auxiliaries, for example, the "good angel,"[7] but notwithstanding the apparent spiritual mediations, the identity of the source is unique: the Holy Spirit. It is God in action, discreetly, in one's life. The final speaker in that inner realm is the "*evil spirit*," which Ignatius qualifies as the "*enemy* of our human nature,"[8] presenting him as a personified principle. The evil spirit unfortunately can interfere and even mimic some imprints that God can leave in our interiority. Such potential forgery forces the development of a more detailed grammar beyond the basic signs of consolation and desolation, taking into consideration, for example, the context of a specific consolation or desolation as well as the alternation between them.

It is worth noting here that Teresa also experienced both the inner movement of the Spirit and the challenge of discernment. In her early years of robust spiritual life, following her rededication to contemplative prayer, Teresa was advised by her confessors to reject vehemently her visions of Christ, which they attributed to the devil.[9] It happened in a religious context that was suspicious of women's spiritual experiences and conscious of the risks of unregulated experiences of the Spirit.[10] While obedient, Teresa never wavered in her conviction that the spiritual impulses she experienced were coming from God. The soundness of her judgment was finally confirmed when she encountered a confessor who—in her assessment—knew the "language of the Spirit."[11]

The challenge of discerning the voice of God must be engaged on two fronts. On the one hand, one must track the inner movements daily, and over time. For that purpose, Ignatius promoted the "examen," the daily examination of one's inner self.[12] The examen is the central spiritual tool for discernment in the Ignatian tradition. Ignatius himself presented various "versions" of the examen and spiritual writers continue to follow that lead.[13] At its core, the examen is a reality check of one's relationship with God in a spirit of thanksgiving, truth, and desire for a greater union. As part of the examen, the following questions can be addressed: Am I in desolation or in consolation? How do I fare in my relationship with God and others? If I am considering an important decision, have I perceived some inkling of God's confirmation for one option or another? Over time, the discerner gains through the daily examen a greater acuity of perception of those inner movements, and can also see the unfolding of one's inner life: How do consolation and desolation alternate over time? Where and when do I experience consolation or desolation? Ignatius himself kept a diary where he would write down in a few words the daily movements of his inner self, especially in prayer.

In addition, Ignatius offers a grammar as to the way the Spirit usually speaks. He draws upon the long tradition of discernment in the church, as well as his own experience as a learner and a teacher, to offer some "rules" about God's language of interiority.[14] These rules guide us in reading the signs of one's inner life, and discern both the source of those signs, as well as their usual unfolding. Ignatius's rules are divided into two sets: for beginners, and then for more subtle discerners. This suggests that the hearer of God's voice can become more conversant with that language over time through experience and guidance. The potential development of fluency leaves open the possibility of reaching a level that goes beyond the grammar, while respecting its rules. This would be the "poetry" of the saints, whose lives in the Spirit exceed grammatical exercises to reach an original sense of beauty. Saints bear witness to the vast horizon beyond the basic grammar of interiority.

GOD IN ACTION

The rules for discernment in the *Spiritual Exercises* present the interplay of God's action and the individual's response from the vantage point of the inner life, although they also illuminate the particulars of the Spirit's action.[15] Taking a different path, the dynamics of the Spirit can be uncovered in the testimonial teaching of Teresa of Avila as a threefold movement of disjunction, emptying/incarnation, and inspiration.[16] This movement is also confirmed in an essential locus: peace. Let us unpack these various insights.

The Spirit *disjoints, disrupts, shakes up, urges, brings newness.* This is the first moment of the Spirit's movement, a movement that reflects the "ecstatic" dimension of experiences of the Spirit that was noted in chapter 7. On the negative side, the disruptive component of the action of the Spirit is highlighted by Ignatius when he states that the good spirit would prick the conscience of individuals who are on the path from bad to worse,[17] attempting to waken them. The disruption of the Spirit also plays in a positive key. When Teresa narrates experiences of spiritual ecstasy (*arrobamiento*), her vocabulary underlines the disruption of the everyday realm:[18] a strong impulse (*ímpetu*), a feeling of being "outside" oneself and without natural forces, as well as a distortion of time, since the ecstasy is as short as its content is dense.

These descriptive elements of the experience of the Spirit imply a clear change or disjunction from the preceding state. In the realm of action, the Spirit would also initiate a movement by disruption. For example, an unexpected and troubling vision of hell constituted the initial event that ultimately led Teresa on her way to establish a reformed monastery.[19] In a similar vein, the seemingly innocuous talk of a missionary about the souls lost in India for lack of missionaries brought Teresa to deep sorrow and eventually prompted the foundation of a series of monasteries as a way to cooperate to God's desire of salvation.[20] The disruption (by the Spirit)—either by an inner intervention or through the agency of others—of Teresa's rest constitutes a theme of her narratives describing the foundation of new convents: at a time when she could legitimately enjoy the fruits of her labor, a request for a new foundation appears, whose unfolding and final realization bears the providential mark of the Spirit.[21] Disruption by the Spirit creates a crack, an opening into which the Spirit can enter and create a new space.

The second moment of the dynamic of the Spirit is a concomitant movement of *emptying and incarnation*, inviting a configuration to God in Christ.[22] The paradigmatic example is that of Christ himself, whose own movement of self-emptying, or *kenosis*, is expressed powerfully in Paul's letter to the Philippians (Phil 2:5–11). However, that movement of emptying is not an end in itself, but a means to free up space to allow a new reality to take shape. Luke's story of the incarnation highlights the role of the Holy Spirit for the "becoming-human" of Christ; its narrative structure inspired Teresa's account of the foundation of the first reformed Carmel, San José, a new space of and for God.[23] Like Mary, Teresa was called to prepare a place for Christ to inhabit, grow, and be revealed. For all human beings, the (usually) slow process of being configured to the image and likeness of the image of God—Christ himself—is guided by the Holy Spirit, the same Spirit that filled Mary, accompanied Jesus, and was then bestowed on the disciples after Christ's death and resurrection. The Spirit strives to create something new in human beings.

The final moment of this dynamic is *inspiration*; the Spirit inspires, guiding toward action. This action could take the form of deeds or words—not excluding prayer. For active saints, like Ignatius, this does not come as a surprise. The Acts of the Apostles also underlines the agency of the Spirit in guiding the early church in its proclamation of the gospel. Even Teresa, whose call was to a strict contemplative life, was inspired to take on the very active roles of founder, reformer, and writer.[24] Hence, the Spirit, after the inner workings of emptying and incarnation, thrusts the believer into a renewed active life, this time guiding him or her into words and deeds that would manifest God's presence to the world.

At the heart and at the end of the interaction between Spirit and believer lies *peace and intimacy*. Peace is listed as one of the fruits of the Spirit in Paul's writings, but Teresa would elevate it to the pinnacle: it is the sign of God's presence par excellence, even in times of troubles. Such inner peace is the result of the intimacy between the human being and God in the Spirit. One of the last documents from Teresa, written a year before her death, exudes this sense of a peaceful intimacy with God, as the more extraordinary spiritual phenomena had vanished.[25] Ignatius also alludes to that peaceful presence of God when he says toward the end of his life that he could find God any time.[26] The link between divine intimacy and peace is drawn in the seventh rule of discernment of the second week of the *Spiritual Exercises*, where the action of the Spirit in the receptive human being is depicted as soft and gentle, like a drop of water reaching a sponge.[27] We find here, on a personal scale, the "harmony of the Spirit" sought on the ecclesial scale in chapter 12 in part 3.

DISCERNING THE LANGUAGE OF THE SPIRIT

Guidelines are useful on a journey of discerning God's voice. Indeed, one of the main reasons for "fearing" the Holy Spirit throughout history is the risk of mistaking one's fancy for the will of God. The array of inner voices could lead to a disruption, or even a destruction, not intended by God; the Spirit doesn't have the monopoly of disruption! The distinction between God's will and one's own remains even in a context of intimacy and cooperation. One's thoughts should not be confused with the promptings of the Spirit. Nor should the Spirit be relegated to a purely exterior code. The interplay of an evanescent divine imprint and of one's inner self calls for a healthy uncertainty and a continued quest.

French theologian Yves Congar, in his monumental trilogy on the Holy Spirit, identifies three dimensions to discernment: the doctrinal or objective discernment, the subjective or personal discernment, and the discernment within the community.[28] The *subjective* dimension is what comes to mind initially when we talk about discernment, especially in the Ignatian tradition, but the other two dimensions are also essential, even for Teresa and Ignatius. For a genuine discernment, one needs to look beyond oneself. We will rely on Congar's three-part typology as we unfold the other two criteria for discernment in an Ignatian and Teresian key.

The *doctrinal* or *objective* discernment acknowledges that a tradition has arisen from the reality that the Spirit has spoken throughout the years to—and through—countless individuals, groups, and the whole church. The commandments, the Bible, but also a broader tradition, which includes the saints and revered spiritual teachers and movements, are recognized as inspired by the Holy Spirit. All the above provide an objective benchmark by which any personal discernment should be measured. If the subjective discernment and the objective dimension appear to be in disagreement, the matter has to be probed more carefully. The objective dimension was central to any discernment for Teresa, since she declares that she would rather die a thousand deaths than go against the smallest ceremony of the church,[29] highlighting a conviction that the church, as filled with the Holy Spirit, constitutes an absolute criterion for discernment.[30]

The third dimension, that of the *community*, incorporates other living beings in the discernment. They, too, can listen to God's voice, and they might have a say in a discernment regarding a person. The discerning party can be the whole church, for example, in the case of the discernment of a vocation to ordained ministry, but also, on a smaller scale, a spiritual director, who is a genuine discernment partner, not simply a depositary of the objective dimension or a mirror of the personal discernment.

What emerges from Congar's analysis is the need for an "ecclesial referent." That ecclesial referent is not simply constituted by a set of laws or rules, or even only by the tradition—though it integrates all those elements—but constitutes a living and discerning other, embodied paradigmatically in the person of the spiritual director. Ignatius, for one, never envisioned that someone could venture alone into spiritual life and discernment, and Teresa wrote frequently about the care in the choice of a spiritual director.[31] The *Spiritual Exercises* were given by someone who had received them previously, and received by another. The spiritual director is at once teacher, guide, mirror, and fellow hearer of God's voice. She or he brings an element of *otherness* to the living relation at work in discernment. The ecclesial referent provides a mediation— without becoming a "middle man"—of the action of the Holy Spirit, both through his personal discernment while hearing, and through his carrying the wealth of the tradition.

CONCLUSION

The title of this chapter, "Discerning the Action of God," highlights the conviction that God is active in our world and our lives. The activity of God is primordially that of the Spirit, present and at work in every heart. The title also expresses the desire of the believer to find God's will in one's daily life, in one's activity, and to follow it. God is active in one's inner journey, but such presence of God needs to be discerned. One must learn the language of the Spirit.

This quest is lived out in companionship with others whose own act of listening to God's voice forms people into patient hearers and doers. The genuine presence of the Spirit bears fruits and leads forward. God, in the Spirit, is in movement, disrupting and emptying, and inviting human beings to join in the trinitarian dance of the incarnation.

PART 3

Embracing the Holy Spirit

11

Oscar Romero

Renewed by the Spirit

O. Ernesto Valiente

In the course of his pastoral ministry, Oscar Romero was transformed from a cautious and traditional priest into a prophet and martyr. This chapter explores the action of the Holy Spirit in the process of that transformation. It considers Romero's formation and early pastoral work, then focuses on his episcopal ministry in Santiago de María and the first six months of his tenure as archbishop of San Salvador. This is a particularly fruitful period in which to examine the Spirit's agency in Romero's life because it marks a transition in how he perceived his ministerial role.

Instead of an approach that considers only Romero's direct references to the Holy Spirit in his preaching and writings, we will also examine the guiding presence of the Spirit through Romero's appropriation of the theological virtues, which the *Catechism of the Catholic Church* teaches are "the pledge of the presence and action of the Holy Spirit in the faculties of the human being" (1813). Hence, taking an approach that stresses Romero's experience within his own situation, we will examine how his appropriation of the virtues that flow from grace—faith, love, and hope—shaped him as a "heroic witness of the kingdom of God."[1] While acknowledging the deeply interrelated nature of the three theological virtues, we will also argue for the primacy of the Spirit's incarnating love as the main source and reason for Romero's transformation.

THEOLOGICAL AND SPIRITUAL FOUNDATIONS

By all accounts, Romero was, from early in his life, a person firmly grounded in the Christian faith. Oscar Arnulfo Romero was born on August 15, 1917, in Ciudad Barrios, a small town in eastern El Salvador. He grew up in a modest home cared for by a very religious mother. At the age of thirteen, young Oscar entered the minor seminary and six years later the diocesan seminary in the province of San Miguel. Because of his maturity and intellectual promise, he was sent in 1937 to complete his priestly formation in Rome, where he studied at the Jesuit-run Gregorian University.

Like any other Catholic seminarian in the 1930s and '40s, Romero's theological training reflected the language and approach of neo-Scholasticism, an ahistorical method that conceived theology as a deductive science, one that drew conclusions from principles that were regarded as divinely revealed. Theological reflection began with church teaching and applied the implications of this teaching to concrete experiences of the lived faith. Neo-Scholastic theology also tended to emphasize the mission of Christ over that of the Holy Spirit, and to overstress the separation between the world and God—that is, between the natural and the supernatural orders of reality. Romero's notebooks from that time reveal a preference for classics in spirituality including St. Teresa of Avila, John of the Cross, and especially the sixteenth-century Jesuit Luis de la Puente.[2]

From 1937 to 1943, Romero lived in the Collegio Pio-Latino-Americano Pontificio, which was also run by the Jesuits. There, he was introduced to Ignatian spirituality and to the austere and demanding version of the *Spiritual Exercises* practiced by the Spanish Jesuits in Rome at that time.[3] Romero was planning to continue doctoral studies in ascetical theology and had decided to write his dissertation on the work of Fr. de la Puente.[4] Theologian Damian Zynda argues that, for Romero, de la Puente "symbolized an ideal of holiness focused interiorly—on theological ideas, spiritual practices of piety, and body-denying penances."[5]

Whatever influence de la Puente might have had, it seems that Romero's way of encountering God and the world was, at least until he became archbishop, largely influenced by some of the negative features of neo-Scholastic theology. His actions evinced a spirituality that tended to separate reality into two planes of existence—the divine and the human; the sacred and the profane. Such a tendency intimates that to live a rich spiritual life, a person needs to escape from the materiality of the daily world. As exemplified throughout most of Romero's priestly life, he showed a propensity to prioritize the interior and individual dimension of his personal relationship with God at the expense of the social and political dimensions of his faithfulness. For our purposes, it is also important to note that the proclivity to escape the world can distort the dispositions (faith, hope, and love) that mediate the Spirit's presence in our lives and, in a manner of speaking, prevent the Spirit from fully incarnating therein.

A HOLY AND TIRELESS PRIEST WITH HIS HEAD IN THE CLOUDS

Romero was ordained in Rome in 1942, but his advanced theological studies in spirituality were interrupted by the Second World War, which forced him to return to El Salvador the following year. Back in the city of San Miguel, Romero assumed diverse ministerial and administrative responsibilities in the diocese. Romero himself would later attest that throughout these twenty-three years in San Miguel, he was "buried under paper work."[6] During this time, Romero was widely known as a kind, traditionalist, and austere priest. Nobody questioned his faith commitment—he was what people often call "a holy priest."

Romero's privileged position as a church leader in San Miguel—an agrarian province with a few magnificent coffee plantations and large numbers of impoverished peasants—allowed him to move effortlessly between different social circles and nurture many lasting friendships among both the rich coffee growers and the poor. It is striking that, despite Romero's personal austere piety, his pastoral approach toward the poor majority was not that different from that of the Salvadoran church hierarchy: he was charitable toward the poor but did not seriously question the reasons for their plight. Theologian Martin Maier recalls the words of a parishioner during Romero's time in San Miguel: "Father Romero was a friend of the poor and the wealthy. To us, the poor, Romero said to love God because God knows what he is doing by placing you last in the line. For later on, you will receive heaven."[7] Such sanguine and naive hope differs radically from the prophetic and transformative hope that Romero would proclaim during the last three years of his life.

Having been appointed secretary of the Episcopal Conference of El Salvador in 1967, Romero, now a monsignor, left San Miguel and moved to San Salvador. His exemplary administrative work soon led to his promotion, in 1968, as Executive Secretary of the Episcopal Secretariat of Central America and Panama. Then, in 1970, at the age of fifty-three, Romero was appointed auxiliary bishop of San Salvador.

In San Salvador, Romero continued to make the Ignatian spiritual exercises regularly while he also drew closer to the Opus Dei community. Indeed, "[He] admired Opus Dei for its fidelity to the church, its commitment to work, and its 'supernatural sense': traits that he cultivated in his own life."[8] Romero's discipleship was largely exercised by attending to his ministerial responsibilities and the development of his interior life: prayer, devotions, and an array of ascetic practices. Considering his forthcoming episcopal ordination, Romero decided to do a week of Ignatian spiritual exercises. His spiritual notebook offers a small window into his concerns and priorities at the time. There, he comments on his experiences of "sweet intimacy with Jesus" and jotted down his commitment to "know the Church and my place and duty to her each day more. Fidelity to the magisterium. Her doctrine is my criterion."[9] There he also outlined his immediate resolutions: "(1) celebrate Mass with more fervor; (2) better preparation of confession; (3) faithfulness to the breviary; spiritual guidance; midnight matins."[10] Irrespective of what one might think of his devotional practices, Romero was without doubt a man of faith, hope, and love dedicated to serve God and Christ's church. And yet, these virtues did not seem to take into consideration or question his surrounding social reality.

A VOLATILE SITUATION

As auxiliary bishop of San Salvador (1970–74), Romero witnessed a period of rapid change and social deterioration that paved the road for a looming civil war. After decades of fraudulent elections, many Salvadorans had lost confidence in the electoral process. Hence, they began to affiliate with different types of revolutionary organizations to bring to the streets the grievances of the population at large. At the same time, the Salvadoran church had engaged a process of deep renewal fueled first by the Second Vatican Council (1962–65), and later by the Second Conference of Latin American Bishops at Medellín (1968). The bishops at Medellín had examined the structural injustice in which the Latin American people lived and condemned its "dismal poverty, which in many cases becomes inhuman wretchedness."[11] The then archbishop of San Salvador, Luis Chávez y González, along with a significant number of local priests and religious, had begun to implement the new pastoral directives from Medellín, but most other bishops, including Romero, viewed these directives with suspicion. The renewal caused a rift within the Salvadoran church hierarchy that for many years had sided with the authoritarian governments that protected the interests of the Salvadoran oligarchy. Old alliances and interests persisted within much of the local church, and many of its leaders remained deaf to the pleas of the poor.

In 1971, Romero was appointed editor of *Orientación*, the diocesan biweekly newspaper, which gave him a platform to address the national situation. He described the country as threatened by a situation of widespread confusion. In a famous editorial piece, he wrongly accused the Jesuit high school, which had begun to implement the principles of Medellín, of leading their students "down the path of demagogy and Marxism."[12] In a 1972 editorial, Romero's traditional view of the church was on clear display when he rhetorically asked, "In the whirlwind of struggles, contradictions, ideologies, opinions, theories, and interpretation...who should [the regular Christian] believe?...The answer is to believe, listen, and obey the magisterial teaching, which resides mainly in the Vicar of Christ."[13] In different editorials, Romero lavishly enlisted Paul VI's pronouncements, the documents of Vatican II, and the declaration of the Salvadoran Episcopal Conference to shed light on the current Salvadoran situation.[14]

Conspicuously absent from his sources are the documents from the Latin American Bishops Conference at Medellín, which Romero complained were often misinterpreted and whose manipulation could lead to violence.[15] Thus, while the bishops at Medellín had identified the *signs of the times* in the experience of the poor who were beginning to organize for their rights, Romero saw in those same events only confusion and threat. It was as if his faith—misinformed by the prevailing ecclesial culture and the political interpretation of the dominant social class—had impeded his capacity to discern the movements of the Spirit working in his immediate history. Put in the contemporary words of Pope Francis, one could say that, at this stage, Romero exhibited a spirituality of illusion that "sees things only as we wish them to be...but does not accept what the Lord places before our eyes."[16] This illusory and escapist spirituality prevents the theological virtues from being properly actualized. Hence, up to this time, Romero largely evinces an abstract and idealized faith that was seemingly blind to the *signs of the times*, a hope that robbed Christ's promises from their critical and prophetic function in the present, and a generic love that prevented him from taking a preferential option for those in most need.

THE SPIRIT'S INITIATIVE

After four years as auxiliary bishop in San Salvador, Rome appointed Romero bishop of the diocese of Santiago de María on October 15, 1974. With this sojourn to the eastern part of the country, Romero would embark on a slow but intense process of personal transformation. Some theologians who collaborated closely with Romero, such as Ignacio Ellacuría and Jon Sobrino, have described this process as one of "conversion," but Romero himself preferred to speak of an "evolution" of his overall availability to the Spirit of God.

Romero's new see had a population of around half a million people. It was mostly rural with various plantations owned by a few, while 70 percent of the rest of the population lived in poverty.[17] Traveling by Jeep, and, whenever necessary, horse or mule, to remote villages and hamlets, Romero embraced his pastoral responsibilities in earnest and began to reacquaint himself with his people.[18] Years later, in conversation with Fr. Cesar Jerez, the Jesuit provincial, Romero succinctly described the impact of his time in Santiago de María on his "evolution":

> It's just that we all have our roots, you know…I was born into a poor family. I've suffered hunger. I know what it's like to work from the time you're a little kid….When I went to seminary and started my studies, and then they sent me to finish studying here in Rome, I spent years and years absorbed in my books, and I started to forget about where I came from. I started creating another world. When I went back to El Salvador, they made me the Bishop's secretary in San Miguel. I was a parish priest for 23 years there, but I was still buried under paperwork….Then they sent me to Santiago de María, and I ran into extreme poverty again. Those children that were dying just because of the water they were drinking, those campesinos killing themselves in the harvest.…You know Father, when a piece of charcoal has already been lit once, you don't have to blow on it much to get it to flame up again….So yes, I changed. But I also came back home again.[19]

Romero's personal reencounter with his people also rekindled his love for them. Their precarious situation elicited a compassion that drew him closer to them and prompted him to look beneath the ideologies that were attempting to justify his people's social and economic plight. Suffering, as noted in the final chapter, can make us most attentive and open to the Spirit's creative activity; this was certainly true for Romero. It is noteworthy that the influence of the Spirit upon Romero during this transformative time did not manifest primarily through his faith or his hope, but through his love—that is, through compassion. As his conversation with Fr. Jerez above reveals, love appeared as the origin of Romero's transformation. Such love would be instrumental in reshaping his faith and hope, as well as his overall engagement with his nation's reality. In other words, in Romero's process, love functioned as an epistemological condition for a renewed faith and hope, and led to what later would unfold as a deeply incarnational spirituality.

Perhaps because the Spirit respects the person's integrity and accommodates herself to the circumstances of the person's life, Romero's transformation was not instantaneous. In Santiago de María, he enlisted the diocesan newspaper, *El Apostol*, to criticize the local coffee landlords for not paying fair wages to their laborers, but leveled his complaints in a rather general and indirect fashion. After the National Guard tortured and massacred six peasants in a town close to Santiago de María, Romero wrote to the nation's president in protest, but chose not to denounce the action publicly. Nevertheless, clearly Romero's theological faith and pastoral practices were in a state of transition. Two Passionist priests, who were running a pastoral center in the diocese and worked closely with Romero at that time, attest that, when confronted by the pastoral needs of the local communities, Romero began to reexamine the texts from Medellín and to reflect on the insights of liberation theology.[20]

THE INCARNATED SPIRIT

On February 23, 1977, as the political and social situation continued to deteriorate throughout the country, Oscar Romero was appointed archbishop of San Salvador with the full support of the government and the dominant class. Less than three weeks later, on March 12, 1977, one of his best friends, Fr. Rutilio Grande, SJ, was assassinated. This tragic event marks a turning point in the new archbishop's life. Grande had been working as a pastor in Aguilares, a poor rural parish thirty miles north of San Salvador, where peasants had organized and were now asking for fair wages and better working conditions, angering local landlords. Grande and two of his parishioners were killed when their car was riddled with bullets as they were driving to a church service.

Theologian Jon Sobrino accompanied Romero to Aguilares after Grande's murder and later described how shocked the archbishop was when he first saw his friend's lifeless body, as "hundreds of campesinos [stared] at him wondering what he was going to do about what had happened."[21] Romero himself later recalled his own thoughts: "When I saw

Rutilio dead, I thought, 'if they killed him for what he was doing, it's my job to go down that same road.'"[22] At Grande's funeral the following day, Romero preached about Grande's life and ministry: "True love is what brought Rutilio Grande to his death....A priest with his peasants, going to his people to identify himself with them, to live with them...because love is what inspires us, brothers and sisters."[23] If Romero's experience in Santiago de María had enkindled his love for the poor, it was Grande's martyrdom and his grieving community that lifted up the demands—and the possible cost—of such incarnated love.

It is not surprising that Romero's Sunday homilies in the following weeks emphasized the agency and transformative power of the Holy Spirt. On April 7, he reminded his church that "as prophetic people anointed by the Spirit," they are called "to announce and encourage goodness and to denounce and condemn evil."[24] On May 15, Romero preached that Christ sends his Spirit "so that the politician...will transform politics into an instrument of God...so that the capitalist...will transform and humanize his capital...so that the workers, the poor, the outcast...will see in this church something that transforms their poverty into redemption, so that they are not led down paths of resentment and class struggle."[25]

As Romero began to enter more deeply into the reality that surrounded him, and assumed what Theresa O'Keefe describes in her chapter as a more *relational* way of seeing the world, his theological faith began to shift accordingly. Three months after his friend's death, Romero was compelled to return to the town of Aguilares to console its community once again after the military had violently occupied the town and killed dozens of peasants. In his homily to the battered survivors, Romero not only connects their sufferings to those of Christ, he also identifies them with Christ crucified. Drawing on the readings from Zechariah 12:10–11 and Luke 9:18–24, the archbishop told the peasants gathered before him, "You are the image of the divine one who was pierced...of Christ nailed to the Cross."[26] Guided by the Spirit of truth who leads us to Christ (John 16:13), Romero discerned Christ present in the life of his suffering brothers and sisters—incarnated in those crucified. This new light marked a watershed in the process of Romero's spiritual transformation and set the direction in which his pastoral ministry would evolve.

A NEW BEGINNING

Just two months later, on August 6, 1977, Romero celebrated the Feast of the Transfiguration with the publication of his Second Pastoral Letter, *The Church, the Body of Christ in History*. In the letter, Romero articulates, in a programmatic fashion, the new incarnational ecclesiology and the renewed mission that would set the direction for the Salvadoran church.

Romero opens his letter by stating his desire to offer a word of faith and hope to all Salvadorans: faith to shed light on the crisis of the Salvadoran situation and the hope of the good news of the gospel. Romero acknowledges that for a long time the church thought of human history as something provisional and ephemeral: "It seemed that the history of humankind and the history of salvation ran along parallel lines... but Medellín put an end to...the dichotomy between the temporal and the eternal, the secular and the religious, between the world and God."[27] With a renewed understanding of his ecclesial community as transcendent but firmly rooted in history, Romero writes, "The church is the flesh in which Christ makes present down the ages his own life and his personal mission."[28] Mindful that the church partakes of the trinitarian mission, Romero adds, "She therefore understands Christ's preference for the poor, because the poor are, as Medellín explains, those who *place before the Latin American Church a challenge and a mission that she cannot sidestep and to which she must respond with a speed and boldness adequate to the urgency of the times* (Medellín Documents, *Poverty*, #7)."[29] Romero concludes this programmatic letter by encouraging the church's fidelity to Christ and his mission to thus become "with him, the builders of his kingdom here in El Salvador, for the happiness of all Salvadorans."[30]

As is well documented, for the next three years and up to his martyrdom on March 24, 1980, Romero's exemplary leadership set the pace for a prophetic church that placed the most vulnerable at the center of its concerns, while he put his life and his church in the hands of the Spirit who led him to Christ incarnated in the lives of his persecuted church. Romero's faithfulness to this incarnated Spirit became evident in a love that denounced injustice, sought reconciliation, and stood in solidarity with Christ's poor. Although these actions of love and solidarity always came at a cost, they generated hope for an entire nation, because they began to express in a limited but real manner Christ's eschatological promises. Romero's hope was none other than the hope of his people— the hope for justice, forgiveness, and reconciliation. This same love also informed the deepening of Romero's faith, which continued to illuminate and respond to the demands of the nation's critical situation. Thus, he defended Christ's truth and struggle against the idols that preyed on the nation: the absolutizing of wealth, the ideological manipulation of national security, and the delusion of violence.

In the end, Romero's faithfulness attests to a freedom that is willing to make itself utterly available to God. His transformation testifies to the Spirit of compassion who breaks through our limited conceptions of the divine to offer us new eyes, to create us anew in Christ, and to mission us as church to recreate the world.

12

Spiritual Charisms in the World Church

Margaret Eletta Guider, OSF

The Holy Spirit would appear to create disorder in the Church, since he brings the diversity of charisms and gifts; yet all this, by his working, is a great source of wealth, for the Holy Spirit is the Spirit of unity, which does not mean uniformity, but which leads everything back to harmony.

—Pope Francis, *Homily on the Solemnity of the Holy Spirit*
(May 19, 2013)

This chapter draws attention to the role and function of religious orders and ecclesial movements in the world church today, highlighting the action of the Holy Spirit in the living out of the spiritual charisms associated with those orders. While holding fast to hope in the harmony of charisms as envisioned by Pope Francis, we cannot ignore the existing tensions and unreconciled divisions between, among, and within religious orders and ecclesial movements, as well as the toll that such discord takes on the people of God. Though some members of the church are unaware or unaffected by this reality, others have direct knowledge and experience of the disruption and disunity it generates and sustains over time. By way of concrete examples, a few come to mind:

- Parishioners impacted by a radical change in parish life when a religious order of priests withdraws from the parish and an ecclesial movement assumes parochial leadership

- Diocesan clergy resentful about the appointment of bishops who are members of a religious order or ecclesial movement, rather than priests from their own ranks

- Young people drawn into the posturing for prominence and competition for popularity exhibited by some members of ecclesial movements and religious institutes at international events such as World Youth Day

Experiences such as these serve as reminders of how easily communities of faith can become casualties of the discord of charisms. They also highlight the need for more intentional ecclesial efforts to reflect critically on the nature of charisms and the way they are discerned *from above* and *from below*.

Mindful of these experiences and the contemporary ecclesial concerns to which they draw attention, we begin with some background on spiritual charisms followed by an explanation of how these charisms became a subject of ecclesial interest and concern in the aftermath of World War II and during the years leading up to Vatican II. We will then explore some specific consequences of Vatican II for religious institutes and ecclesial movements. A case study then stimulates thinking on one of the contemporary challenges facing religious institutes and ecclesial movements, namely making meaning of the Spirit-driven dynamics of vocation in terms of growth and diminishment. The chapter concludes with a modest proposal for ecclesial discernment based on a few key insights of Pope Francis.

DISCORD OR HARMONY?

Throughout the world church, particular spiritual charisms have been regarded as special gifts of the Holy Spirit "given for the common good, that is, for the benefit of the whole Church."[1] Yet, despite efforts on the part of the people of God to listen attentively "to what the Spirit is saying to the churches" (Rev 2:7), specifically through the outpouring of such gifts, church leaders, along with the faithful, are often puzzled, unsettled, and disturbed when those claiming to live out these spiritual charisms present competing and sometimes contradictory spiritual, theological, and ministerial claims. Inevitably, such discord gives rise to questions and theories as to why these spiritual charisms, instead of fostering communion and cohesion, appear to contribute to disunity and division. How is it that the same spiritual charism can be viewed by some as prophetic and transformative and by others as problematic, even perverse?

Contemporary efforts to answer this provocative question are not without precedent. In fact, the roots of this question can be traced back to the public ministry of Jesus at Capernaum where John declared, "Teacher, we saw someone casting out demons in your name, and we tried to stop him, because he was not following us" (Mark 9:38; Luke 9:49) and Jesus responded, "Do not stop him" (Mark 9:39; Luke 9:50). As evidenced throughout church history, charisms in the church are often assessed differently, depending upon the vantage point of those doing the assessment. From the earliest councils of the church to twenty-first-century apostolic visitations, ecclesial discernment *from above* has carried with it an institutional obligation to "test the spirits to see whether they are from God" (1 John 4:1). Similarly, from the house churches of early Christianity to Christian base communities, ecclesial discernment *from below* has endeavored to engage the prophetic imaginations of the faithful in discovering how *not* to quench the Spirit or despise prophesy, but rather to "test everything; hold fast to what is good" (1 Thess 5:19–21).

In the effort to reflect upon the Spirit's holy manner of working in today's church and world, it is helpful to consider some of the reasons why ecclesial discernment must be undertaken both from above and from below. First, experiences of discord, whether real or perceived, require the church to be mindful not only of the mystery of spiritual charisms in the life of the church, but also of the paradox of their inherent tensions. Second, such experiences call into question the way those who embrace these charisms succeed or fail in living them out authentically. Third, such experiences serve as sobering reminders that while the popular papacy of Pope Francis has brought an atmosphere of magnanimity to church life, disharmony persists. Finally, the negative consequences of discord on the well-being of persons and institutions should not be underestimated in the life of the world church.

A PRE–VATICAN II PERSPECTIVE

Prior to Vatican II, spiritual charisms were understood as extraordinary gifts of the Holy Spirit poured out upon men and women embracing the call to follow Christ according to a specific form of Christian life. Theologically, these charisms were distinguished from the general or ordinary graces, which were poured out upon every baptized Christian for the sanctification of everyone. In the years preceding Vatican II and immediately in its wake, attentiveness to spiritual charisms—those identified with various forms of religious life as well as those associated with ecclesial movements—increased throughout the church; the charisms also became a focus of theological investigation and debate. The following account provides some insight into the shifts of consciousness that took place in the church regarding spiritual charisms.

In 1950, at the invitation of Pope Pius XII, general superiors from around the world gathered in Rome to attend the First General Congress of the States of Perfection. Speaking to those assembled, Arcadio Larraona, CMF, Secretary of the Congregation for Religious, identified two key dynamics of spiritual renewal that were present during the Congress: *aggiornamento* (that is, openness to new ways of thinking and acting) and *charisma*.[2] His exhortation to religious leaders and to their respective religious institutes can be summarized as follows: *Return to your origins. Rediscover the charisms of your founders and foundresses. Allow yourselves to be transformed by the question: How is the Spirit at work within your institute today?* Two years later, at the First World Congress of Mothers General, Larraona issued a similar exhortation to the sisters who gathered in Rome: "Do not concern yourselves with what your founder did in times past; consider rather what he [*sic*] would do if today he were alive and acting."[3]

According to witnesses, the power of the Holy Spirit was evident during both congresses and in the subsequent assemblies and activities that they inspired. With Larraona's words—"We must live in our times and according to the needs of our times"[4]—lingering in their ears, many renewal-oriented superiors recognized that the pursuit of a more adequate and appropriate understanding of particular spiritual charisms was inextricably linked to the capacity and competency of men and women religious to scrutinize the signs of the times, to interpret them in the light of the gospel (cf. Luke 12:56), and to experience the newness of their charisms by rediscovering them as if for the first time.

This charismatic impulse, attributed to the Holy Spirit, gave rise to research and reflection on religious founders, foundresses, and their early followers. As spiritual writings, autobiographies, hagiographies, and histories became available in translation, access to these publications contributed to a new enthusiasm, interest, and historical consciousness regarding the origins, spiritualities, and ministerial legacies of diverse religious families. Greater attention was given to the fact that some spiritual charisms were not restricted to vowed religious alone, but also lived out by monastic oblates, mendicant tertiaries, members of lay confraternities and sodalities, apostolic lay cooperators, and associates of congregations who embraced these spiritual charisms, charisms *to which* they felt personally called and *through which* they gave expression to their baptismal commitment in the secular world.

During the late 1940s and 1950s, as international support for the lay apostolate was growing among bishops, clergy, and religious, the church's awareness of ecclesial movements was intensified. This focused attention and concern for the laity found expression in the proceedings of the First and Second World Congresses of the Lay Apostolate, which were held in Rome in 1951 and in 1957 respectively.[5] As evidence suggests, the Holy Spirit had been engaged for decades in the outpouring of *new* spiritual charisms upon men and women who were neither members of religious institutes nor lay persons directly affiliated with religious institutes. As the proceedings from both congresses attest, this surprise of the Spirit was far more than a European phenomenon. Representatives from eighty countries gave witness to experiences of vocational graces and commitment in service of the church and the world. Many gave expression to their growing concern that Catholic Action, the official instrument for coordinating lay involvement in the church and society, was being used by ecclesial authorities as an overarching organizational structure to which all lay movements were expected to conform. This way of proceeding, in the estimation of lay apostolate leaders as well as some bishops, clergy, and religious, was becoming increasingly problematic and an impediment to the Spirit's movement and to mission.

By 1961, as preparation for the Second Vatican Council was under-way, Leon-Joseph Suenens, a Belgian cardinal and a member of the Central Preparatory Commission of the Council, emerged as a leading spokesperson among the bishops. Suenens asked "for the suppression of the monopoly of *Action catholique*," which, he argued, "hindered the activities of all other apostolic movements."[6] Soon, the subject of spiritual charisms found its way to the center of discussions on *renewed* and *new* ways of being church, of understanding the universal call to holiness and the centrality of the baptismal vocation of every Christian. By November 1964, the council fathers gave expression to a captivating theology of mission centered on the Trinity. That theology, coupled with a robust theology of the Holy Spirit, provided the foundations and criteria for understanding charisms in the life of the church; it was articulated in the first chapter of *Lumen Gentium*, the Dogmatic Constitution on the Church.

A POSTCONCILIAR PERSPECTIVE

In 1965, the proclamation and reception of the Vatican II document· *Perfectae Caritas*, the Decree on the Adaptation and Renewal of Religious Life, added momentum to the complex processes of renewal and aggiornamento in religious life, processes attributed to the Holy Spirit and set in motion a decade prior to the Council. For many institutes, these processes coincided with an unanticipated decrease in the number of new vocations, a consequence of which was a decline in the number of members available to serve in their institutional ministries. While numbers only captured part of the story, they were nonetheless indicators of the long-term implications of these post–Vatican II demographic shifts and their implications for religious life and the church in subsequent decades. In addition, the late 1960s ushered in a time of internal and external divisions within and among institutes, as religious endeavored to interpret their respective charisms authentically. Questions and discussions regarding the real meaning and permanent validity of religious life in the modern world gave rise to ongoing tensions, debates, and controversies.

Mindful of the waning of some religious institutes, especially in Europe and North America, there is a value in remembering that the decline in members is not only a matter of statistical analysis, but also ecclesial interpretation. Given the limitations of our human abilities to account for the action of the Holy Spirit (John 3:8), market theory and prosperity theology do not offer the most fruitful ways of interpreting diminishment in relation to religious institutes. More constructive and accurate are interpretations that focus on religious life continuing to be an expression of self-giving love,[7] irrespective of numbers, or that focus on the Spirit's outpouring of gifts for a period according to the needs of the age. Might it be that completion is another way of describing the process by which an extraordinary gift is gradually poured out until it has accomplished the end for which it was given according to God's good will and purpose? Stewarded with creative fidelity to God by those who received it, might it be that the measure of a loving commitment cannot be quantified in human terms by numbers of members or institutions or longevity? As the history of religious life illustrates, many groups do not endure more than a century or two. Who else but the Spirit can render a judgment on the measure of authenticity with which women and men religious embrace their respective charisms and dare to live with the question, "What would our founders and foundresses do today?"

As some men and women religious were led by the Spirit to the peripheries of the church and society, to live and minister in both traditional and nontraditional ways, often among persons and communities from which there would be little likelihood of attracting vocations, they began to realize the deeper meaning of their charisms and God's plan for their unfolding futures. Well aware of the fact that their supporters and critics alike frequently had their own measures of success for assessing how religious should be stewarding their particular charisms for the good of the church and service to the world, men and women religious recognized that with open hearts and hands and minds, those who have been entrusted with the gift must render an honest accounting for their discernments, their choices, and their actions, individually and collectively, to the Giver of the gift. Such was the experience of Archbishop Romero and Rutilio Grande, SJ, as discussed earlier in chapter 11.

In coming to such consciousness, ongoing discernment always means facing two questions: Regarding the living out of a spiritual charism entrusted to an institute's care, what decisions and actions are authentic responses to movements of the Holy Spirit? And what choices and activities are neither attuned to the Spirit nor authentic expressions of the charism?

Our focus now shifts from the lives and commitments of men and women religious to those of members of ecclesial movements composed primarily of laypeople. Here, it is important to underscore the significance of *Apostolicam Actuositatem*, the Decree on the Apostolate of the Laity, which was promulgated at the conclusion of Vatican II. That document added momentum to the complex processes of growth and development manifested in new communal forms of witness and proclamation, forms that also involved laymen and laywomen and sometimes clergy. In addition, there are certain parallels, in terms of reception and resistance within various ecclesial arenas, between the dynamics set in motion by *Perfectae Caritatis*, with its implications for diverse forms of religious life, and the impact that *Apostolicam Actuositatem* had on lay movements.

Though some ecclesial movements—such as *Opus Dei*, *Focolare*, *Communion and Liberation*, and *Cursillo*—were well established prior to the Council, the emergence of the Catholic Charismatic Renewal Movement in 1967, as discussed in the next chapter, cannot be underestimated in terms of its global influence and significance. Attributing its international reception to the power of the Holy Spirit, this experience of a "New Pentecost" within the Roman Catholic Church took on a vibrancy and power similar to experiences of the Holy Spirit recounted in the Scriptures as well as those experiences manifested in rapidly growing Pentecostal churches and charismatic communities within mainline Protestant denominations.[8] As this phenomenon spread quickly throughout the world church, it not only fostered spiritual renewal through intense devotion to the Holy Spirit, it also affirmed the charismatic ethos of many other emerging ecclesial movements and new communities, often referred to as the *Movimenti*.[9]

As growing numbers of adherents to ecclesial movements and new communities began to exercise power and influence, not only in ecclesial spheres but in social and political ones as well, both critics and supporters of these *Movimenti* often viewed them as responses to certain tendencies present in the churches of Europe and North America. Likewise, they were viewed as a response to new ways of being church that emerged in parts of Latin America, Africa, and Asia. Though charismatic movements have often been regarded as quite distinct from one another and from other noncharismatic ecclesial movements, the *Movimenti* have been perceived as serving similar ends, particularly in terms of spiritual renewal and evangelization.

For over forty years, in contrast to the decline in vocations to religious life, ecclesial movements have experienced rapid growth in membership and in ministries. Given the energy and vibrancy of the *Movimenti*, there is an unquestionable appeal and attraction to these spiritual charisms that cannot be reduced to successful recruitment strategies or ecclesiastical favor. While recognized throughout the world for their contributions to the building up of local churches and faith communities, they also have been censured for contributing to ecclesial divisions and polarizations. The findings of ecclesial investigations into the activities of some movements and their leaders, notably the Legionaries of Christ, have been sobering and devastating. Those tragic realities, however, have not diminished the authentic witness of countless members of the *Movimenti*, who have continued to respond to the urgings of the Spirit by bringing signs of life and hope to the world and to the future of global Catholicism.

Still, the scandals underscore the need for ongoing ecclesial discernment not only from above and from below, but also from within the movements themselves. Like the questions faced by men and women religious regarding their attentiveness to the Spirit and the authenticity with which they have lived out their spiritual charisms, the leaders and members of the *Movimenti* have been challenged to face with integrity and transparency a critical scrutiny of their own authentic living out of their spiritual charisms. What truly has been the action of the Spirit in their lives? And what of their commitments—ecclesiastical, social, and political—have been the products, not of the Spirit's action, but rather of their own desires, designs, and self-interest?

THE WAYS OF
THE HOLY SPIRIT

Several years ago, a story circulated in Rome among general supe-riors of men religious. A well-known cardinal, a high-ranking member of the curia, declared that the age of the historical religious orders was waning throughout the world, while the age of the ecclesial movements and new communities, the *Movimenti*, was waxing. The cardinal then proceeded to make a cause-and-effect analogy between fidelity and flourishing: inferring that the decline in vocations among men and women religious was a consequence of their failure to live out their charisms authentically. A non-European superior general, shepherding one of the largest religious families in the world, was indignant at the cardinal's inference. He took issue with the cardinal's prognostications and reminded him that the work of the Holy Spirit unfolds according to the will of a gracious God whose thoughts are not our thoughts and whose ways are not our ways (cf. Isa 55:8–9).

Though this story has no definite conclusion, it nonetheless serves as an instructive lesson on the nature and meaning of spiritual charisms and the church's need for ongoing discernment. It reveals how impres-sionistic evidence alone is not sufficient for capturing the mystery and paradox that are at the core of every spiritual charism. When it comes to evaluating the authentic living out of spiritual charisms within the Roman Catholic Church, therefore, a judgment cannot be rendered sim-ply based on their waxing or waning.

That principle suggests that neither the cardinal nor the superior general got it right. Each in his own way sought to substantiate his respective position on the apparent vitality (or lack thereof) of spiritual charisms in the life of the church using an argument based upon num-bers indicative of temporal notions of "flourishing." For whatever reason, neither of them seems to have considered the fundamental insight that when it comes to ecclesial discernment of the authentic living out of spiritual charisms, more criteria are needed than flourishing alone.

CONCLUSION

Diverse forms of religious life and various types of ecclesial movements are understood by the church to be among the most important means through which the Holy Spirit reforms, renews, and revitalizes the church. Consequently, it is necessary for church leaders as well as the faithful to conscientiously engage in processes of ecclesial discernment—from above as well as from below—that promote critical reflection on the ways in which spiritual charisms are being lived out in the everyday life of the church.

In offering a concrete proposal for such critical reflection, we can draw upon three key insights of Pope Francis, insights to which he often refers when speaking about the action of the Holy Spirit in the life of the church.[10] Hopefully, the following questions can serve as a practical resource and starting point for identifying the criteria needed in today's world church for discerning the authentic living out of spiritual charisms:

- What is the "newness" that those living out a spiritual charism offer the church in ways that enable the people of God to be "surprised by the Spirit" and experience the fullness of life in the Spirit (John 10:10)?

- How do those living out a spiritual charism manifest the "harmony of the Spirit" by building up the people of God (Rom 14:19; 1 Cor 14:26; 1 Thess 5:11) in ways that foster unity and inclusion amidst great variety and diversity?

- How do those living out a spiritual charism continue to "move with the Spirit" by courageously reliving the experience of Pentecost, setting the world on fire, creatively sustaining a passion for mission and joyfully proclaiming the gospel in ways that are attuned to God's plan for the flourishing and fulfillment of all creation (Rom 8:22)?

13

The Catholic Charismatic Renewal in the Hispanic Parish

Hosffman Ospino

Moving quickly toward the front of the lower church, Diana walks with confidence to deliver the *enseñanza* (teaching) before the *círculo de oración* (prayer circle). Everyone in the parish knows her well. Diana was first introduced to the spirituality of the Catholic Charismatic Renewal while a member of the parish youth group in her home country.

A mother of four, two adult and two teenage children, Diana's journey has not been easy. She separated from her husband long ago and raised her kids mostly on her own. Not having much education, she has held many odd jobs. Her unwavering faith, however, gives her the certainty that God walks with her. She does not have much but gives generously. Tonight, she will share her *testimonio* (witness). People raise their hands and pray out loudly asking that the Holy Spirit come upon Diana. She lowers her head, closes her eyes, and prays with them. The moment gains intensity. Some people pray in what they call "tongues," neither Spanish nor English. Musicians start playing a few chords, then a familiar song brings everyone together: *Espíritu Santo, ven, ven en el nombre del Señor* ("Holy Spirit, come, come in the name of the Lord"). A new air invades the worship space. Diana opens her Bible to read the passage of the Syrophoenician woman in Mark 7:24–30. During the next forty-five minutes, she will break open the passage, share her thoughts about it, connect it to her own life and the life of the community, and help the group discern what God is saying to them this very evening. Diana has never received theological formation or formally studied the Scriptures, yet this evening she exudes a unique sense of confidence and authority, one that comes from the community gathered in prayer and…the Spirit.[1]

This scene is quite familiar in thousands of Catholic parishes in the United States. It is estimated that half of the nearly 4,500 parishes with Hispanic ministry have a Catholic Charismatic Renewal (CCR) group.[2] The CCR is a major contemporary movement of spirituality in the Catholic Church; it emphasizes the work of God's Holy Spirit in the lives of the baptized through charisms that build the Church community and empower believers to openly witness their faith in Jesus Christ. The CCR is the largest and most influential ecclesial movement among the more than thirty million United States Hispanic Catholics today.

There is no doubt that the United States' Catholic experience is being profoundly transformed by the Hispanic presence. About 43 percent of all Catholics in the country share a Hispanic background. If the Catholic Church in the United States is to remain vibrant in the twenty-first century, it needs to intentionally understand the various dynamics shaping the spiritual lives of nearly half its population. The CCR is one such dynamic. In this chapter, we will examine key possibilities and contributions of the CCR to the renewal of parish life in the United States, particularly as a venue to identify, mentor, form, and promote Hispanic Catholic leaders nurtured by this spirituality.

CATHOLIC CHARISMATIC RENEWAL COMMUNITIES

To better understand the possibilities and contributions of the CCR, it is important to highlight a few core characteristics that identify communities associated with this spirituality. CCR groups often embody the characteristics of what sociologist Danièle Hervieu-Léger calls "emotional communities." Among such characteristics are voluntary association, personal commitment (usually after some form of "conversion" experience), relational bonds sustained by the sharing of personal testimonies and the following of a charismatic figure, prayer that involves the body (not just the mind), environments that favor the engagement of the emotions (e.g., music, light), distrust of an intellectualized faith, primacy of individual experience, flexible gatherings, attention to collective feelings, and spontaneous interpretation of Scripture.[3] The vignette at the beginning of this chapter captures many of these qualities.

Catholics committed to the spirituality of the CCR model, in various ways, the drive to share the gospel with renewed energy in our day as part of the New Evangelization.[4] Three indicators illustrate this: the emphasis on intentional openness to the work of the Holy Spirit among the baptized, the conviction that the Spirit gifts *all* Christians with charisms to build the church as the Body of Christ, and the thrust to share with fellow Catholics—and others—the joy of being a Spirit-led community.

In various contexts around the world, the CCR exhibits certain autonomy vis-à-vis parish structures that allows for some level of "dispersion," as scholar of religion Manuel Vasquez suggests, thus "increasingly becoming an ecclesial and worship style rather than a highly structured and centralized movement."[5] In the United States, however, such a level of dispersion is more an exception than the norm, since the CCR enjoys a strong presence in Catholic parishes. The movement uses these established communities as home bases for gatherings and activities. Most Hispanics associated with CCR groups are regular members of their parishes. About seventy dioceses and archdioceses in the United States have offices that support the work of CCR groups with formation, administrative oversight, and relationships with other organizations in the local church. For these tasks, many dioceses have designated pastoral leaders (e.g., spiritual directors or vicars) as liaisons.[6] Furthermore, various national organizations support the work of CCR leaders at different levels.[7]

BACK HOME, YET DISTINCTIVELY LATIN AMERICAN/HISPANIC

The rise of apostolic movements in our day has been interpreted as a gift of the Holy Spirit to the church. What is God telling us through the CCR? Why is this movement important for the church in the United States at a time when thousands of our faith communities are becoming increasingly Hispanic? The origins of the CCR as a contemporary ecclesial movement are associated with a group of Catholic students gathered at Duquesne University in Pittsburgh, Pennsylvania, in 1967. Group members were deeply influenced by the *Cursillo* spirituality. The students "received the Holy Spirit" in a way that, for many Catholics at the time, was rather foreign and resembled more the signs of a spirituality born in the context of Pentecostal Christianity: they felt and surrendered to the Spirit; they spoke about being "baptized in the Holy Spirit"; some spoke "in tongues"; several claimed to have received the "gifts" of healing and prophecy.[8] They were convinced that other Catholics needed to experience this and thus promised to share the experience. Soon this Spirit-led movement spread like fire.

The Duquesne experience did not happen in a vacuum. With the backdrop of the Second Vatican Council (1962–65), Catholics throughout the world were engaged in a major process of discernment exploring where the Holy Spirit was leading the church. There was no doubt that Vatican II signaled a time of renewal for the church. Was what happened at Duquesne another sign of the Holy Spirit wanting to renew it? Catholics had to trust and let the Spirit guide them, as the early Christians did at Pentecost.

It did not take much to see glimpses of Pentecostal spirituality in this Catholic "charismatic" movement. The origins of Pentecostalism as a spiritual renewal movement in the United States go back to the very early days of the twentieth century. Fifty-one years before the Duquesne experience, the events at a small Protestant mission church led by a young, black minister, William J. Seymour, on Azusa Street in Los Angeles signaled that something new was taking place. It was something not easy to describe in conventional terms, yet it was clear that this was different from most standard expressions of Christian worship: "Weird Babble of Tongues. New Sect of Fanatics Is Breaking Loose. Wild Scene Last Night on Azusa Street. Gurgle of Wordless Talk by a Sister," announced rather despairingly the front page of the *Los Angeles Times* on April 18, 1906.[9] It was the early days of the Azusa Street Revival. Seymour and his church were not the first to embrace a Pentecostal-like spirituality, yet they became paradigmatic.

Pentecostalism quickly spread throughout the United States and various parts of the world. Millions of people embraced it. Latin America proved to be a fertile ground for this movement of spiritual renewal, as it would later be for the CCR. Pentecostal communities placed the Bible at the center of their reflection, welcomed women and nonordained men into positions of leadership, including preaching and managing churches, and were constituted by mainly working class people of color who often struggled with poverty and other social ills.[10] These characteristics also came to identify many CCR communities in Latin America and Hispanic Catholic communities in the United States, while remaining rooted in the Catholic sacramental tradition and in communion with the hierarchy.[11]

Though most historical accounts trace the origins of the CCR movement worldwide to the United States, there are indications that around the same time of the Duquesne experience, some Catholic groups in Latin America were also engaged in instances of spiritual renewal with similar characteristics.[12] This was not surprising since Pentecostalism had already been spreading throughout the world for half a century. What matters, nonetheless, is that the Holy Spirit was inspiring one of the most exciting movements of renewal among Christians during the twentieth century, and Latin America was to be a major hub for that movement. Catholic missionary priests, vowed religious women and men, and lay-people from the United States and Canada promoted the CCR spirituality in various parts of Latin America through their work in parishes, congresses, and retreats. As of 2013, about seventy-four of the 130 million Catholics who identify with the CCR lived in Latin America.[13] The countries with the largest number of Catholic charismatics are Brazil, Colombia, Mexico, and the Dominican Republic.

During the first half of the twentieth century, about 90 percent of all Latin Americans self-identified as Catholic. Today only 69 percent of adults do so.[14] The expansion of the CCR has coincided with the rapid growth of Protestant Pentecostalism in Latin America. Among the 16 percent of Christians who self-identify today as Protestant—or *evangélicos*, a term used in Spanish and Portuguese almost interchangeably—in Latin America, roughly two-thirds see themselves as Pentecostal Christians "either because they belong to a Pentecostal denomination (median of 47%) or because they personally identify as Pentecostal regardless of their denomination (median of 52%). Some Protestants identify as Pentecostal in both ways."[15]

Catholics tend to read the growth of Pentecostal Protestantism among Latinos/Hispanics in the continent in terms of losses. But perhaps we are being invited to read this phenomenon with ecumenical eyes as a powerful movement of renewal ignited by the Holy Spirit and carried out via two sister streams: the CCR and Pentecostalism. Or are we to say that the Holy Spirit is divided? For Catholics, this has been the perfect opportunity to revise outmoded practices and assumptions that take for granted the allegiance to the institutional church among Hispanic Catholics, recognizing that many of those practices and assumptions fall short of meeting the spiritual longings of this population.

While the Latin American religious landscape is being reshaped by Pentecostalism and the expansion of movements within the church like the CCR, millions of Catholics from Latin American and Caribbean countries have been engaged in a major migration journey toward the north. Currently, 20 million (Hispanic) immigrants from Latin America and the Caribbean reside in the United States, two-thirds of them are Catholic. Many of these Catholics were influenced by the spirituality of the CCR in their home countries. They often settle in parishes that focus on the ministry to immigrant populations and offer services largely in Spanish.[16]

How many United States Hispanic Catholics self-identify as Charismatic or as associated with the CCR? Estimates range from one to fourteen million.[17] This discrepancy calls for further research, better criteria to name this reality in the church, and intentional accompaniment on the part of Catholics who do not call themselves Charismatic. A common source of tension in parishes with Hispanic ministry is the lack of commitment on the part of the clergy and other pastoral leaders to work with Catholics affiliated with this apostolic movement. As indicated above, most Hispanics associated with the CCR in parishes are immigrants. Little is known about US-born Hispanics affiliated with the movement. One thing is certain, however: the Spirit-led movement that crossed international frontiers to find a major stronghold in Latin America and the Caribbean, today crosses borders back into the United States to continue to give life, renew, and transform—this time with a distinctive Latin American and Hispanic identity.

TRANSFORMING AND ENRICHING CATHOLIC PARISH LIFE

The life of the Spirit among Hispanic Catholics becomes manifest through a wealth of spiritual traditions that are intimately associated with many Hispanic cultures, histories, and experiences. Edwin David Aponte observes, "Just as the Latino/a population of the United States is more diverse than commonly perceived, so are the many Latino/a concepts of spirituality and what is holy, of what is *santo*."[18] Technically speaking, there is no such thing as a homogeneous "Hispanic Catholic spirituality." Rather, there are many expressions of Hispanic Catholic spiritual life that share some common elements.

Parishes with Hispanic ministry that welcome and support CCR groups are familiar with the transformative influence of this movement of spiritual renewal. These communities are among the first to benefit from the gifts that the Holy Spirit bestows upon those who pray to receive the grace to live their baptism with more intentionality. They also harvest the fruits of renewal that are giving new life to the entire American Catholic experience.

Hispanic Catholics associated with the CCR are more likely to attend Mass on a weekly basis, read the Scriptures, and engage in moments of prayer beyond Sunday.[19] They are twice as likely to volunteer in parish ministries as lectors, extraordinary ministers of holy communion, and serve on church committees.[20] The CCR is, therefore, a major vehicle to strengthen the spiritual experience of Hispanic Catholics and a way of being Christian that empowers them with leadership skills that may be helpful for their lives and the life of the church.

Fostering Leadership

That there is only a small number of Hispanics serving in formal positions of leadership in Catholic parishes, dioceses, and organizations remains a major concern.[21] One main reason preventing Hispanics from rising to positions of leadership in a church that often requires professional credentials to serve in that capacity is their low levels of educational attainment: only 14 percent of Hispanic adults older than twenty-five have completed a bachelor's degree.[22] This does not mean that Hispanics lack the drive to lead or the desire to train to assume leadership roles in ecclesial contexts and beyond. In fact, half of all Catholics in programs of lay ecclesial ministry formation in the United States are Hispanic, although most are enrolled in programs that grant neither degrees nor the credentials to be hired as professional ministers.[23] Tens of thousands exercise leadership in small groups and parish communities, yet they lack clear pathways and resources to bring their leadership skills beyond those contexts.

One important step in the process of mentoring Hispanic Catholic leaders is to identify spaces in the life of the parish where these women and men discern their gifts. For the majority of white, Euro-American Catholic priests, religious sisters and brothers, deacons, lay ecclesial ministers, and school leaders, that space has been Catholic education, especially Catholic schools and colleges.[24] Unfortunately, Hispanics remain scandalously absent from Catholic educational institutions.[25] However, data from the *National Study of Catholic Parishes with Hispanic Ministry* indicates that the CCR is presently one of the most effective resources in parishes serving Hispanic Catholics to accomplish the goal of fostering ministerial leadership.[26]

CCR groups are excellent spaces for Hispanic Catholics in parishes to discern a vocation to leadership and service. Such discernment starts by opening one's life to the work of the Holy Spirit and the decision to embrace the call to holiness received by all the baptized. Already in the Hebrew Scriptures, as noted in chapter 6, the Spirit enlivens *and* empowers believers. The conviction that the Holy Spirit grants charisms (gifts of grace) to those who profess with faith that Jesus Christ is the Lord is a major incentive to discern not only which gift one has been given, but also what gifts to ask for.[27]

The experience of the "baptism in the Spirit" serves as a catalyst for this discernment. CCR members prepare and pray intensely for it.[28] This baptism in the Spirit (cf. Acts 1:5; 11:16), according to Paul Josef Cordes, is a grace that is possible because of Pentecost, a grace from God that is experienced by the individual in the present-day life of the church. Among the fruits of this baptism are a rediscovery of the Scriptures, a renewed interest in prayer and the sacraments, the desire to pray for deliverance and renewal, love for and commitment to the church, and a sense of mission.[29]

Reception of the gifts of the Holy Spirit does not require formal training or educational degrees or even ordination, nor are there gender, racial, or social restrictions. The Spirit is for all who believe and so are the charisms. It is tempting to focus only on those "extraordinary"[30] gifts that Catholics associate with the CCR such as speaking in tongues (glossolalia), healing, and prophecy.[31] But there are many other "ordinary" gifts, as the New Testament attests (e.g., 1 Cor 12:4–10; Rom 12:6–8; Eph 4:7–13), that relate to service to others in light of one's relationship with Jesus Christ. Such gifts are expressed usually in the day-to-day practice of the faith.

Offering one's thoughts about a Scripture passage, leading a prayer of healing, visiting families at their home to pray with them, leading the rosary in a small community, singing in front of a large group, sharing one's testimony, and so on are all small steps that can lead into larger experiences of service and leadership. Many CCR Hispanics eventually join programs of faith and pastoral leadership formation in diocesan pastoral institutes. A few join seminaries, universities, and houses of formation, but most do not. Failing to cultivate the leaders and the energy emerging from this apostolic movement is a grave loss for the entire church. The Holy Spirit is speaking loudly and inspiring generously. Bishops, diocesan personnel, pastors, religious sisters and brothers, deacons, and lay ecclesial ministers, among others need to do much more to support Hispanic leaders being nurtured by the spirituality of the CCR— and other ecclesial movements—and develop appropriate pathways to identify, mentor, form, and promote them.

Living in Tension

Tensions about worship style, the exercise of authority to interpret elements of the faith (especially the Scriptures), roles within established structures in the church, and even theological controversies have been part of the history of the CCR during its fifty years of existence as a movement. But the overall response and embrace of the CCR has been extensively positive.[32] Nearly every other movement in the history of

Christianity claiming to be guided by the Holy Spirit has faced similar challenges—the next chapter in this book, for example, notes that it is not unusual for faithful Christians who received charisms from the same Spirit in the same church to appear as embracing contradictory and competing claims. Mainstream Catholicism still wrestles with a movement like the CCR that paradoxically affirms the individual person's autonomy through religious expression, yet manages through communal discernment to bring such energy into the realm of the Charismatic group and its internal norms without leaving the larger ecclesial communion.[33] Perhaps this is a way for Catholics to recognize that living in paradox is very much of the Spirit.

Lack of knowledge and expertise about the movement is a common reason that prevents the clergy and other pastoral leaders from getting more involved with the CCR. Some simply feel uncomfortable with the expressive characteristics of CCR spirituality. The large numbers of international priests, who do not have the knowledge or the appreciation for this spirituality, arriving in the United States to serve Hispanic Catholics—and others—may exacerbate this tension. Recent research revealed that merely 21 percent of international diocesan priests and 14 percent of international religious priests are associated with an apostolic movement. Only half of them mentioned that such movement is the CCR.[34] Unless ecclesial structures affirm and embrace the potential of this spiritual movement in parish and diocesan life, thousands of CCR groups and potential leaders will continue to move along unaccompanied. To take this for granted is to miss a unique opportunity to advance the New Evangelization effectively in our day.

LISTENING TO THE SPIRIT

This is a time for the Catholic Church in the United States to carefully *listen* and *discern*, guided by God's Holy Spirit. The listening required is tantamount to reading the signs of our time. Most Hispanic Catholics are very young (median age twenty-nine); most Catholics in the United States under eighteen are Hispanic (60 percent). Despite the winds of secularization and disenchantment with institutional religion that waft through our neighborhoods and institutions, most Hispanics remain Catholic.

Half of all parishes with Hispanic ministry are being energized by the presence of the CCR. Most Hispanic groups nurtured by the CCR spirituality work in close collaboration with parishes. More than half of all Catholics identified with the CCR reside in Latin America and the Caribbean, currently the largest sources of Catholic immigrants making the United States their new home. Hispanic Catholics are more likely to practice their faith when affiliated to the CCR. A growing number of Hispanic pastoral leaders going to seminaries, houses of formation, and university-based ministerial programs have been nurtured by CCR communities. Countless more who were "baptized in the Spirit" are developing leadership skills to bring to life the gifts that the Spirit has given to them and long for the appropriate pathways to bring those gifts to further fruition in the church and beyond.

Are we listening to what the Spirit is saying to the church in our day?

14

The Adolescent and
the Transforming Spirit

Theresa O'Keefe

We have all witnessed the dancing of a small child. Happy to twirl in the center of a room, she is simultaneously confident and unconscious of others' attention. It is a fun, joyful thing that makes us smile. In time, this dance is replaced by another dance taken up as a young adolescent. At that time, she starts a dance that alternately seeks out an audience and dismisses it. One moment she wants to be invisible and the next she steps to center stage. She is, in turn, generous and shy, flamboyant and unsure, self-conscious and self-forgetting, vulnerable and confident. It is alternately easy and awkward, and sometimes grace filled. In all her dancing, she is placing herself before the world, looking to be seen, loved, and to love. She dances forward, demonstrating her new-found desire to be recognized, known, and valued for who she is. She then steps back, sensing her vulnerability in her search. If we are honest, it is a dance we have all done as we grew into a sense of ourselves and our place in the world. In fact, it is a dance we never stop doing, for we are always looking to love and be loved. What makes the dance special in adolescence is that it is the first time we are learning these steps. It is the first time we are conscious of ourselves, such that we might give our-selves to another and receive another in kind.

The metaphor of dancing is aptly associated with the Spirit, as the words used to describe the Spirit are those of action and movement. The *Catechism of the Catholic Church* (CCC) uses words such as *awakening, communicating, touching, outpouring,* and *speaking.*[1] They reflect movement, being drawn forward or shown. But what is shown to us by the Spirit is not the Spirit, but God's word. "We do not hear the Spirit….[The Spirit] reveals the Word to us and disposes us to welcome him in faith" (CCC 687). The Spirit draws us to see and know the Incarnate One, to recognize Christ and welcome Christ, wherever Christ may be found. Our efforts of searching for more, seeking more—not in an acquisitive way, but in a manner of awe and wonder—are evidence of the Spirit acting. We see such seeking in adolescence. As an individual grows out of childhood toward adulthood, we see evidence of the Spirit at work in the adolescent, as she begins to seek out and discover more in herself and seek and discover more in those around her. Her seeking is the Spirit drawing her to discover the person of Christ, both in herself and in others.

In this chapter, we will note that the cognitive changes of adolescence—in particular, the rise of self-consciousness—are an occasion for transformation through which the adolescent begins to see herself as a person. She is coming to know herself as unique and valuable. By the same process of growth, she begins to recognize others as full and unique persons, to whom she may give herself in love. This transformation is facilitated by the Holy Spirit. For the Holy Spirit, drawing all to Christ, draws her to seek her unique personhood and calls her to recognize the uniqueness of another. The mutual validation happens in the love experienced in the relationships with others. The ecstatic movement of the Holy Spirit, working within the adolescent and the other, draws the adolescent from the self-interest of childhood toward self-giving adulthood. Thus, loving relationships with others are essential for the adolescent to accomplish this important transformation.

THE DESIRE TO BE KNOWN

What prompts this seeking? The neurobiological changes initiated in puberty and refined through the following decade of life support the adolescent's new capacity to ideate and make connections among concrete categories.[2] In what is described as "formal operational thinking," the adolescent begins to perceive what were once "invisible" ideas, connections, and themes; he gains the capacity for what developmental theorist

Robert Kegan calls "cross-categorical knowing."[3] For example, an eight-year-old can recognize actions that have been named as good and bad by others, but is not able to make moral determinations. It is not until the cognitive capacities of adolescence come on board that those actions can begin to be classified within thematic values, like truthfulness, honesty, loyalty, care. Thinking thematically is the capacity of "cross-categorical knowing" that takes years to refine once initiated, and is only initiated in adolescence. Once recognized, the thematic and categorical can gain greater nuance and depth with opportunity and attention over the next several years. The new capacity of the adolescent to see beyond the concrete examples and instructions, and thereby recognize connections among and across the concrete, becomes essential as he moves toward adulthood. This capacity enables him to think and act with greater consistency and responsibility without explicit directions each step of the way. These abilities of ideation and seeing connections reflect a leap over the cognitive capacities of childhood; they take practice and encouragement to master. This awareness and attentiveness to the inner life, particularly emotional life, are essential for developing an ethical sense, as will be argued in the next chapter. Yet once begun in his teen years, these capacities carry on for the rest of his life; they are never outgrown.[4]

Perhaps the most dramatic sign of the adolescent's new capacity for perception is in the social realm of his life. He gains the ability to see himself anew and appreciate that he is connected to others, like family, friends, and groups. With the development of self-consciousness, he becomes newly aware of his seeing, feeling, acting, emotions, and thoughts. He begins also to make judgments about his thoughts, feelings, and actions. As he begins to see and judge himself, he begins to sense that others are seeing and judging him too. James Fowler offers the following little couplet to summarize this self-consciousness:

I see the you seeing me:
I see the me I think you see.

Fowler names self-consciousness as a "new burden" because it prompts an "egocentrism" that keeps the adolescent preoccupied with what he believes the other sees in him.[5] While burdensome, self-consciousness is a sign of the Holy Spirit, drawing the adolescent to both acknowledge himself and to look outside of himself for acknowledgment from others.

LOOKING FOR SOMEONE

In adolescence, the young person gains the capacity to see herself, as a person, connected to other people, distinct and unique in her own right. The prior givenness of life that children assume is replaced by a sense of particularity, uniqueness. "I am someone," she realizes, "or at least I hope I am." Theologian John Zizioulas claims that it is the human capacity for personhood, being uniquely known in relationships of love, that reveals the human is in the image of God.[6] Zizioulas, looking to the theological breakthroughs of the fourth-century Cappadocian fathers, writes that we do not share in God's nature, which is uncreated, because we are creatures. Rather, we share in God's personhood, God's "way of being," which is to "*be truly*" a person, unique and freely given.[7] "The person," Zizioulas insists, "cannot exist in isolation," for God "is communion." So, we come to know ourselves as persons in relationship:

> It is the other and our relationship with him that gives us our identity, our otherness, making us "who we are," i.e., persons; for by being an inseparable part of a relationship that matters ontologically we emerge as *unique* and *irreplaceable* entities. This, therefore, is what accounts for our being, and our being ourselves and not someone else: our personhood. It is in this that the "reason," the *logos* of our being lies: in the relationship of love that makes us unique and irreplaceable *for another*.[8]

It is the Holy Spirit who draws the adolescent to seek more in himself. The paradox is that he must look outward toward another to confirm that he is unique, distinct, and irreplaceable.

Yet from whom does he find such validation? Who among the many people around him is going to be the "relationship that matters"? This is where the dancing begins as the young person, drawn by the Spirit, moves forward in hope. Yet he also learns to retreat in hurt or embarrassment, perhaps too shy to risk again, for not all relationships are validating. In fact, some will be hurtful. The Holy Spirit is not only active in drawing the adolescent out in order to have his personhood acknowledged; the Spirit is also working in the loving encounter with another.

FINDING VALIDATION

As this discussion suggests, among the new capacities of the adolescent is the perception of value, especially social value. Self-consciousness becomes the entryway by which the adolescent begins to perceive herself as valuable—or not. And as Zizioulas claims, she naturally looks to others for recognition and validation. In the desire to be validated, the adolescent dances forward hoping for recognition, looking for almost anyone to look back at her and acknowledge her as someone. However, if she has contrast experiences of true care and reliability, she will find that not all recognition is loving and not all validation is reliable. For this is a learning process for her, with missteps along the way, whereby she learns to discern what is truly valuable from what is not.

Child development theorist David Elkind notes that the adolescent will seek out peer relationships in the hopes of inclusion and belonging, but along the way she will encounter her first moments of exclusion, betrayal, or disillusionment.[9] Peer groups may not deem her worthy of inclusion; supposed friends may abandon her at strategic moments; romantic attachments may prove to be impermanent. It takes some time to recognize that simply gaining attention is not validation. In fact, much attention can be painful or embarrassing. So here we see the adolescent retreat, scared of risking painful attention.

Likewise, it takes time to realize that validation is insufficient if it is based on a false or incomplete portrayal of who you really are. Youth ministry writer Chap Clark notes that too often adolescents feel that they are not valued for who they are as persons. Clark discovered that many adolescents often presume that the praise and encouragement they receive from important people, like parents, coaches, and teachers, are for their athletic or academic accomplishments, not for themselves as persons. Rather than disappoint the people who are investing in the adolescents' success, they learn to hide what is contrary or potentially disappointing.[10] Similarly, technology researcher Sherry Turkle found many adolescents curate their social media image to garner approval from those who would read their posts, both those known and unknown to them. Yet these same adolescents feel unsure of the value or truth of the affirmation those images receive.[11] In both cases, these adolescents develop habits of simultaneously burnishing their public selves while hiding their more inner thoughts and feelings. In these cases, they dance expertly, while hiding the fact they would rather dance to a different tune or not dance at all. In each of these instances, whether through avoidance or hiding, the adolescent misses out on the deep validation of being known and loved. Instead, they are just another pretty face in the sea of adolescent humanity; they suffer what Zizioulas calls "the hell of anonymity."[12]

The real win for the adolescent—and for any of us—is to be seen, known, *and* valued for who we really are. This happens in "the relationship that makes us unique and irreplaceable for another." Zizioulas writes, "As a person you exist as long as you love and are loved."[13] Coming to see and value herself as a person requires the adolescent to risk being vulnerable and learn to trust others with her true self. This is learned incrementally with trial, error, and sometimes forgiveness. Furthermore, as affirmed by Clark and Elkind, it takes caring adults to intentionally invite and teach the adolescent these relational skills. To return to the metaphor of dance, a caring adult needs to invite her to dance, to engage her seriously and grace-fully, to teach her the steps the adult has learned, and to invite her to show her own steps. The Holy Spirit works in the dancing, drawing the adult to really see and value the adolescent partner, whereby she comes to see and value herself.

VALUING THE OTHER

But it cannot be all about the adolescent. As she acknowledges her inner life—her unique personhood—it becomes possible for the adolescent to acknowledge the unique personhood of someone else. Furthermore, she becomes able to acknowledge the *relationship* that exists between her and others. She is increasingly able to move from seeing others as instrumental actors in her world to seeing them relationally. With that acknowledgment, she is better able to contribute to and benefit from her relationships. Kegan writes, she becomes "capable of loyalty and devotion to a community of people or ideas larger than the self," and to subsume her immediate interests to the interests of the relationship and community.[14] Once accomplished, she can be trusted to act independently and planfully, mindful of the concerns of others as well as her own. This is a major transformation. Just as Ernesto Valiente describes how Oscar Romero was transformed by his recognition of the profound personhood of the poor in his care, so too can the adolescent be moved to see beyond herself.

Educational theorist Jack Mezirow writes that transformational learning happens when the whole "meaning perspective" out of which the learner is functioning is replaced by one that is more inclusive and satisfying. In this case, the adolescent shifts from a more *instrumental* way of seeing the world—wherein others serve as functionaries—to a more *relational* way of seeing the world—whereby others are regarded as whole persons, with whom the adolescent is in relationship. Such transformation, according to Mezirow, is triggered by a "disorienting dilemma." Something causes the person to be dissatisfied with her current "meaning perspective" such that she begins to look for a wider, more satisfying perspective.[15] In this case, there are two factors contributing to the disorienting dilemma of adolescent transformation. The first is the inner stirrings that cause the adolescent to see herself differently—to begin to see herself as a unique person. The second factor is the presence of robust relationships in the adolescent's life, which challenge her to recognize these others as unique persons too.

A robust relationship is one in which the adolescent is sufficiently seen, known, and valued for who she is, while also calling her to respond in kind. The other calls her to attentiveness, vulnerability, trust, and accountability while making their perspective more apparent, distinct from, but connected to hers. "I'm your father; I'm not just the taxi service, you know! Have some consideration." For example, if her father calls her to pay attention to him (or the family) and he offers some insight into his life (or the family's), the adolescent is less likely to keep her new self-consciousness focused on herself. She may begin to imagine what it is like to be in her father's position. This is not to suggest that parents unduly burden the adolescent with the full weight of their adult concerns, rather that they call the adolescent to recognize that the adults *have* concerns of which the adolescent is unaware. Kegan argues that the repeated effort to name and take on the point of view of another is a valuable way for the adolescent to recognize the particularity of her own point of view and to imagine the possibility and validity of others.[16] This continual effort to jog her out of her self-centered perspective to see and account for the realities of others and the relationship between herself and others is an essential element for transformational change of the adolescent.

To speak theologically about this same process, it is the Spirit *within* the adolescent calling him to look outside of himself to another for his own validation; and it is the Spirit from *within* the other calling the adolescent to recognize and validate them. In both movements, it is the Spirit drawing him to see Christ, within himself and the other. Theologian Catherine Mowry LaCugna, looking to those same fourth-century Cappadocians, writes, "The identity and unique reality of a person emerges entirely in relation to another person."[17] What is made possible in the cognitive development of adolescence is that the individual human is first able to recognize personhood, his own and that of another, and recognize the relationship between them. Thus, him freely giving his life—his person—in love to another is made possible.

THE ESSENTIAL NEED FOR THE OTHER

The adolescent needs robust relationships with others to recognize his worth and to discover the worth of another. However, one of the challenges of twenty-first century life in the United States is that adolescents have little access to long-term, diverse relationships with adults. There are two contributing factors: one structural, the other cultural. Structurally, it has been the practice of the past two centuries that adults spend their working day away from their homes; similarly, the extension of mandatory secondary education in the early twentieth century means that adolescents spend much of their days in school with their age peers. The upshot of these two factors has meant that adolescents and adults spend most of their waking hours separated from one another.[18]

Culturally, adults and adolescents have come to expect that such age segregation is normal, good, and should be perpetuated.[19] Influential developmental theorist Erik Erikson posited adolescent identity discovery is an individual project in which others "reflected" the adolescent's "diffused self-image."[20] His conception of the other is static, suggesting they serve as mirrors that reflect, not persons who respond or challenge. Furthermore, Erikson's call for a "moratorium," by which he means an opportunity for the adolescent to try out identity expressions without being prematurely locked into an identity, has been interpreted as cultural license to leave the adolescent alone to figure things out on his own.[21] Thus, a project he does *for* himself becomes one he does *by* himself; the search for his sense of self becomes an experience of isolation.

Subsequent psychological voices have challenged that dominant view. Judith Jordan and Jean Baker Miller argue that one comes to know oneself, not apart from relationships, but within the context of relationships. According to their argument, the adolescent comes to know herself in distinction from, in contrast to another who is close at hand. The better she can see the other as a full person, the better able she is to recognize her self-in-relation to that other.[22] Reflecting the dancing metaphor, at one moment the adolescent lurks on the edges of gatherings and the next she steps into the center, looking to her dance partners for feedback; she does not leave the dance hall altogether. Thus, rather than judge the adolescent as pushing away from her family so as to be left alone, we can see her as suddenly self-conscious that she *has* a family. They have not lost their influence; it is just that now she sees they *have* an influence. Consequently, she steps back to consider their perspective before claiming it herself. In a similar fashion, she reshuffles her friends; they are no longer playmates determined by circumstance, but full people with likes, dislikes, opinions, and cares. She can now choose friends and be chosen by them. Awareness of these relational spaces is new territory for the adolescent, and among them she comes to see and value herself more clearly. Here, we hear echoes of Zizioulas: "As a person you exist as long as you love and you are loved."[23]

Finally, where does the adolescent find such relationships? It is natural to expect that they are found primarily and exclusively with parents or adolescent peers, but those are not always the best or only places. On the one hand, age peers, while essential, frequently do not know how to call one another to greater maturity. On the other hand, the relationship with parents is so loaded with history, hopes, and emotions that it is frequently difficult for the adolescent to feel that he is recognized and valued for who he is. The adolescent frequently reads parental affirmations as "what they are supposed to say" rather than genuine. Or he may feel compelled to show his parents his "best self" in response to the parents' investment.[24] For the parents' part, it is difficult for them to hear their son without his words somehow reflecting back on their choices and hopes for him. It is also noteworthy that adolescents may feel more at ease turning to therapists or other professionals to reveal themselves, but they do so with the presumption that such revelations remain secret. All these factors point to the value of other adults—aunts, uncles, neighbors, congregation members, and family friends. Any one of them can function without the expectation of parents, with greater maturity than age peers, and with more credibility than those "paid to care." These potential sources of relations, outside the immediate circle of expected sources, may be the most helpful for the adolescent, and through them the Holy Spirit may be able to act most effectively.

Through the cognitive development of adolescence, particularly the gift of self-consciousness, the Holy Spirit invites and empowers the dance that helps the adolescent recognize her value and her place in the world. Adolescence is a potentially transformative moment in life; a shift from the self-interest of childhood to the self-giving of adulthood. It is a move from an instrumental engagement in the world to a relational engagement. But it is not automatic. It is prompted and made possible by the ecstatic love of the Holy Spirit. The Spirit draws the adolescent to look within herself and to look beyond herself to find her value. The promptings within her must be met by love expressed by another, who recognizes her uniqueness and calls her to do likewise. Thus, her dance is not one she can do alone. She needs attentive and responsive partners who value what she brings to the dance—herself—and call her to value them. The love of the Holy Spirit between them completes the circle and binds them together, such that their dance becomes one of grace and beauty that transforms their world.

15

Empowered by
the Holy Spirit

Andrea Vicini, SJ

The Holy Spirit is at the heart of the moral life and empowers persons and communities to discern, judge, decide, and act by promoting just relationships as well as personal and social flourishing. For today's readers, the previous sentence is not likely to be contentious. Since the Second Vatican Council, with its invitation to recognize the signs of the divine in history, believers and theologians have been attuned to discerning the presence, gifts, and action of the Holy Spirit. Writing before the Council, however, the distinguished scholar Henlee Barnette (1911–2004) lamented that "one of the surprising things that strikes the student of Christian ethics is the fact that ethicists almost universally ignore the essential relationship of the Holy Spirit to Christian morality."[1]

Barnette rightly stressed that "the Spirit is the source of all moral excellencies" and, as portrayed in Scripture, "the fruit of the Spirit is love, joy, peace, patience, kindness, generosity, faithfulness, gentleness, and self-control" (Gal 5:22–23). In Christian life, the Holy Spirit is "the spring of ethical power."[2]

In creation and throughout history, the Spirit sanctifies every creature. In moral life, the Spirit forms and informs one's conscience,[3] and "contributes to the 'enrichment and expansion of our moral subjectivity' by entering the hearts of people and empowering 'the ways we function cognitively, volitionally, and affectively.' […Moreover,] the Spirit is present volitionally as the power of conviction in our decision making."[4] Hence, "without the energizing of the Spirit the Christian ethic would be irrelevant and impracticable."[5] Finally, the Spirit also "works in the dynamic personal relationship with the believer to bring immediate understanding and insight into one's consideration. This forms the positive foundation of a confident and creative process of moral deliberation."[6]

While affirming the Spirit's work in the human processes of making moral decisions, Barnette also notes, "The fruit (note the singular use of the word 'fruit' to denote the unity of Christian morality) of the Spirit is morality not magic, ethics not emotionalism."[7] Since "emotionalism" has a negative connotation, is Barnette implying that Christians should beware of emotions?

Emotions can unsettle, trouble, and overwhelm the moral agent. Nonetheless, in the Christian tradition, many authors argue for a holistic approach that recognizes the importance of one's emotions to the moral life, and seeks to integrate them into living one's discipleship and in announcing the good news. Even in relation to social contexts and interactions, both individual and collective emotions play relevant roles in discerning, making judgments, deciding which course of action should be taken, actuating what has been decided, and assessing the final outcomes. In such a way, emotions contribute to articulate individual and communal moral life.

Both in the case of individuals and communities, how we live ethically could benefit from exploring how the Holy Spirit reaches out to human beings by graciously illuminating their emotions, by strengthening or purifying people's emotional lives, or by leading to conversion or reform.

EMOTIONS AND MORAL LIFE

Historical Insights

In reflecting on emotions, what insights can be gained from history? In turning to history, however, a problem should be acknowledged. The ancients referred to passions, not to emotions. As Thomas Dixon indicates, "The *pathe*, *passiones*, or passions of the soul were a major mental category for thinkers from the ancient Greeks to the early moderns, until the 'emotions' came into existence in the nineteenth century."[8]

Anastasia Scrutton agrees: "The term [emotion] did not crop up in English until the mid-sixteenth century, when it was used to denote a public disturbance, and was not given its current meaning until the early nineteenth century."[9] By contrast,

> The predominant scholarly attitude towards the emotions in recent decades has been one of loving restoration. Long maligned by moralists and theologians as irrational and harmful, so the story goes, it has fallen to modern philosophers, neuroscientists and psychologists in recent years to retrieve the emotions from centuries of neglect and abuse and to restore their intellectual lustre.[10]

Any historical exploration needs to avoid simplifications. With this warning in mind, there are three key historical turning points that could be illuminating.

In Athens, in the early third century BCE, the Stoics understood emotions to be judgments concerning the uncontrollable. The Stoic quest for equanimity (that is, *apatheia*) represented a strategy to decrease emotions by reevaluating material things and lessening any attachment to them. A Stoic approach would stress that people need to distance themselves from emotions—whether they arise in individuals, institutions, or communities. For a Stoic, the emotions would be a dimension where the Holy Spirit could not interact with human beings.

In Judaism and Christianity, the Bible distances itself from the Stoic approach. Scripture can be read by focusing on emotions, both in the Hebrew Bible and in the New Testament. In other words, the Spirit relates with and reaches out to human beings even in what concerns their individual and collective emotions. For example, in the Gospels, emotions help readers to figure out how, in Jesus, the divine is deeply moved out of love for humankind and for the whole creation. In John's Gospel, we read that "Jesus began to weep" (John 11:35). This is a very concise statement showing Jesus's emotional response to the announcement of the death of his friend Lazarus. In Jesus and because of him, emotions are integral to both the incarnation and redemption.

Theologians also discuss whether it would be possible to ascribe emotions to God the Creator, with the theological challenge that this hypothesis poses to thinking about God's immutability and impassibility.[11] In any case, emotions are integral to the lives of the disciples, and shape the loving responses of God's people to divine love and to the Spirit's action in their lives within the Christian community, society, and history.

Within Christianity, the great medieval theologian Thomas Aquinas (1225–74) considered how emotional responses relate to human rationality and how they might affect one's will.[12] For Aquinas, emotions can be ordinate or inordinate, depending upon their fittingness to humanity's true end. As a consequence, "Emotions are praiseworthy or blameworthy when they involve the distinctively human powers of reason and will."[13] As interpreted by the theologian William Mattison, "In describing the different ways that emotions may be governed by reason and will, Thomas offers a developmentally sensitive model for the habituation of emotions into virtuous components of the Christian life."[14] In other words, emotions can contribute to, or hinder the progress of human beings toward their goal; that is, living the commandment to love and, at the end of times, receiving the gift of eternal relational intimacy with God that is expressed by Aquinas as beatific vision, as seeing God face-to-face and enjoying God's friendship for eternity within the Communion of Saints. Illuminated by the Spirit, "the habituation of emotions into virtuous components of the Christian life"[15] helps people to strive toward their true end. Each virtue is an amalgam of thought, habit, and ordered passion, that is, of ordered emotions and of what they generate in the moral agents.

What are the important implications of Aquinas's approach for us today when we reflect on human agency? *Becoming aware* of one's emotional life, *cultivating* and *tutoring* the emotions, as well as *educating the imagination* become essential tasks and responsibilities, both for human development and for strengthening one's ethical capabilities to do what is right. Contemporary authors agree. For Patricia Lamoureux, the emotions are important for moral development and conscience formation. For example, emotions are a motivational force—"we do things because we emotionally care about them and are personally invested; when we stop being moved, we stop moving." Emotions are also integral to the way people understand situations and issues: they convey information. The emotions need tutoring, however, because they do not always have a positive effect on moral development.[16]

Defining Emotions

The preceding brief and limited historical exploration shows that defining emotions is not an easy task. As Scrutton indicates,

> While the term is etymologically derived from the Latin *motus*, *motus* denotes "movement" and is only indirectly related to the current meaning of emotion. Furthermore, no exact translation or equivalent is found in Latin or any of the ancient languages. In contrast to the preference of the modern world for a single overarching category, the ancient and mediaeval worlds had a diversity of descriptions of human experiences.[17]

A descriptive way of defining emotions, which is based on *etymology*, focuses on moving and on being moved, with an emphasis on physical responses. But emotions are not merely episodic and limited bursts of activity. They can also be more prolonged, even long-term processes rooted in one's desires and personality.[18] In positive terms, because the Holy Spirit inspires, illuminates, and prompts us through our emotions, emotions are integral to what moves moral agents to act justly—hopefully, after having carefully assessed and judged the situation, and decided wisely.

In popular parlance, however, an ethical argument that is defined as "emotive" is considered unsound. Emotions are suspect because they affect the person, make people passive, susceptible, vulnerable, and remain outside one's control.[19] This mistrust of human emotions could depend on a rationalistic account of ethical action that associates emotions with unruliness and considers them as a threat to the rigor of moral reasoning and acting.

Emotions depend on what happens *to* people, to their bodies, minds, conscience, and souls, that is, to their whole selves. At the same time, emotions are also one of the many ways in which people respond to what happens *around* them, to what is exterior to their being. This ability of relating the self and the external environment—what is interior and what is exterior—shows how emotions have a dynamic component that encompasses both the self (that is, the personal dimension) and what is outside the self (that is, the external context, which includes other people, creatures, things, situations, and even the environment). An example is given by events that, through the media, affect millions, and probably the whole world.[20] The spiritual tradition also affirms that the Holy Spirit reaches out to us through our whole self and in what happens in history.

In summary, two points can be made: First, emotions are anthropologically and experientially shaped, and "embody a sense of ourselves and our situations."[21] They influence and manifest who the moral agents are, and how they discern and act. Emotions can strengthen or undermine all aspects of human agency: the assessment of what one is facing, the discernment concerning how to respond to one's situation and its specific circumstances; the choice of the possible means to address one's condition; the evaluation of what happened; the determination of what was right or wrong, what could be done better, and what needs to be corrected and how.

The importance of emotions in moral discernment, decision making, ethical judgments, and in performing right actions is strengthened by the current understanding of the relation between emotions and rationality, where emotions are considered integral to our reason. Together with many philosophers, theologians, psychologists, and neuroscientists, the philosopher Martha Nussbaum argues that emotions have cognitive content, an intelligence of their own.[22] Thomas Dixon agrees: "The standard view now is that emotions are cognitive states which constitute intelligent appraisals of the world. They are neither mere feelings, nor obstacles to reason."[23]

If emotions are cognitive, people need to learn how to express the rationality that is associated with their emotions, just as they learn how to articulate their speculative reasoning and to channel its power to avoid experiencing reasoning as a disturbance to right discernment, decision making, and action.

Emotions, and being attentive to them, allow for a more accurate *assessment* of the moral agent and, at the same time, of the situations lived by the moral agent involved and how the moral agent is responding to those situations, interacting with them, and even transforming them. People could become aware of the multiple emotions that they experience in the various situations that they face. Such *awareness* could help them by inspiring decisions or by leading them to reassess and reformulate their ethical responses. In such a way, emotions can play a *formative role* whenever they are examined critically.

With its many gifts, the Holy Spirit empowers the moral agent and enlightens the disciples' ethical lives. Emotions are inseparable from the traditional elements that intervene in moral assessment, in making judgments, in deciding, and in acting—for example, critical analysis, principles, rules, and virtues. Therefore, emotions should be added to other moral resources that help people to act ethically.

Second, as Paul Lauritzen affirms, "Emotions are culturally mediated or constructed experiences that are shaped by, and crucially dependent upon, cultural forms of discourse such as symbols, beliefs, and judgments."[24] Consequently, emotions should be examined critically. At the same time, because "emotions are culturally mediated or constructed,"[25] cultures and historical periods might be assessed by understanding and interpreting how emotional reasoning and responses influence diverse contexts.

Racial discrimination and persecution stand as troubling examples of how racist cultures relied on emotions (for example, fear of those with different skin color) to foster discriminatory social attitudes and oppressive policies. Individual and collective emotional responses to racial diversity further promoted and consolidated those racist societies. Emotions, however, also contributed to reject racially biased preconceptions gradually. In the United States, during the African American civil rights movement, Martin Luther King Jr.'s powerful preaching and evocative speeches testify to the inspiring action of the Holy Spirit, and exemplify how emotions were essential in promoting the individual and collective emotional conversion that advanced the recognition of basic civil rights to all citizens. Other positive examples abound. One of them is the emotional and generous response that usually occurs in the aftermath of natural tragedies (for example, earthquakes and tsunamis). In those emergencies, giving to those who are in dire need shows how solidarity is socially valued and promoted.

Various authors explore the social and political dimensions of emotions, for example, by focusing on groups, or on civil society and the political arena, or on religious public discourse. In her book *Political Emotions*, Nussbaum argues that love is a political emotion with motivational capacity that can lead citizens to construct a good society.[26] In the pursuit of justice, love matters. Human beings should cultivate appropriate sentiments of love, with its affiliated emotions, such as compassion and sympathy.

THE HOLY SPIRIT AND EMOTIONS

In contributing to the shape and direction of the moral life, emotions can lead believers to recognize and experience the presence and action of the Holy Spirit in personal, ecclesial, and social contexts. The Spirit interacts with emotions in three ways—companionship, mentorship, and friendship—to generate, strengthen, and support empowering relational dynamics.

Discerning Companion

First, as a dedicated, discrete, and respectful *companion*, the Holy Spirit accompanies, promotes, and supports the discernment of both single moral agents and communities. Being a gift giver, the Spirit helps individuals and communities to receive the gifts that characterize and accompany the presence of the Spirit. Discernment is one among these gifts.

"Etymologically discernment means sorting," as Jean-René Bouchet indicates.[27] In the case of both individual believers and communities, however, discernment is more than sorting. Discernment can be presented both as a gift given by the Spirit and as a skill empowered by the Spirit. As a gift, discernment interacts with all human capabilities including emotions. As a skill, "discernment can be improved through careful exercise. In this manner, it is a skill that can be taught and learned."[28] Like a trusted companion, "discernment advises, invites, arouses but never imposes."[29] The whole being is engaged in discerning: "Discerning the leading of the Spirit will not mean ignoring our emotions and physical responses, nor, on the other hand, will it mean ignoring reason and argument in order to wait for an intuited 'leading of the Spirit.'"[30] For individuals and communities, "discernment is the secret to living a creative and loving lifestyle with people we want to live with and to work with; it is the key to making good choices when we are walking on paths where no one has posted signs to tell us where to go."[31]

For Kirsteen Kim, the action of the Holy Spirit is characterized by openness, "because of the unpredictability of the Spirit's movements," and humility, "since the Spirit is the Spirit of the Almighty God."[32] Therefore, discernment presupposes virtuous moral agents who strive to live virtuous lives. Discernment guides practical moral reasoning. The Holy Spirit strengthens the discerning ability of seeing the signs of divine presence and action in one's life and in history, as well as listening to what the Spirit is communicating through God's word in one's life experiences, within the Christian community, and in society—as noted already in chapter 10, which examines Teresa of Avila and Ignatius of Loyola, two key figures in the spiritual tradition.

Finally, accompanied by the Spirit of discernment, communities seek

> light on a direction to take or a choice to be made. The sign that the decision has been a true exercise of discernment will never be given solely by the unanimity or absolute majority with which it was taken. The decision must also depend on listening to each other and being involved with each other and the relationship with the other communities to which this community is organically linked, the coherence of the direction taken and the fundamental intention of the community.[33]

Empowering Mentor

Second, as a wise and skilled *mentor*, the Holy Spirit guides moral action by empowering discerned personal and collective emotional responses and commitments that will lead to strengthening moral agency and to living the gospel by being with those who are poor, caring and serving them, promoting social justice and the common good. As was stressed in chapter 6, the Hebrew Bible makes clear that the divine spirit empowers human beings and communities to live God's commandments.

Spiritual and moral empowerment is "the central motif of an ethics of the Spirit."[34] Concretely, "it is primarily through deeper knowledge of, and an intimate relationship with, God, Jesus Christ and the community of faith that people are transformed and empowered by the Spirit for religious-ethical life."[35] As a mentor, the Spirit empowers individuals and communities by making them mentors for others and for one another in diversified ways depending on situations and contexts.

Compassionate Friend

Third, as a compassionate, generous, and loving *friend*, the Holy Spirit supports moral agents in their striving, successes, failures, and disappointments. In his encyclical letter *Dominum et Vivificantem*, "On the Holy Spirit in the Life of the Church and the World," Pope John Paul II stressed how the Spirit is "giver of life," "counselor," "intercessor," and "advocate" (D&V 2–3). In light on the teaching of the Second Vatican Council (see *Dei Verbum* 2),[36] John Paul II also added that "'the gift of the Spirit' ultimately means a call to friendship, in which the transcendent 'depths of God' become in some way opened to participation on the part of man [*sic*]" (D&V 34). Friendship is a further way to experience the intimate emotional closeness of the Spirit.

The Holy Spirit is a very engaged and committed friend of every human being, of humanity, and of the entire creation. As a compassionate friend, the Spirit helps humanity with the light of the Spirit's discerning wisdom and with the warmth of the Spirit's purifying fire. All the gifts of the Spirit make human beings more and more able to transform the whole world by making it a better place for each person—particularly those who are more in need—and for all living creatures and nonliving forms (see *Laudato Si'* 80, 88).[37] Experiencing the Spirit's compassionate friendship, human beings also become more compassionate[38] because "the Spirit instills within us 'the *longing* for justice…a *love* for the poor, a *compassion* for the needy, a heart that *desires* the good of the widow and orphan and prisoner and sojourner.'"[39]

CONCLUSION

The Holy Spirit empowers persons and communities to discern, judge, decide, and act by promoting just relationships as well as personal and social flourishing. These pages focused on how this empowerment occurs through the interaction of the Holy Spirit with human emotions. In the case of individuals, emotions are integral to who moral agents are and how they act ethically. In social contexts, emotions are shaped by culture and history, while, at the same time, they influence them. In profound ways, by touching emotions, the Holy Spirit relates with each one and with the various social contexts as a dedicated, discrete, and respectful *companion*; as an experienced, wise, and skilled *mentor*; and as a compassionate, generous, and loving *friend*. In people's lives, the joy and the beauty of those situations in which authentic companionship, mentorship, and friendship have been experienced give to single persons and to communities a glimpse of the grace of the Holy Spirit in human history and in the history of salvation.

16

The Holy Spirit as Dynamic Meaning Maker

Melissa M. Kelley

On October 31, 2015, a Russian airliner crashed in Egypt, killing all 224 people on board. Twelve days later, forty-three people were killed and hundreds injured by twin suicide bombers in Beirut, Lebanon. On the following day, a terrorist group attacked several sites in Paris, France, killing 130 people and wounding hundreds more. The Islamic State of Iraq and Syria (ISIS), the violent extremist group that operates out of bases in Syria and Iraq, claimed responsibility for all three attacks.

In the wake of this terrorist violence, focus in the United States turned immediately to Syrian refugees, those millions of people who had fled the four-year civil war in Syria and were desperately seeking refuge somewhere in the world. Strong voices in the United States, including many in the United States Congress, governors, mayors, and candidates for the presidential nomination, insisted that the United States must declare an immediate and perhaps permanent halt to resettling any Syrian refugees, because potential or actual terrorists could enter the United States under the guise of refugee status and inflict great harm on the country. Within one week of the Paris attacks, the United States House of Representatives passed a measure significantly tightening the process for acceptance of Syrian refugees in the United States.

In response to this strong opposition to the resettlement of Syrian refugees in the United States, other prominent voices expressed the imperative that concern and compassion for the refugees must not be sacrificed to unrealistic fears, particularly given the careful refugee vetting process in the United States. Speaking at the G–20 Summit in Turkey in November 2015, President Barack Obama urged compassion toward the refugees:

> The people who are fleeing Syria are the most harmed by terrorism. They are the most vulnerable as a consequence of civil war and strife. They are parents. They are children. They are orphans. And it is very important…that we do not close our hearts to these victims of such violence, and somehow start equating the issue of refugees with the issue of terrorism.[1]

Similarly, Bishop Eusebio Elizondo, chair of the US Conference of Catholic Bishops' Committee on Migration, exhorted,

> These refugees are fleeing terror themselves—violence like we have witnessed in Paris. They are extremely vulnerable families, women, and children who are fleeing for their lives. We cannot and should not blame them for the actions of a terrorist organization….We must work with the world community to provide safe haven to vulnerable and deserving refugees who are simply attempting to survive.[2]

Such urgings toward compassion seemed substantially ineffectual; as measured by various polls conducted in November and December of 2015, a majority of the United States' citizens seemed increasingly opposed to the resettlement of Syrian refugees within the country.[3]

How might we understand such strong opposition in the United States to resettlement of Syrian refugees? While this complex question defies an easy answer, we might consider people's responses as flowing, at least in part, from a crisis of meaning in the wake of tremendous loss. Times of loss can usher in experiences of "narrative disruptions,"[4] whereby one feels that the narrative or story that one has constructed for the present and future is challenged or even destroyed, leaving one in a crisis of meaning and facing the great challenge of making new meaning for one's life.

This chapter presents an overview of theoretical work in narrative, narrative disruption, and meaning making in times of loss and crisis and suggests connections between this work and the responses of people in the United States to the Syrian refugees in the wake of terrorist activity. It then considers how Christians might understand the dynamic work of the Holy Spirit in the activity of making meaning following narrative disruption and the critical role of the pastoral minister in encouraging the faithful to participate in this meaning-making work of the Holy Spirit. Finally, it suggests how consideration of and participation in the meaning-making activity of the Holy Spirit might help Christians make faithful decisions following loss, including the losses attached to violent terrorist activity.

NARRATIVE, NARRATIVE DISRUPTION, AND MEANING MAKING

Humans are people of stories. One of the primary ways we think and communicate about our lives is in the form of stories, or narratives. For instance, when we are forming a new friendship, we often share aspects of our personal stories with one another, such as wonderful or challenging dimensions of our childhood, important moments in our work or parenting journey, and dreams for our future. Certainly, we can and do communicate in ways other than stories—for instance, at a business meeting, we may simply share information or discuss a topic. But almost instinctually, we seem to think of and communicate about our lives in the form of stories, an instinct that seems to occur across cultures and across the ages.[5] The narratives we hold and tell about our lives typically contain the elements of all stories, such as major and minor characters, settings, and plots. These elements and more form the personal, familial, and communal narratives that we come to know and tell about ourselves. Importantly, our stories may also describe important aspects of our faith lives.

Why are we so inclined to consider and communicate about our lives in the form of narrative? One important reason is the connection between narrative and meaning. The life narratives that we tell often communicate what is most important to us. We might call this the meaning of our lives. *Meaning* is a vague and complex term. Elsewhere I have expressed my understanding of *meaning* as follows:

> Meaning is the deep sense we make of things, the way we understand the world, how we articulate the overarching purpose or goal of our lives, the significance we seek in living, the core values by which we order our lives. Meaning also includes theological dimensions such as how we understand God's activity in the world, God's feelings about and responses to us, and God's role in suffering. Meaning, including theological meaning, helps to create order, sense, and purpose out of experiences and events that could otherwise seem random, nonsensical, disordered, or chaotic.[6]

The ways we articulate our life stories reflect and shape how we understand the meaning of our lives.[7] For example, in articulating my story, I might emphasize the ways I have experienced God's Spirit in my life, as well as how I have tried to respond to the Spirit. This emphasis reflects a critical source of the meaning around which I have tried to build my life.

Of course, sometimes events occur that do not fit easily into our chosen life narratives. Robert Neimeyer, a psychologist and researcher who works extensively in grief, has described such events as "narrative disruptions"[8] because they disrupt the stories that we are living or hope to live. Everyone's story is vulnerable to narrative disruption. For example, my story may include the dream of a long and happy retirement after a lifetime of work, and this dream may be disrupted and even rendered senseless by a dire medical diagnosis. Such narrative disruption may leave me unsure of how to move forward, since my planned future story now seems impossible. Thus, narrative disruption can create great struggle and pain. It can be terribly painful for another reason, also. Earlier, I described the connection between narrative and meaning: our ways of constructing our narratives reflect something of the meaning or meanings on which we try to ground our lives. When narrative disruption occurs, not only might my story be shaken, but so also might the meaning embedded therein. For instance, many people seem to build their story around the meaning that if they live a good life, nothing bad will happen to them.

This meaning may work well for a time, but when a loved one dies unexpectedly, not only is the story disrupted but an essential meaning is also undermined. This potential threat to core meanings is a prime source of the great pain that can follow narrative disruption.

What are we to do when narrative disruption occurs and we face shaken or even lost meaning? Contemporary work in grief understands the affirmation or reconstruction of meaning as the central task in responding to loss.[9] When I feel my story and the embedded meaning are threatened, I face a choice. I may find that, at least gradually, I can reaffirm my meaning as viable and important, even in the wake of the narrative disruption. For example, a primary meaning of my life may be that bad things sometimes happen but the Holy Spirit is present to us in loving ways through everything. When I experience disruption, I may suffer the pain of the disruption but my sense of meaning may hold. Over time, I may even see the narrative disruption as an affirmation of my meaning, as I feel the Spirit's loving presence in the struggle.

Sometimes, however, this affirmation of meaning following narrative disruption does not seem possible or even desirable. For instance, if I have constructed my life around the meaning that bad things don't happen to those whom God loves, I will likely face a significant threat to this meaning during terrible loss. I will struggle to reaffirm my meaning unless I conclude that a bad thing happened to me because God does not love me. Clearly this would be an awful outcome of the narrative disruption. A better—although quite challenging—response would be to shape a new meaning that can hold both my suffering and my overall life story. For example, gradually I might begin to see suffering as part of the human journey through which we are sustained by God's loving Spirit.

Let us now consider the contentious struggles in the fall of 2015 over whether the United States should receive Syrian refugees following terrorist attacks around the world. Work in narrative, narrative disruption, and meaning making can help us frame these struggles. Violence on a grand scale seems to be increasingly the norm in the United States and worldwide. Indeed, within weeks of the Paris attacks, the United States endured the killing of fourteen people at their workplace in San Bernardino, California and then, in June 2016, the death by shooting of forty-nine people in a single incident in Orlando, Florida. In recent years, the United States has experienced a significant increase in the frequency of active shooter incidents, in which "an individual actively engaged in killing or attempting to kill people in a confined and populated area."[10] According to the US Federal Bureau of Investigation, there were on average 6.4 such incidents annually in the United States between 2000 and 2006. Between 2007 and 2013, this average rose to 16.4 such incidents each year.[11] In 2014, all terrorist activity around the world accounted for 32,700 deaths, almost double the number killed in 2013.[12] In confronting such grim realities, we might easily conclude, "Yes, terror is the new normal."[13]

Such widespread and mounting violence exacts a significant toll. Twentieth-century American psychologist Abraham Maslow posited that humans confront a hierarchy of needs, the most primary needs being our physiological imperatives (for example, air, food, sleep) and safety concerns (that is, security, stability). Only when these most essential needs are satisfied will a person be motivated to address other needs, such as relational connection and self-actualization.[14] Drawing on this understanding, we might consider that a core narrative theme for everyone is fundamental safety. No one wants to incorporate *terrorist attack* into one's life story. Further, the "story" of the United States has been embedded from its origins in values of life, liberty, safety, and happiness.[15] The terrorist attacks in the United States on September 11, 2001, dealt an awful blow both to the national narrative and the embedded meanings. We might think of the subsequent wars in Iraq and Afghanistan as functioning in significant ways to reestablish the national narrative and to restore these meanings.

For many in the United States, the violence in 2015 may again have deeply shaken both personal and national narratives and the embedded meanings, challenging them to reconstruct or reaffirm meaning for their lives. Perhaps for many, the struggle to reestablish a narrative of safety led directly to a rejection of the Syrian refugees. The critical question to consider next is how Christians might respond to such narrative disruption and threatened meaning; specifically, how we might attend to and participate with the Holy Spirit in the work of meaning making following narrative disruption to shape our responses to others as well as to live into a hopeful future.

THE MEANING-MAKING WORK
OF THE HOLY SPIRIT

When narrative disruptions occur, people of faith must consider and respond to these disruptions in the light of their faith story and related meanings. Of course, for Christians this requires an explicit focus on the presence and work of the Holy Spirit. In this section, we highlight three aspects of the work of the Holy Spirit that speak directly to the crises and challenges that unfolded in the fall of 2015.

First, the Holy Spirit is the instrument of God's continuing work of creation in the world. Creation continues to unfold through the Spirit, although we may not always have eyes to see it. It may be especially difficult for us to see the creative activity of the Spirit at a time of death, destruction, and loss. Yet, our resurrection faith compels us to see life even in death, through the Spirit, who is "the Lord, the giver of life."[16] And paradoxically, it is sometimes precisely through suffering and loss that we are most attentive and open to the Spirit's creative activity. Theologian S. Bruce Vaughn expresses something of this paradox as he describes his grief following the death of his young son:

> I do not recall when I first noticed this, but as I mustered the courage to suffer my own grief something very subtle began to happen. I discovered in the chaos, at the edge of the abyss, an unnamable creative energy. It began to dawn upon me that Genesis 1 is not a commentary about some primeval era: "In the beginning God created the heavens and the earth. The earth was without form and void, and darkness was upon the face of the deep." This is where anything that deserves the name life must begin—in the void, in the darkness of chaos. It is into this darkness that we descend whenever we mourn. And if we keep our eyes open in this darkness, we find there what the text of Genesis 1 asserts: That the breath of life, the Spirit of the Creator, is moving around in there: "and the Spirit of God was moving over the face of the waters."[17]

This focus on the Spirit's creative activity, even in death, is an essential faith act and constitutes a critical corrective to the doomsday mentality so prevalent in our world, driving fear and self-protection.

Second, the creative work of the Holy Spirit may generate new life for individuals and communities.

> When the Spirit breaks in, old ways of thinking and living are left behind and new ways of thinking and living begin to take over....It may not happen all at once, but when the Holy Spirit comes there is the dawn of a new day, hope for a new and different future, and courage and strength to move toward it.[18]

The possibility of newness through the Spirit is an essential theme of the Christian story and challenges narrative themes of human making that generate fear or despair, such as "terror is the new normal." While terrorism may now be a regular part of our national and global narratives, this destructive plotline cannot ultimately foil the newness of life created by the Spirit. Trusting that the Spirit is constantly active, "making all things new" (Rev 21:5), we have hope that our individual and communal narratives will continue to unfold in new ways, even as we reckon with difficult realities. Somewhere, somehow, the Spirit may break in, offering new plot material that generates hopeful meaning for the present and future.

A third aspect of the Holy Spirit's work is its inherent relationality. We can consider this relationality first as it pertains to the work of meaning making following narrative disruption. Contemporary work in meaning making following loss suggests that none of us makes meaning in a vacuum. Meanings are co-constructed in relationships with others.[19] For instance, following a loss I might turn to friends as I sort out the meaning of my experience. These others may significantly influence my meaning making, such as how I understand God's role in my suffering and what I think is possible for my future. For Christians, the most important partner in the co-construction of meaning is the Spirit: "When the Spirit of truth comes, he will guide you into all the truth" (John 16:13). As we seek to reaffirm or reconstruct meaning following narrative disruption, the Spirit will lead us to the truths on which to ground our present and future stories.

Relationality also describes how we participate in the work of the Spirit. In making meaning, our role is more than being led by the Spirit. Our role is also to attend to and participate in the dynamic work of the Spirit. This sort of mutuality in meaning making requires both action and discernment. We must work actively in the realm of meaning making following disruption, and we must also be wise regarding the meanings we embrace and promulgate. From a Christian faith perspective, all meanings are not created equal. As noted throughout this book, we must practice discernment as we participate in the meaning-making work of the Spirit.

How do we discern the work of the Spirit in which we should participate? The Spirit's activity today will be consistent at heart with what it has always been, as evidenced in Scripture and throughout history, albeit perhaps expressed in a new way for a new day.[20] Essentially, we might say that the new thing the Spirit is doing will be grounded in and expressive of God's love for all. "'God is Love' and love is his first gift, containing all others. 'God's love has been poured into our hearts through the Holy Spirit who has been given to us.'"[21] As Catherine Mooney's chapter demonstrates through consideration of the spirituality of Bernard of Clairvaux (d. 1153), the Christian spiritual tradition has emphasized the Spirit's role in communicating God's love. This relational love defines the Spirit's work and must be a hallmark of our efforts to cooperate with the Spirit. Our call is to advance work that proffers God's love as the source of ultimate meaning, for ourselves and for all.

THE ROLE OF
THE PASTORAL MINISTER

As Christians seek to discern and participate in the work of the Holy Spirit, pastoral ministers have a significant role to play. There are four aspects of this role regarding the violence in the fall of 2015, as well as the plight of the Syrian refugees. First, ministers must reassure the faithful that the Spirit's presence and ongoing creative activity cannot be truncated by destructive human effort. Even when significant narrative disruptions occur, such as horrific terrorist attacks, the Spirit is present, offering continuity to individual and communal faith narratives: "the Advocate, the Holy Spirit, whom the Father will send in my name, will teach you everything, and remind you of all that I have said to you" (John 14:25–26). Second, as we struggle for faith meaning following devastating events, ministers must remind us that not all meanings are created equal. The meanings we claim following narrative disruption must be consonant with the meanings that flow from the Spirit's work; that is, we must embrace meanings that communicate God's constant love for all. Further, inadequate meanings may emerge from deficient stories, and ministers must challenge faulty or problematic stories, such as the national myth so dominant in the United States that emphasizes safety for the United States at all costs. Such myths must be appraised in light of gospel perspectives on compassion and love of neighbor.

Third, ministers must encourage the faithful to participate in the work of the Spirit as best they can. This may require surrendering an old story that does not adequately reflect God's love for all. For instance, members of a faith community could prayerfully consider how they might concretely respond to the Syrian refugees in ways that powerfully communicate God's love and care in their suffering. Such reflection might yield the wrenching decision to reshape the community's core identity and purpose in order to better reflect this love and care. While such work may be painful, people might experience courage and freedom knowing that they are truly engaged with the very Spirit of God. The fact that communities need to respond to challenges to meaning as they arise in the changing events of history reinforces that the Spirit guides and moves with the church on its pilgrimage of faith, as Richard Lennan and Nancy Pineda-Madrid discuss in chapter 5.

Finally, such participation in the loving work of the Spirit best flows from a vital relationship with the Spirit, and thus ministers must help the faithful to cultivate and live out of this relationship as much as possible. In this age of terror, all individuals and communities are vulnerable to anxiety about safety. Only a living relationship with God's Spirit offers a sense of ultimate safety, one that allows us, even when terrible events occur, to feel secure in hope and trust that the Spirit is at work in creative and loving ways. When this security, hope, and trust become bedrock meanings of our life stories, we may be less driven to seek safety at all costs. As Jesus gave his life for the many, we may even choose to risk safety in order to extend compassion and love to all those who suffer and seek the face of God.

> *Come Holy Spirit, fill the hearts of your faithful and kindle in them the fire of your love. Send forth your Spirit and they shall be created. And you shall renew the face of the earth.*

Epilogue

The goal of this book has been to orient readers to experience and embrace the Holy Spirit. Both themes summon us to greater depths in our turning toward the Holy Spirit. The sixteen chapters are an invitation to become more in tune with the Spirit's movements in our lives, in the church, and in the world. Becoming ever more in tune with the Spirit requires a deliberate intention on our part, and is also the work of a lifetime. The Spirit, with abundant generosity, graces those who openly seek the Spirit. However, to welcome the Spirit with open arms invites ongoing transformation; the never-ending process of conversion.

Even though responding to the summons of the Spirit opens a pathway to a deeper engagement with God and a richer appreciation of God's presence in the world, our response to the Spirit is often fraught with ambiguity. Such ambiguity arises from the fact that so much of human inclination is given to reducing the Spirit to a mere support for our own desires and goals, on a personal and social/collective level. In other words, we can want to respond to the Spirit, while also wanting to guarantee that the Spirit does not take us beyond the limits of our own designs.

The movement of the Spirit and our own goals can, of course, be interrelated, but each must be considered and discerned carefully. How often our ego diminishes or limits our ability to listen to the Spirit. This complexity presents a delicate challenge. On the one hand, our ego needs to be invested in whatever we do or we would fail to accomplish anything; we must want, therefore, to respond to God's movement. On the other hand, our ego can insist that the world must be as we would have it; that insistence can make us reluctant to respond positively when we are challenged to open ourselves to the Spirit in a specific way, when we are called to greater trust in the Spirit who leads us to life.

Growing in the grace of the Holy Spirit, therefore, involves growing in what the Jesuit tradition of spirituality describes as "holy indifference." That indifference is the opposite of disengagement and apathy. Paradoxically, it is an indifference that is active; it embodies the willingness to trust in the Spirit, to allow that the Spirit might "interrupt" our best-laid plans, our most compelling visions and riveting goals, not to punish or humiliate us, but to lead us to a deeper relationship with the God who is always "bigger," and with the world that God loves. The grace of the Holy Spirit can surprise us, but intends, always and only, what gives life.

The Spirit leads us as pilgrims. The Spirit seeks constantly to invigorate all that is tired and spent, to nourish the neglected corners of our faith, and to captivate us with every grace we need to be sustained through life's vicissitudes. The presence of the Spirit, who is inseparable from all that God promises through the life, death, and resurrection of Jesus Christ, assures us that our pilgrimage will not be in vain, but will end in the fullness of God's own life. These pages echo the long history of the Christian community's faith that trust in the Spirit leads to life. With St. Catherine of Siena, the book proclaims, "Be who you were created to be, and you will set the world on fire."

Notes

Introduction

1. The full text of the Sequence for Pentecost can be found at http://www.catholicity.com/prayer/sequence-for-the-solemnity-of-pentecost.html.

2. Bernard Cooke, with Bruce Morrill, *The Essential Writings of Bernard Cooke: A Narrative Theology of Church, Sacrament, and Ministry* (Mahwah, NJ: Paulist Press, 2016), 104.

1. The Spirit and the Nearness of God

1. Denis Edwards, *Breath of Life: A Theology of the Creator Spirit* (Maryknoll, NY: Orbis Books, 2004), 12.

2. J. A. Draper, "The Tip of an Ice-Berg: The Temple of the Holy Spirit," *Journal of Theology for Southern Africa* 59 (1987): 57.

3. Jürgen Moltmann, *The Spirit of Life: A Universal Affirmation* (Minneapolis, MN: Augsburg Press, 1992), 12.

4. Anne Claar Thomasson-Rosingh, *Searching for the Holy Spirit: Feminist Theology and Traditional Doctrine* (London: Routledge, 2015), 121–22.

5. N. T. Wright, *What Saint Paul Really Said: Was Paul of Tarsus the Real Founder of Christianity?* (Grand Rapids, MI: Eerdmans, 1997), 158.

6. This is the central thesis of Gupta's essay, and he establishes it most effectively. See Nijay K. Gupta, "Which 'Body' Is a Temple (1 Corinthians 6:19)? Paul beyond the Individual/Communal Divide," *The Catholic Biblical Quarterly* 72, no. 3 (July 2010): 518–36.

7. Bernard Cooke, *Power and the Spirit of God: Toward an Experience-Based Pneumatology* (New York: Oxford University Press, 2004), 189.

8. Yves Congar, *I Believe in the Holy Spirit*, vol. 1 (New York: Seabury Press, 1983), 151.

9. Basil of Caesarea, *On the Holy Spirit*, 26.61, in *St. Basil the Great on the Holy Spirit*, trans. David Anderson (Crestwood, NY: St. Vladimir's Seminary Press, 1980), 94.

10. Cooke, *Power and the Spirit of God*, 119.

11. For this notion of the Spirit's "creative blessing" as well as the notion of the Spirit's "eschatological blessing," I am indebted to David Kelsey. See *Eccentric Existence: A Theological Anthropology*, vol. 1 (Louisville, KY: Westminster John Knox Press, 2009), 447–50.

12. John Ruusbroec, *The Sparkling Stone in John Ruusbroec: The Spiritual Espousals and Other Works*, intro. and trans. by James A. Wiseman, OSB (New York: Paulist Press, 1985), 168.

13. Ibid., 184.

14. Edwards, *Breath of Life*, 107.

15. For a rich description of the work of the midwife to which I am indebted, see Margaret Guenther's *Holy Listening: The Art of Spiritual Direction* (Lanham, MD: Rowman and Littlefield, 1992), 87–89.

16. Edwards, *Breath of Life*, 112.

17. Elizabeth Johnson, *She Who Is: The Mystery of God in Feminist Theological Discourse* (New York: Crossroad, 1993), 128–29.

18. Kelsey, *Eccentric Existence*, 451.

19. For the notion of "the more" in the real, see Jon Sobrino's "Presuppositions and Foundations of Spirituality," in *Spirituality of Liberation: Toward Political Holiness* (Maryknoll, NY: Orbis Books, 1985), 13–22.

20. Kelsey, *Eccentric Existence*, 449.

21. This is a strong accent in David Kelsey's work. See ibid., 450.

22. Ibid., 450.

23. See ibid., 443–46.

24. I am reminded of this passage by José Comblin, for whom the experience of the Spirit is always tied to a concern for justice and the building up of the community. See *The Holy Spirit and Liberation* (Maryknoll, NY: Orbis, 1989), 42.

2. The Holy Spirit Makes Us Divine

1. See, e.g., Gregory of Nyssa, *Catechetical Oration*, 24, on God's "tricking" Death by having him consume Christ the "Life" on the Cross.

2. See, e.g., Ambrose of Milan, *On the Mysteries*, 9.55.

3. Irenaeus, *Against the Heresies*, 5, prologue.

4. Athanasius, *On the Incarnation*, 54.3 For a major study, see Norman Russell, *The Doctrine of Deification in the Greek Patristic Tradition* (New York: Oxford University, 2004).

5. Origen, *On First Principles*, trans. G. W. Butterworth (New York: Harper & Row, 1966), 1.3.1; note that Origen does not adhere strictly to this schema in all of his writings.

6. Ibid., 1.3.2.

7. Ibid., 1.3.5.

8. See especially Athanasius, *Letter 1 to Serapion*, 1.24.

9. On Christ's humanity as the "instrument" of his divinity, see Athanasius, *On the Incarnation*, 8.3.

10. See Peter Brown, *The Body and Society: Men, Women, and Sexual Renunciation in Early Christianity* (New York: Columbia University, 1988), 66.

11. Ambrose of Milan, *On the Sacraments*, 6.1.4, my translation.

12. Kathleen Miles, "Ray Kurzweil: In the 2030s, Nanobots in Our Brains Will Make Us 'Godlike,'" *Huffington Post*, October 1, 2015, http://www.huffingtonpost.com/entry/ray-kurzweil-nanobots-brain-godlike_560555a0e4b0af3706dbe1e2.

3. Matter Matters: Saintly Relics and the Holy Spirit

1. See Jean-Pierre Torrell, *Saint Thomas Aquinas, Vol. 1. The Person and His Work*, trans. Robert Royal, rev. ed. (Washington, DC: The Catholic University of America Press, 2005), 293; and William of Tocco, *Vita S. Thomae Aquinatis*, ch. 65, in *Fontes Vitae S. Thomae Aquinatis*, ed. D. Prümmer (Toulouse: Privat, 1911), 138.

2. William of Tocco, *Vita*, ch. 61, in *Fontes*, 134.

3. See the introduction to *Thomas Aquinas: Selected Writings*, ed. and trans. Ralph McInerny (London: Penguin Books, 1998), ix.

4. See, e.g., Patrick J. Geary, *Furta Sacra: Thefts of Relics in the Central Middle Ages*, rev. ed. (Princeton: Princeton University Press, 1990).

5. Quotation taken, with slight modifications, from Robert Bartlett, *Why Can the Dead Do Such Great Things? Saints and Worshippers from the Martyrs to the Reformation* (Princeton: Princeton University Press, 2013), 269–70.

6. Ibid., 270.

7. Taken from Prayer A over the Place of Committal, Rite of Committal, in *Order of Christian Funerals* (New York: Catholic Book Publishing Co., 1989), 114.

8. Geoffrey Wainwright, "The Holy Spirit," in *The Cambridge Companion to Christian Doctrine*, ed. Colin E. Gunton (Cambridge: Cambridge University Press, 1997, 273.

9. *Cathechism of the Catholic Church*, 2nd ed. (Vatican City: Libreria Editrice Vaticana, 1994, 1997).

10. English translation taken from *Decrees of the Ecumenical Councils*, ed. Norman P. Tanner, 2 vols. (London: Sheed and Ward, 1990), 1:54.

11. Geary, *Furta Sacra*, 30–31.

12. Ibid., 25.

13. See canon 1237 §2 of the Code of Canon Law, in *Code of Canon Law: Latin-English Edition* (Washington, DC: Canon Law Society of America, 2012 [2nd printing]), 381.

14. *Councils and Ecclesiastical Documents Relating to Great Britain and Ireland*, ed. Arthur W. Haddan and William Stubbs, vol. 3 (Oxford: Clarendon Press, 1872), 580 (my translation and emphasis). See Geary, *Furta Sacra*, 35 and 160n14.

15. John Dillenberger, *Images and Relics: Theological Perceptions and Visual Images in Sixteenth-Century Europe* (New York: Oxford University Press, 1999), 14.

16. Lateran IV mandated, e.g., that the Eucharist and the chrism are "to be kept locked away in a safe place in all churches, so that no audacious hand can reach them to do anything horrible and impious" (Constitution 20; Tanner, *Decrees of the Ecumenical Councils*, 1:244).

17. Chapter 5; Tanner, *Decrees of the Ecumenical Councils*, 2:695.

18. See, e.g., part 3 of Luther's *Confession concerning Christ's Supper* (1528), in *Martin Luther's Basic Theological Writings*, ed. Timothy F. Lull, 2nd ed. (Minneapolis: Fortress Press, 2005), 68.

19. *Decree on Invocation, Veneration and Relics of the Saints, and on Sacred Images*, my translation (Tanner, *Decrees of the Ecumenical Councils*, 2:774–75).

20. Thomas Aquinas, *Summa theologiae* III q. 25 a. 6 co., my translation (*Summa theologiae*, vol. 4: Pars IIIa et Supplementum, ed. Rubeis, Billuart, P. Faucher, et al. [Turin: Marietti, 1948], 175 [hereafter, "Marietti ed."]).

21. Thomas Aquinas, *Summa theologiae* III q. 25 a. 6 obj. 2 and ad 2, my translation (Marietti ed., 174–75).

22. See André Vauchez, *Sainthood in the Later Middle Ages*, trans. Jean Birrell (Cambridge: Cambridge University Press, 1997), 427–43; and Charles Freeman, *Holy Bones, Holy Dust: How Relics Shaped the History of Medieval Europe* (New Haven: Yale University Press, 2011), 15–23.

23. For a brief history of the six occasions on which the coffin of St. Cuthbert was opened and his remains examined—from March 20, 698 to March 1, 1899—see David Willem, *St. Cuthbert's Corpse: A Life after Death* (Durham, UK: Sacristy Press, 2013).

24. See Victoria Tudor, "The Cult of St. Cuthbert in the Twelfth Century: The Evidence of Reginald of Durham," in *St. Cuthbert, His Cult and His Community to A.D. 1200*, ed. Gerald Bonner, David Rollason, and Clare Stancliffe (Woodbridge, UK: Boydell Press, 1988), 447–67, here 452–53.

25. Freeman, *Holy Bones, Holy Dust*, 141.

26. Vauchez, *Sainthood in the Later Middle Ages*, 428; and Freeman, *Holy Bones, Holy Dust*, 22. Cf. 2 Cor 2:15–16, where Paul describes the faithful as "the aroma of Christ to God among those who are being saved and among those who are perishing; to the one a fragrance from death to death, to the other a fragrance from life to life."

27. Wainwright, "The Holy Spirit," 287.

28. Quotation taken, with slight modifications (e.g., italics mine), from James Monti, *A Sense of the Sacred: Roman Catholic Worship in the Middle Ages* (San Francisco: Ignatius Press, 2012), 613–14.

29. Thomas Aquinas, *Summa theologiae* III q. 25 a. 6 ad 2.

30. See Augustine, *On Nature and Grace*, esp. 3.3–6.6 (English translation in *Answer to the Pelagians I*, WSA I/23, trans. Roland J. Teske, SJ, ed. John E. Rotelle, OSA [Hyde Park, NY: New City Press, 1997], 225–75, here 226–27).

31. See, e.g., Augustine, *On Nature and Grace* 17.18 (WSA I/23, 233).

4. The Holy Spirit in the Eucharistic Prayers of the Roman Rite

1. On the development of the Eucharistic Prayers, see John Baldovin, "Eucharistic Prayer," in *The New Westminster Dictionary of Liturgy and Worship*, ed. Paul Bradshaw (Louisville, KY: Westminster/John Knox Press, 2002), 192–99.

2. The most comprehensive treatment to date is Anne McGowan, *Eucharistic Epicleses, Ancient and Modern: Speaking of the Spirit in Eucharistic Prayer* (Collegeville, MN: Liturgical Press, 2014).

3. For translations of the *Didache* and other early EPs, see English translation in Ronald Jasper and Geoffrey Cuming, eds., *Prayers of the Eucharist: Early and Reformed*, 3rd ed. (Collegeville, MN: Liturgical Press, 1990), 35 (hereafter PEER).

4. PEER, 53.

5. Ibid, 35.

6. Ibid., 77–78.

7. Ibid., 43.

8. For a recent thorough treatment, see McGowan, *Eucharistic Epicleses*, 50–86.

9. See Enrico Mazza, *The Celebration of the Eucharist: The Origin of the Rite and the Development of Its Interpretation* (Collegeville, MN: Liturgical Press, 1999), 143.

10. PEER, 145.

11. Ibid., 164–65.

12. For a review of the dossier on the question of the epiclesis and the Roman Canon, see McGowan, *Eucharistic Epicleses*, 96–101; also, John McKenna, *The Eucharistic Epiclesis: A Detailed History from the Patristic to the Modern Era*, 2nd ed. (Chicago: Liturgy Training Publications, 2009).

13. See Annibale Bugnini, *The Reform of the Liturgy 1948–1975* (Collegeville, MN: Liturgical Press, 1980), 448–50.

14. See Nathan Mitchell, *Cult and Controversy: The Worship of the Eucharist outside Mass* (Collegeville, MN: Liturgical Press, 1982), 151–57.

15. St. Thomas Aquinas, *Summa theologiae* IIIa, 78, 1, ad 4; see IIIa, 80, 4, resp. where Thomas describes the entire Mass ritual.

16. Denziger-Hünermann, *Enchiridion symbolorum definitionum et declarationum de rebus Fidei et morum*, 43rd ed., with English trans. (San Francisco: Ignatius Press, 2012), no. 1320. The text reads, "It is by the power of these words that the substance of bread is changed into the body of Christ, and the substance of wine into his blood" (my emphasis).

17. PEER, 197–98.

18. See Yves Congar, *I Believe in the Holy Spirit*, vol. 3 (New York: Crossroad, 1995), 233–34. For a classic statement of this position, Nicholas Cabasilas, *A Commentary on the Divine Liturgy* (Crestwood, NY: St. Vladimir's Seminary Press, 1977), no. 29.

19. Addai and Mari, PEER, 42–44; Cyril, PEER, 84–87; Theodore, PEER, 135–37; see Mazza, *Origins*, 301–31.

20. John Chrysostom, *Homily on the Betrayal of Judas 1: 6*, cited in Congar, *I Believe in the Holy Spirit*, 3:233.

21. See John McKenna, *Become What You Receive: A Systematic Study of the Eucharist* (Chicago: Liturgy Training Publications, 2011), 224–28.

22. See McGowan, *Eucharistic Epicleses*, 264; Aidan Kavanagh, "Some Thoughts on the New Eucharistic Prayers," *Worship* 43 (1969): 9.

23. *The United Methodist Book of Worship* (Nashville: United Methodist Publishing House, 1992), 38.

24. Congar, *I Believe in the Holy Spirit*, 3:240.

25. Ibid.

26. *Baptism, Eucharist and Ministry* (Faith and Order Paper 111) [The Lima Document], (Geneva: World Council of Churches, 1982), *Eucharist* no. 15; see *Commentary* on no. 14.

27. Congar does this particularly well, see *I Believe in the Holy Spirit*, 3:234–37.

5. The Holy Spirit and the Pilgrimage of Faith

1. Pope Francis, *Evangelii Gaudium*, The Joy of the Gospel: On the Proclamation of the Gospel in Today's World (Washington, DC: USCCB Publishing, 2013).

2. Pope John Paul II, *Dominum et Vivificantem*, On the Holy Spirit in the Life of the Church and the World, (Homebush, NSW: St. Paul Publications, 1986), no. 26.

3. For the contribution of one of those theologians, Yves Congar, see Gabriel Flynn, "*Ressourcement*, Ecumenism, and Pneumatology: The Contribution of Yves Congar to *Nouvelle Théologie*," in *Ressourcement: A Movement for Renewal in Twentieth-Century Catholic Theology, ed. Paul Murray and Gabriel Flynn* (Oxford: Oxford University Press, 2012), 219–35.

4. Pope Paul VI, *Ecclesiam Suam*, Paths of the Church (1964) (Boston: St. Paul Books and Media, n.d.), no. 26.

5. See also *Catechism of the Catholic Church* (New York: Image Books, 1995), nos. 737–40.

6. All references to the Council's documents in this chapter come from Austin Flannery, ed., *Vatican Council II: Constitutions, Decrees, Declarations* (Collegeville, MN: Liturgical Press, 2014).

7. Vatican II, *Dei Verbum*, The Constitution on Divine Revelation (1965).

8. On the role of the Spirit in the formation and interpretation of Scripture, see *Dei Verbum*, especially nos. 11 and 23; on the Spirit's relationship to the eucharistic community, see Vatican II's *Sacrosanctum Concilium*, The Constitution on the Liturgy (1963), no. 6.

9. Vatican II, *Gaudium et Spes*, Pastoral Constitution on the Church and the Modern World (1965).

10. Karl Rahner, *Kritisches Wort: Aktuelle Probleme in Kirche und Welt* (Freiburg: Herder, 1970), 54; Richard Lennan's translation.

11. Vatican II, *Unitatis Redintegratio*, Decree on Ecumenism (1964).

12. Karl Rahner, *Nature and Grace*, trans. D. Wharton (London: Sheed and Ward, 1963), 79.

13. Víctor Codina, SJ. *Creo en el Espíritu Santo: Pneumatología Narrativa* (Santander, Spain: Sal Terrae, 1994), 11–27.

14. Ibid., 11–27; Víctor Codina, SJ, *Los Caminos del Oriente Cristiano: Iniciación a la teología Oriental* (Santander, Spain: Sal Terrae, 1997); Víctor Codina, SJ, *No extingáis al Espíritu: Una iniciación a la Pneumatología* (Santander, Spain: Sal Terrae, 2008), 229–42. His dissertation was titled, "El aspecto cristológico en la espiritualidad de Juan Casiano" (1966).

15. Víctor Codina, SJ, "Eclesiología de Aparecida," in *Aparecida: Renacer de una Esperanza*, ed. Amerindia Fundación (n.p.: Indo-American Press, 2007), 105–25; Victor Codina, SJ, "Las Iglesias del Continente 50 Años Después de Vaticano II: Cuestiones Pendientes," unpublished paper, 2012.

16. Codina, SJ, *Creo en el Espíritu Santo*, 42–44; Codina, SJ, *No extingáis al Espíritu*, 161–62.

17. Codina, SJ, *Creo en el Espíritu Santo*, 37; Nancy Pineda-Madrid's translation, 38.

18. Ibid., 39; Nancy Pineda-Madrid's translation.

19. Ibid., 41; Nancy Pineda-Madrid's translation.

20. Ibid., 189; Nancy Pineda-Madrid's translation.

21. Ibid., 187; Nancy Pineda-Madrid's translation.

22. Ibid., 185; Nancy Pineda-Madrid's translation.

23. Elizabeth A. Johnson, "Elizabeth A. Johnson CSJ, Distinguished Professor of Theology, Biography." Fordham University faculty page, http://www.fordham.edu/info/23704/faculty/6347/elizabeth_a_johnson (April 28, 2016); Elizabeth A. Johnson. "Forging Theology: A Conversation with Colleagues," in *Things Old and New: Essays on the Theology of Elizabeth A. Johnson*, ed. Phyllis Zagano and Terrence W. Tilley (New York: Crossroad, 1999), 121–22; J'annine Jobling, "Elizabeth A. Johnson, CSJ (1941–)," in *The Student's Companion to the Theologians*, ed. Ian S. Markham (West Sussex, UK: Blackwell Publishing, 2013), 427–30.

24. Jamie L. Manson, "Feminism in Faith: Sister Elizabeth Johnson's Challenge to the Vatican," *BuzzFeedNews* (March 6, 2014), https://www.buzzfeed.com/jamielmanson/feminism-in-faith-catholicism?utm_term=.ceyP3AAGk#.xu3VKRRpm (April 28, 2016); Elizabeth A. Johnson, "Elizabeth A. Johnson CSJ, Distinguished Professor of Theology, Biography"; Wikipedia, "Elizabeth Johnson (Theologian)," https://en.wikipedia.org/wiki/Elizabeth_Johnson_(theologian) (April 28, 2016).

25. Elizabeth A. Johnson, *Abounding in Kindness: Writings for the People of God* (Maryknoll, NY: Orbis Books, 2015), 231.

26. Elizabeth A. Johnson, *Ask the Beasts: Darwin and the God of Love* (London: Bloomsbury Academic, 2014), 132, 133; Johnson, *Abounding in Kindness*, 228.

27. Elizabeth A. Johnson. *She Who Is: The Mystery of God in Feminist Theological Discourse* (New York: Crossroad, 1993), part 3, chaps. 7—9, 124–87.

28. Helen Bergin, "Feminist Pneumatology," *Colloquium* 42, no. 2 (2010): 195.

29. Ibid., 188–93.

30. Pope Francis, *Laudato Si'*, Praise Be to You: On Care for Our Common Home (Washington, DC: USCCB Publishing, 2015).

31. Johnson, *Ask the Beasts*, 17, xviii.

32. Ibid., 16, 133.

33. Ibid., 228.

34. Ibid., 176, 177.

35. Ibid., 179.

6. Spirit, Wind, or Breath:
Reflections on the Old Testament

1. For a comprehensive overview, see S. Tengström, "רוח *rûaḥ*," in *Theological Dictionary of the Old Testament*, ed. G. Johannes Botterweck, 15 vols. (Grand Rapids, MI: Eerdmans, 1974), 13:65–96.

2. See also Athanasius's discussion of Isaiah 61:1 and other scriptural references to the Holy Spirit in his *Letter to Serapion*, 1.23; the text can be found in C. R. B. Shapland, *The Letters of Saint Athanasius Concerning the Holy Spirit* (London: Epworth Press, 1951), 124.

3. See Christopher Seitz, "The Trinity in the Old Testament," in *The Oxford Handbook of the Trinity*, ed. G. Emery and M. Levering (Oxford: Oxford University Press, 2011), 29.

4. See Jon D. Levenson, *Creation and the Persistence of Evil: The Jewish Drama of Divine Omnipotence* (Princeton: Princeton University Press, 1988), 84.

5. See Naomi Seidman, "Translation," in *Reading Genesis: Ten Methods*, ed. R. Hendel (Cambridge: Cambridge University Press, 2010), 158–60.

6. Cf. Seitz, "The Trinity in the Old Testament," 37.

7. Richard Lennan, *Risking the Church: The Challenges of Catholic Faith* (Oxford: Oxford University Press, 2004), 93.

7. The Holy Spirit and the New Testament in Light of Second Temple Judaism

1. Solomon's temple (the first temple) was built in the tenth century BCE and later destroyed by the Babylonians in the early sixth century BCE.

2. It is fitting that today, a little more than fifty years after *Nostra Aetate* (1965), we remind ourselves of the relative newness of the teachings in this watershed conciliar document about how Catholics should understand their relationship to Judaism.

3. Meredith B. McGuire, *Lived Religion: Faith and Practice in Everyday Life* (Oxford: Oxford University Press, 2008), 97.

4. M. David Litwa, *We Are Being Transformed: Deification in Paul's Soteriology* (Berlin: De Gruyter, 2012), 133–34. According to Litwa, the ancients understood the soul to be a kind of "fiery" or "hot" pneuma (134).

5. For a discussion of the Spirit in 1 Corinthians, see chapter 1 in this volume.

6. Jörg Frey and John R. Levison, "The Origins of Early Christian Pneumatology," in *The Holy Spirit, Inspiration, and the Cultures of Antiquity: Multidisciplinary Perspectives*, ed. Jörg Frey and John R. Levison (Berlin: de Gruyter, 2014), 6. Many have written on the anti-Jewish legacy of the biblical scholarship of the late nineteenth and early twentieth centuries; most recently, Kelley Coblentz Bautch, "*Kyrios Christos* in Light of Twenty-First Century Perspectives on Second Temple Judaism," *Early Christianity* 6 (2015): 30–50; D. Krause and Timothy K. Beal, "Higher Critics on Later Texts: Reading Biblical Scholarship after the Holocaust," in *A Shadow of Glory: Reading the New Testament after the Holocaust*, ed. T. Linafelt (New York: Routledge, 2002), 18–26.

7. Readers could do no better than the insightful presentation by Jack Levison, *Inspired: The Holy Spirit and the Mind of Faith* (Grand Rapids, MI: Eerdmans, 2013).

8. Sejin Park, *Pentecost and Sinai: The Festival of Weeks as a Celebration of the Sinai Event* (New York: T&T Clark, 2008).

9. Daniel K. Falk, "Festivals and Holy Days," in *The Eerdmans Dictionary of Early Judaism*, ed. J. J. Collins and D. C. Harlow (Grand Rapids, MI: Eerdmans, 2010), 636–45, esp. 638–39.

10. Levison, *Inspired*, 88–91.

11. Levison says that "ecstasy occupies a modest or minimal place in Israel's literature. In contrast, Hellenization, and Roman culture in its train, brought the allure of ecstasy to center stage" (ibid., 78).

12. F. H. Colson and G. H. Whitaker, trans., *Philo*, vol. 2, LCL (Cambridge: Harvard University Press, 1929), 471.

13. Volker Rabens, "*Pneuma* and the Beholding of God: Reading Paul in the Context of Philonic Mystical Traditions," in Frey and Levison, *The Holy Spirit, Inspiration, and the Cultures of Antiquity*, 293–329, here 303.

14. Ibid., 302.

15. Ibid., 303.

16. Levison, *Inspired*, 153–54.

17. E.g., the New Revised Standard Version (NRSV) and the New American Bible Revised Edition (NABRE).

8. Three Sightings of the Holy Spirit in the Early Church

1. For general historical background, see Justo Gonzalez, *The Story of Christianity: The Early Church to the Dawn of the Reformation*, rev. and updated, vol. 1 (New York: Harper Collins, 2010).

2. Christine Trevett, "Gender, Authority, and Church History: A Case Study of Montanism," *Feminist Theology* 17 (1998): 9–24 is a good introduction to the New Prophecy and women's prophetic authority.

3. See Susanna Elm, "Montanist Oracles," in *Searching the Scriptures: A Feminist Commentary*, ed. Elisabeth Schüssler Fiorenza, vol. 2 (New York: Crossroad, 1994), 131–38.

4. Eusebius, *The History of the Church*, trans. G. A. Williams, rev. and ed. Andrew Louth (New York: Penguin Books, 1965, 1989).

5. Epiphanius, *Panarion* 49.2, 3–5, in *Women in Early Christianity: Translations from Greek Texts*, ed. Patricia Cox Miller (Catholic University of America, 2005), 40.

6. Both accounts are in *The Acts of the Christian Martyrs*, trans. Herbert Musurillo (Oxford: The Clarendon Press, 1972). See *Marytrs of Lyon*, 62–85; *Martyrdom of Perpetua and Felicitas*, 106–131.

7. Tertullian, *Treatises on Penance: On Penitence, On Purity*, trans. and annotated William P. LeSaint, SJ (New York: Newman Press, 1959). See Bernhard Poschmann, *Penance and the Anointing of the Sick*, trans. and rev. Francis Courtney (New York: Herder and Herder, 1964).

8. Justin Martyr, *First and Second Apologies*, trans. with intro. and notes by Leslie William Barnard (Mahwah, NJ: Paulist Press, 1997).

9. See Hippolytus, *On the Apostolic Tradition*, I.2–9, trans., intro., and comm. Alistair Stewart-Sykes, Popular Patristics Series 22 (Crestwood, NY: St. Vladimir's Seminary Press, 2001), 54–94.

9. Medieval Writers:
Women, Men, and the Holy Spirit

1. M.-D. Chenu, *Nature, Man, and Society in the Twelfth Century: Essays on New Theological Perspectives in the Latin West*, trans. Jerome Taylor and Lester K. Little (Chicago: University of Chicago Press, 1968).

2. Bernard of Clairvaux, *On the Song of Songs I*, trans. Kilian Walsh (Kalamazoo, MI: Cistercian Publications, 1977), sermon 18.

3. Ibid., Sermon 8; see John 20:22.

4. Ibid., Sermon 3.1.

5. *Scivias*, trans. Columba Hart and Jane Bishop (New York: Paulist Press, 1990), 163–64.

6. Ibid., 59.

7. *The Letters of Hildegard of Bingen*, trans. Joseph L. Baird and Radd K. Ehrman, vol. 3 (Oxford: Oxford University Press, 2004), respectively, Letter 241, p. 40; and Letter 240, p. 38.

8. Joy A. Schroeder, "A Fiery Heat: Images of the Holy Spirit in the Writings of Hildegard of Bingen," *Mystics Quarterly* 30 (2004): 83–85.

9. "Earlier Rule," ch. 1, vv. 1–3, p. 75; "Later Rule," ch. 10, v. 8, p. 105; "Admonitions," I, v. 14, p. 129, in *Francis of Assisi: Early Documents*, ed. Regis J. Armstrong, J. A. Wayne Hellmann, and William Short, vol. 1 (New York: New City Press, 1999). All references to Francis's writings come from this volume.

10. E.g., "Earlier Rule," ch. 17, v. 14. Francis echoes various scriptural references; see, e.g., Rom 8:9; 2 Cor 3:17; Acts 5:9.

11. Optatus van Asseldonk, "The Spirit of the Lord and Its Holy Activity in the Writings of Francis," trans. Edward Hagman, *Greyfriars Review* 5 (1991): 135.

12. "First Version of the Letter to the Faithful," ch. 1, vv. 7–10, pp. 41–42.

13. Catherine M. Mooney, *Clare of Assisi and the Thirteenth-Century Church: Religious Women, Rules, and Resistance* (Philadelphia: University of Pennsylvania Press, 2016), 19–25, 30–48.

14. Francis is quoted in "The Form of Life of Clare of Assisi," ch. 6, v. 3, in *The Lady: Clare of Assisi; Early Documents*, ed. Regis J. Armstrong (New York: New City Press, 2006). All references to Clare's writings come from this volume.

15. "Office of the Passion," Antiphon, v. 2, p. 141.

16. "First Letter," v. 12, p. 44; and see v. 24, p. 46; on the letters, see Mooney, *Clare of Assisi*, 89–116, 197–202.

17. "First Letter," vv. 7, 12, p. 44; v. 24, p. 46; "Second Letter," v. 1, p. 47; vv. 20, 24, p. 49; "Third Letter," v. 1, p. 50; "Fourth Letter," vv. 4, 7, p. 54; v. 15, p. 55; v. 30, p. 57.

18. Catherine M. Mooney, "*Imitatio Christi* or *Imitatio Mariae*? Clare of Assisi and Her Interpreters," in *Gendered Voices: Medieval Saints and Their Interpreters*, ed. Catherine M. Mooney (Philadelphia: University of Pennsylvania Press, 1999).

19. "Second Letter," v. 14, p. 48; for the meaning of "perfection," see vv. 5–7, p. 47; see also "Form of Life," ch. 6, v. 3, p. 118, and p. 118 n. b.

20. Clare, "Form of Life," ch. 10, v. 9; Francis, "Later Rule," ch. 10, v. 8, p. 105.

21. "Fourth Letter," v. 35, p. 57.

22. "Fourth Letter," vv. 7–8, p. 54.

23. André Vauchez, *Sainthood in the Later Middle Ages*, trans. Jean Birrell (Cambridge: Cambridge University Press, 1997), 523.

24. See, e.g., Donald Weinstein and Rudolph M. Bell, *Saints and Society: The Two Worlds of Western Christendom, 1000–1700* (Chicago: University of Chicago Press, 1982), 181, 228–29, 232; Vauchez, *Sainthood in the Later Middle Ages*, 378–81, 407–12.

25. Barbara Newman, "The Heretic Saint: Guglielma of Bohemia, Milan, and Brunate," *Church History* 74 (2005): 1–38.

26. Dyan Elliott, *Proving Woman: Female Spirituality and Inquisitional Culture in the Later Middle Ages* (Princeton: Princeton University Press, 2004), 265–96. On Joan's voices as spirits, *The Trial of Joan of Arc*, trans. Daniel Hobbins (Cambridge, MA: Harvard University Press, 2005), 107, 208.

10. DISCERNING THE ACTION OF GOD

1. Teresa of Avila, *Interior Castle*, 5th dwelling place, ch. 4, § 6.

2. Ignatius Loyola, *Spiritual Exercises*, § 15 (hereafter SpEx, followed by the paragraph number).

3. Teresa of Avila, *Life*, ch. 34, § 17 (hereafter V [for *Vida*, "life," in Spanish] followed by the relevant chapter and paragraph).

4. SpEx 316–17.

5. Cf., e.g., SpEx 328.

6. Ignatius had issues with the Inquisition and wrote at the time of the Reformation, so it would have been imprudent of him to overemphasize the language of the Holy Spirit, as this was often viewed as more Protestant than Catholic.

7. SpEx 331.

8. SpEx 136.

9. V 23:14.

10. The sixteenth century was the time of the multifaceted "movement" of the *Alumbrados* in Spain, whose claim of guidance by the Holy Spirit led sometimes to clashes with church authorities.

11. V 23:16.

12. See especially SpEx 43 for the general examen, but also the prior paragraphs for other examens.

13. Cf. Mark E. Thibodeaux, *Reimagining the Ignatian Examen* (Chicago: Loyola Press, 2015).

14. SpEx 314–27.

15. Elements of the dynamics of the Spirit emerge: encouragement, strengthening, gentleness, and an irruption without cause (SpEx 315, 320, 335, and 330).

16. I rely here on research in the pneumatology of St. Teresa of Avila that aimed at making explicit an implicit theology; for an in-depth research on the dynamics of the Spirit in St. Teresa of Avila, see my *Le lieu du salut: Une pneumatologie d'incarnation chez Thérèse d'Avila* (Paris: Cerf, 2014), ch. 3, pp. 167–215.

17. SpEx 314.

18. An emblematic example can be found in V 38:10 where there is contemplation of the Holy Spirit under the guise of the dove.

19. V 32:1–3.

20. Teresa of Avila, *Foundations*, ch. 1, §§ 7–8 (hereafter F, followed by chapter and paragraph).

21. Cf., e.g., F 9:2–3; 10:1; 15:3. The most striking example being F 17:1–2.

22. Both Ignatius and Teresa have a very christocentric view of the human person; Christ is the model par excellence of what a human being should be. The core of the *Spiritual Exercises* revolves around important christological contemplations (the "Two Standards" in particular—SpEx 136–48), and the contemplation of the life of Christ, as model for one's life, and confirmation for one's discernment.

23. Brouillette, *Le lieu du salut*, 93–98.

24. E.g., the guiding role of the Spirit in her activity as writer is discreetly underlined in the invocations she makes at important turning points in her *Interior Castle*: 4th dwelling place, 1:1; 5th dwelling place, 4:11; 6th dwelling place, 1:1.

25. Teresa of Avila, *Spiritual Testimony* 65, written from Palencia, in 1581.

26. Ignatius Loyola, *Autobiography*, § 99.

27. SpEx 335.

28. Yves Congar, *I Believe in the Holy Spirit*, trans. D. Smith, vol. 2 (New York: Crossroad, 1997), 182–83.

29. V 33:5.

30. Ignatius integrates the "Rules to Think with the Church" at the end of the *Spiritual Exercises* (SpEx 352–70), for which they act as a backdrop. As for Scriptures, their importance is overwhelming through the many contemplations and meditations of the *Spiritual Exercises*.

31. See, e.g., V 13.

11. Oscar Romero: Renewed by the Spirit

1. Oscar Romero Beatification Formula publicly read by Cardinal Angelo Amato in San Salvador on May 23, 2015, http://www.lastampa.it/2015/05/22/vaticaninsider/eng/world-news/on-the-eve-of-romeros-beatification-a-look-to-the-past-and-to-the-future-1wP2S0COOEsd3KeBes3UVP/pagina.html.

2. Jesús Delgado, "La Cultura de Monseñor Romero," in *Oscar Romero: Un Obispo entre Guerra Fría y Revolución* (Madrid: Editorial San Pablo, 2003), 61.

3. Roberto Morozzo, *Monseñor Romero: Vida, Pasión, y Muerte en El Salvador* (Salamanca: Ediciones Sigueme, 2000), 56.

4. James R. Brockman, *Romero: A Life* (Maryknoll, NY: Orbis, 2003), 38–39.

5. Damian Zynda, "Archbishop Oscar Romero: A Life Witness to the Glory of God," in *Archbishop Romero and Spiritual Leadership in the Modern World*, ed. Robert Pelton (Lanham, MD: Lexington Books, 2015), 41–60, at 45.

6. María López Vigil, *Memories in Mosaic*, trans. Kathy Ogle (London: CAFOD, 2000), 158–59.

7. Martin Maier, *Oscar Romero: Mística y Lucha por la Justicia* (Barcelona: Herder Editorial, 2005), 31; my translation.

8. Roberto Morozzo, *Oscar Romero: Prophet of Hope* (Boston: Pauline Books & Media, 2015), 14.

9. Oscar Romero, "Spiritual Notebook," quoted in Monsignor Ricardo Urioste, "The Spirituality of Monsignor Romero," in Pelton, *Archbishop Romero and Spiritual Leadership in the Modern World*, 23–40, at 26.

10. Romero, "Spiritual Notebook," 26.

11. Medellín, "Poverty," 1, 2. Second General Conference of Latin American Bishops, *The Church in the Present-Day Transformation of Latin America*, vol. 2 (Bogotá: General Secretariat of CELAM, 1970).

12. Morozzo, *Oscar Romero*, 34.

13. Oscar Romero, *Orientación*, July 9, 1972, quoted in Morozzo, *Monseñor Romero*, 106; my translation.

14. Morozzo, *Monseñor Romero*, 106.

15. Oscar Romero, "El Verdadero Medellín," *La Prensa Gráfica*, September 13, 1971, quoted in Morozzo, *Monseñor Romero*, 116.

16. Pope Francis, Holy Mass for the Closing of the 14th Ordinary General Assembly of the Synod of Bishops, http://w2.vatican.va/content/francesco/en/events/event.dir.html/content/vaticanevents/en/2015/10/25/chiusurasinodo.html.

17. Morozzo, *Oscar Romero*, 48.

18. Ibid., 51.

19. López Vigil, *Memories in Mosaic*, 158–59.

20. Zacarias Diez y Juan Macho, "En Santiago de María Me Tope con la Miseria," *Dos años de la Vida de Mons. Romero* (San Salvador: Imprenta Criterio, 1995), see http://servicioskoinonia.org/romero/.

21. Jon Sobrino, *Archbishop Romero: Memories and Reflections* (Maryknoll, NY: Orbis Books, 1990), 8.

22. López Vigil, *Memories in Mosaic*, 158–59.

23. Oscar Romero, homily, March 14, 1977, quoted in Morozzo, *Monseñor Romero*, 154–55; my translation.

24. Oscar Romero, homily, April 7, 1977, in *A Prophetic Bishop Speaks to His People*, vol. 1 (Miami: Convivium Press, 2015), 71.

25. Oscar Romero, homily, May 15, 1977, in *A Prophetic Bishop Speaks to His People*, 102.

26. Oscar Romero, homily, June 17, 1977, http://www.sicsal.net/romero/homilias/C/index.html. My translation.

27. Oscar Romero, "The Church, the Body of Christ in History," Second Pastoral Letter of Archbishop Romero, August 6, 1977, accessed April 12, 2017, http://www.romerotrust.org.uk/sites/default/files/second%20pastoral%20letter.pdf.

28. Ibid.

29. Ibid.

30. Ibid.

12. Spiritual Charisms in the World Church

1. Pope John Paul II, "Holy Father's Speech for the World Congress of Ecclesial Movements and New Communities," May 27, 1998.

2. Josu M. Alday, CMF, "The First Claretian Cardinal: Arcadio María Larraona Saralegi," trans. James Curran, CMF (2009), http://www.claret.org/en/library/arcadio-maria-larraona-first-claretian-cardinal.

3. See Lora Ann Quiñones, CDP and Mary Daniel Turner, SNDdeN, *The Transformation of American Catholic Sisters* (Philadelphia: Temple University Press, 1984), 12–13n14.

4. Ibid., 15n16.

5. Pius XII, "Guiding Principles of the Lay Apostolate," Address to the Second World Congress of the Lay Apostolate, Rome, Italy, October 5, 1957.

6. Léon-Joseph Cardinal Suenens, *Memories and Hopes*, trans. Elena French (Dublin: Veritas Publications, 1992), 60.

7. See Pope John Paul II, *Dominum et Vivificantem*, On the Holy Spirit in the Life of the Church and the World (May 18, 1986), no. 11.

8. See Todd M. Johnson et al., "Status of Global Christianity, 2015, in the Context of 1900–2050," *International Bulletin of Missionary Research* 39, no. 1 (January 2015): 29.

9. See Massimo Faggioli, *Sorting Out Catholicism: A Brief History of the New Ecclesial Movements* (Collegeville, MN: Liturgical Press, 2014).

10. Pope Francis, "Address to the Ecclesial Movements on the Vigil of Pentecost," Rome, Italy, May 18, 2013.

13. The Catholic Charismatic Renewal in the Hispanic Parish

1. Vignette is based on my experience at St. Patrick Parish in Lawrence, MA.

2. Hosffman Ospino, *Hispanic Ministry in Catholic Parishes: A Summary Report of Findings from the National Study of Catholic Parishes with Hispanic Ministry* (Huntington, IN: Our Sunday Visitor, 2017), 17.

3. Cf. Danièle Hervieu-Léger, "'What Scripture Tells Me': Spontaneity and Regulation within the Catholic Charismatic Renewal," in *Lived Religion in America: Toward a History of Practice*, ed. David D. Hall (Princeton, NJ: Princeton University Press, 1997), 29–31.

4. See Pope Francis, *The Joy of the Gospel*, nos. 259–61; see also the analysis offered by Allan Figueroa Deck, "Hispanic Ministry: New Realities and Choices," *Origins* 38 (December 2008): 410.

5. Manuel A.Vásquez, "Charismatic Renewal among Latino Catholics," in *Religions of the United States in Practice*, ed. Colleen McDannell, vol. 1 (Princeton, NJ: Princeton University Press, 2001), 348.

6. Cf. the Catholic Charismatic Renewal National Service Committee website, http://www.nsc-chariscenter.org/about-us/other-ccr-groups/.

7. E.g., the Catholic Charismatic Renewal National Service Committee, the Comité Nacional De Servicio Hispano, and the Association of Diocesan Liaisons to the Catholic Charismatic Renewal.

8. See Susan Maurer, *The Spirit of Enthusiasm: A History of the Catholic Charismatic Renewal, 1967–2000* (Lanham, MD: University Press of America, 2010), 23–35.

9. Cited in Robert Owens, "The Azusa Street Revival: The Pentecostal Movement Begins in America," in *The Century of the Holy Spirit: 100 Years of Pentecostal and Charismatic Renewal, 1901–2001*, ed. Vinson Synan (Nashville: Thomas Nelson Publishers), 39.

10. See Maurer, *The Spirit of Enthusiasm*, 8–22.

11. Cf. Manuel A.Vasquez's analysis, "Charismatic Renewal among Latino Catholics," 350. See also Edward L. Cleary, "The Catholic Charismatic Renewal: Revitalization Movements and Conversion," in *Conversion of a Continent: Contemporary Religious Change in Latin America*, ed. Timothy J. Steigenga and Edward L. Cleary (New Brunswick, NJ: Rutgers University Press, 2007), 156.

12. Cf. Cleary, "The Catholic Charismatic Renewal," 161.

13. Cf. Jakob Egeris Thorsen, *Charismatic Practice and Catholic Parish Life: The Incipient Pentecostalization of the Church in Guatemala and Latin America* (Boston: Brill, 2015), 22.

14. Pew Research Center, November 13, 2014, "Religion in Latin America: Widespread Change in a Historically Catholic Region," 4. Available online at www.pewforum.org/files/2014/11/Religion-in-Latin-America-11-12-PM-full-PDF.pdf.

15. Ibid., 8.

16. Cf. Ospino, *Hispanic Ministry in Catholic Parishes*, 14.

17. Cf. ibid., 17; Timothy M. Matovina, *Latino Catholicism: Transformation in America's Largest Church* (Princeton, NJ: Princeton University Press, 2012), 115; Gastón Espinoza, *Latino Pentecostals in America: Faith and Politics in Action* (Cambridge, MA: Harvard University Press, 2014), 4; the Pew Forum on Religion and Public Life, *Changing Faiths: Latinos and the Transformation of American Religion* (Washington, DC: Pew Hispanic Center, 2007), 29.

18. Edwin David Aponte, ¡*Santo!: Varieties of Latino/a Spirituality* (Maryknoll, NY: Orbis Books, 2012), 55.

19. Cf. the Pew Forum on Religion and Public Life, *Changing Faiths*, 29.

20. Ibid., 37

21. See Hosffman Ospino and Elsie Miranda, "Hispanic Ministry and Leadership Faith Formation," in *Hispanic Ministry: Present and Future*, ed. Hosffman Ospino (Miami: Convivium Press, 2010), 175–200; and Matovina, *Latino Catholicism*, 132–61.

22. See "Statistical Portrait of Hispanics in the United States, 1980–2013: Educational Attainment by Race, Ethnicity: 2013," Pew Research Center, http://www.pewhispanic.org/2016/04/19/statistical-portrait-of-hispanics-in-the-united-states/ph_2015-03_statistical-portrait-of-hispanics-in-the-united-states-2013_current-16/, last modified March 11, 2015.

23. Cf. Center for Applied Research in the Apostolate (CARA), *Research Review: Lay Ecclesial Ministers in the United States*, February 2015 (Washington, DC: CARA), 9–10.

24. Cf. Center for Applied Research in the Apostolate (CARA), *Catholic Schools in the United States in the 21st Century: Importance in Church Life, Challenges, and Opportunities*, June 2014 (Washington, DC: CARA), 3–5.

25. Cf. Hosffman Ospino and Patricia Weitzel-O'Neill, *Catholic Schools in an Increasingly Hispanic Church* (Huntington, IN: Our Sunday Visitor, 2016).

26. Cf. Ospino, *Hispanic Ministry in Catholic Parishes*, 18.

27. *Catechism of the Catholic Church*, nos. 767, 768, 798, 801, 951, 2003–4,

28. See Paul Josef Cordes, *Call to Holiness: Reflections on the Catholic Charismatic Renewal* (Collegeville, MN: Liturgical Press, 1997), 11–19.

29. Cf. ibid., 20–27.

30. Cf. *Catechism of the Catholic Church*, no. 2003

31. See Maurer, *The Spirit of Enthusiasm*, 65–68.

32. See ibid., 44–45.

33. See Hervieu-Léger, "What Scripture Tells Me," 32–38.

34. Cf. Dean R. Hoge and Aniedi Okure, *International Priests in America: Challenges and Opportunities* (Collegeville, MN: Liturgical Press, 2006), 155.

14. The Adolescent and the Transforming Spirit

1. *Catechism of the Catholic Church* (Washington, DC: United States Catholic Conference, 1994), nos. 683, 684, 686, 687.

2. Linda P. Spear, *The Behavioral Neuroscience of Adolescence* (New York: W.W. Norton, 2010).

3. Robert Kegan, *In Over Our Heads: The Mental Demands of Modern Life* (Cambridge, MA: Harvard University Press, 1994), 28–29.

4. Kegan's findings indicate that most adults never move beyond 3rd order. Kegan, *In Over Our Heads*, 188, 191.

5. James W. Fowler, *Stages of Faith: The Psychology of Human Development and the Quest for Meaning* (San Francisco: Harper & Row, 1981), 153.

6. John Ziziloulas, "The Doctrine of the Holy Trinity: The Significance of the Cappadocian Contribution," in *Trinitarian Theology Today: Essays on Divine Being and Act*, ed. Christoph Schwöbel (Edinburgh: T&T Clark, 1995), 57.

7. Ibid., 56; original emphasis.

8. Ibid., 56–57; original emphasis.

9. David Elkind, *All Grown Up and No Place to Go: Teenagers in Crisis* (Cambridge, MA: DeCapo Press, 1998).

10. Chap Clark, *Hurt: Inside the World of Today's Teenagers* (Grand Rapids, MI: Baker Academic, 1994).

11. Sherry Turkle, *Alone Together: Why We Expect More from Technology and Less from Each Other* (New York: Basic Books, 2011).

12. Zizioulas, "The Doctrine of the Holy Trinity," 57.

13. Ibid.

14. Kegan, *In Over Our Heads*, 29, 32.

15. Jack Mezirow, *Transformative Dimensions of Adult Learning* (San Francisco: Jossey-Bass, 1991), 168.

16. Kegan, *In Over Our Heads*, 55.

17. Catherine Mowry LaCugna, "God in Communion with Us: The Trinity," in *Freeing Theology: The Essentials of Theology in Feminist Perspective*, ed. Catherine Mowry LaCugna (San Francisco: Harper San Francisco, 1993), 87.

18. Theresa O'Keefe, "Growing Up Alone: The New Normal of Isolation in Adolescence," *Journal of Youth Ministry* 13 (2014): 63–86.

19. David White, *Practicing Youth Discernment: A Transformative Youth Ministry Approach* (Cleveland, OH: The Pilgrim Press, 2005); Clark, *Hurt*.

20. Erik Erikson, *Identity: Youth and Crisis* (New York: WW Norton and Co, 1968), 132.

21. Ibid., *Identity*, 128.

22. Jean Baker Miller, *Towards a New Psychology of Women* (Boston: Beacon Press, 1984). Judith V. Jordan, "Clarity in Connection: Empathetic Knowing, Desire, and Sexuality," in *Women's Growth in Diversity: More Writings from the Stone Center*, ed. Judith V. Jordan (New York: Guilford Press, 1997).

23. Zizioulas, "The Doctrine of the Holy Trinity," 57.

24. Clark, *Hurt*, 108; Elkind, *All Grown Up*.

15. Empowered by the Holy Spirit

1. Henlee H. Barnette, "The Significance of the Holy Spirit for Christian Morality," *Review and Expositor* 52, no. 1 (1955): 5. Barnette served as professor of Christian ethics at Southern Baptist Theological Seminary in Louisville, KY. See also Leon O. Hynson, "Living in the Spirit: Christian Ethics and the Holy Spirit," in *Holiness as a Root of Morality: Essays on Wesleyan Ethics; Essays in Honor of Lane A. Scott*, ed. John Sungmin Park (Lewiston, NY: Edwin Mellen Press, 2006), 181.

2. Barnette, "The Significance," 9.

3. See Anthony Egan, "Conscience, Spirit, Discernment: The Holy Spirit, the Spiritual Exercises and the Formation of Moral Conscience," *Journal of Theology for Southern Africa* 138 (2010): 57–70, at 62. See also John Paul II, *Dominum et Vivificantem* (1986), no. 42, http://w2.vatican.va/content/john-paul-ii/en/encyclicals/documents/hf_jp-ii_enc_18051986_dominum-et-vivificantem.html. Hereafter: D&V.

4. Gene C. Crutsinger, "Discernment in Moral Decision Making: An Ability Enabled by the Holy Spirit," in *Evangelical Theological Society Papers* (Portland, OR: Theological Research Exchange Network, 1997), 4. The author quotes Richard J. Mouw, *The God Who Commands* (Notre Dame, IN: University of Notre Dame Press, 1990), 172.

5. Barnette, "The Significance," 9–10.

6. Crutsinger, "Discernment," 11.

7. Barnette, "The Significance," 9. The sentence within parentheses is in the original.

8. Thomas Dixon, "Revolting Passions," *Modern Theology* 27, no. 2 (2011): 298–312, at 298.

9. Anastasia Scrutton, "Emotion in Augustine of Hippo and Thomas Aquinas: A Way Forward for the Im/Passibility Debate?" *International Journal of Systematic Theology* 7, no. 7 (2005): 169–77, at 170.

10. Dixon, "Revolting," 298.

11. E.g., Richard E. Creel, *Divine Impassibility: An Essay in Philosophical Theology* (Cambridge, UK: Cambridge University Press, 1986); Marcel Sarot, *God, Passibility and Corporeality,* Studies in Philosophical Theology (Kampen, The Netherlands: Kok Pharos, 1992).

12. See Diana Fritz Cates, *Aquinas on the Emotions: A Religious-Ethical Inquiry,* Moral Traditions Series (Washington, DC: Georgetown University Press, 2009).

13. William C. Mattison, "Virtuous Anger? From Questions of 'Vindicatio' to the Habituation of Emotion," *Journal of the Society of Christian Ethics* 24, no. 1 (2004): 159–79, at 160.

14. Ibid., 161.

15. Ibid.

16. Patricia A. Lamoureux, "Emotion, Imagination, and the Role of the Spirit: A Response to Anne Patrick," *New Theology Review* 11 (1998): 57–62, at 57. Within the citation, the quote is from Sidney Callahan, *In Good Conscience: Reason and Emotion in Moral Decision Making* (San Francisco: HarperSanFrancisco, 1991), 101.

17. Scrutton, "Emotion," 170.

18. See Anastasia Scrutton, "Living Like Common People: Emotion, Will, and Divine Passibility," *Religious Studies* 45, no. 4 (2009): 373–93, at 377–78.

19. "We talk of 'falling in love,' being 'paralysed by fear,' 'struck by jealousy,' and 'overwhelmed by sadness.'" Scrutton, "Living," 376.

20. Tragic examples are the terrorist attacks to the Manhattan's Twin Towers on September 11, 2001, those in Beirut and Paris in November 2015, and in Brussels in March 2016, as well as the ordeals of thousands of people fleeing war and poverty looking for a better future in Europe and in the whole global North.

21. Paul Lauritzen, "Emotions and Religious Ethics," *Journal of Religious Ethics* 16, no. 2 (1988): 307–23, at 308.

22. Martha C. Nussbaum, *Upheavals of Thought: The Intelligence of Emotions* (Cambridge and New York: Cambridge University Press, 2001). See also Martha C. Nussbaum, "Compassion: The Basic Social Emotion," *Social Philosophy & Policy* 13, no. 1 (1996): 27–58.

23. Dixon, "Revolting," 298.

24. Lauritzen, "Emotions," 308. See also 316.

25. Ibid., 308.

26. Martha C. Nussbaum, *Political Emotions: Why Love Matters for Justice* (Cambridge, MA: Belknap Press, 2013). She shows that love is a political

emotion by focusing on emblematic figures in the United States (i.e., Abraham Lincoln, Franklin Delano Roosevelt, and Martin Luther King Jr.) and in India (i.e., Mohandas Gandhi, Jawaharlal Nehru, and Bhimrao Ramji Ambedkar).

27. Jean-René Bouchet, "The Discernment of Spirits," in *Conflicts about the Holy Spirit*, eds. Hans Küng and Jürgen Moltmann (New York: Seabury, 1979), 105.

28. Crutsinger, "Discernment," 2.

29. Bouchet, "The Discernment," 106.

30. Steven R. Guthrie, *Creator Spirit: The Holy Spirit and the Art of Becoming Human* (Grand Rapids, MI: Baker Academic, 2011), 164. See also D&V, no. 59.

31. Lewis B. Smedes, *Choices: Making Right Decisions in a Complex World* (San Francisco: Harper & Row, 1986), 97. Quoted in Crutsinger, "Discernment," 6.

32. Kirsteen Kim, "How Will We Know When the Holy Spirit Comes? The Question of Discernment," *Evangelical Review of Theology* 33, no. 1 (2009): 93–96, at 94–95.

33. Bouchet, "The Discernment," 105.

34. Hynson, "Living," 189.

35. Volker Rabens, *The Holy Spirit and Ethics in Paul: Transformation and Empowering for Religious-Ethical Life*, Wissenschaftliche Untersuchungen Zum Neuen Testament 2 Reihe (Tübingen: Mohr Siebeck, 2010), 21. Quoted in Mark Saucy, "How Does the Holy Spirit Change Us? A Review Essay," *Journal of Biblical and Pneumatological Research* 4 (2012): 109–22, at 110.

36. Second Vatican Council, *Dei Verbum*, (1965), http://www.vatican.va/archive/hist_councils/ii_vatican_council/documents/vat-ii_const_19651118_dei-verbum_en.html.

37. Pope Francis, *Laudato Si'* (2015), http://w2.vatican.va/content/francesco/en/encyclicals/documents/papa-francesco_20150524_enciclica-laudato-si.html. See also no. 216.

38. See Elizabeth A. Johnson, *Women, Earth, and Creator Spirit*, The Madeleva Lecture in Spirituality (New York: Paulist Press, 1993), 59.

39. Crutsinger, "Discernment," 5. The author quotes Mouw, *The God*, 174. The emphasis is Mouw's. See also Víctor Codina, *El Espíritu del Señor Actúa desde Abajo*, Presencia Teológica (Maliaño: Sal Terrae, 2015), 45–64.

16. The Holy Spirit as Dynamic Meaning Maker

1. "Obama: Shameful, Un-American to Close Our Hearts to Syrian Refugees," Breitbart News Network, accessed 12/15/2015, http://www

.breitbart.com/video/2015/11/16/obama-shameful-un-american-to-close -our-hearts-to-syrian-refugees/.

2. "Bishops' Migration Chair: U.S. Should Welcome Syrian Refugees, Work for Peace," United States Conference of Catholic Bishops, accessed 4/6/2016, http://www.usccb.org/news/2015/15-157.cfm.

3. See "Americans More Fearful of a Major Terror Attack in the U.S., Poll Finds," *The Washington Post*, accessed 3/11/2016, https://www.washingtonpost .com/politics/americans-more-fearful-of-a-major-terror-attack-in-the-us-poll -finds/2015/11/20/ec6310ca-8f9a-11e5-ae1f-af46b7df8483_story.html; "IBD/ TIPP Poll: 56% in U.S. Oppose Admitting 10,000 Syrian Refugees," *Investor's Business Daily*, accessed 3/11/2016, http://www.investors.com/politics/ editorials/new-ibdtipp-poll-shows-most-americans-oppose-taking-in-10000 -refugees/; "Poll: Most Americans Say Send Ground Troops to Fight Isis," *CNN Politics*, accessed 3/11/2016, http://www.cnn.com/2015/12/06/politics/isis -obama-poll/.

4. Robert A. Neimeyer, "Narrative Disruptions in the Construction of the Self," in *Constructions of Disorder: Meaning-Making Frameworks for Psychotherapy*, ed. Robert A. Neimeyer and Jonathan D. Raskin (Washington, DC: American Psychological Association, 2000), 207.

5. Donald E. Polkinghorne, *Narrative Knowing and the Human Sciences* (Albany, NY: State University of New York Press, 1988).

6. Melissa M. Kelley, *Grief: Contemporary Theory and the Practice of Ministry* (Minneapolis, MN: Fortress Press, 2010), 75.

7. Elliot G. Mishler, *Research Interviewing: Context and Narrative* (Cambridge, MA: Harvard University Press, 1986); Polkinghorne, *Narrative Knowing and the Human Sciences*.

8. Neimeyer, "Narrative Disruptions," 207.

9. Robert A. Neimeyer, "Preface," in *Meaning Reconstruction and the Experience of Loss*, ed. Robert A. Neimeyer (Washington, DC: American Psychological Association, 2001).

10. Pete J. Blair and Katherine W. Schweit, *A Study of Active Shooter Incidents, 2000–2013* (Washington, DC: Texas State University and Federal Bureau of Investigation, U.S. Department of Justice, 2014), accessed 3/11/2016, https://www.fbi.gov/about-us/office-of-partner-engagement/active-shooter -incidents/a-study-of-active-shooter-incidents-in-the-u.s.-2000-2013, 5.

11. Ibid.

12. "The Plague of Global Terrorism," *The Economist*, accessed 12/28/2015, http://www.economist.com/blogs/graphicdetail/2015/11/daily-chart-12.

13. David Von Drehle, "Beating Isis," *Time*, November 30/December 7, 2015, 57.

14. Abraham H. Maslow, *A Theory of Human Motivation* (Mansfield Centre, CT: Martino Publishing, 2013).

15. *Declaration of Independence*, the Charters of Freedom, accessed 12/29/15, http://www.archives.gov/exhibits/charters/declaration_transcript.html.

16. "What We Believe," United States Conference of Catholic Bishops, accessed 3/9/2016, http://www.usccb.org/beliefs-and-teachings/what-we-believe/index.cfm.

17. S. Bruce Vaughn, "Recovering Grief in the Age of Grief Recovery," *Journal of Pastoral Theology* 13 (2003): 39.

18. Shirley C. Guthrie, *Christian Doctrine*, rev. ed. (Louisville, KY: Westminster John Knox Press, 1994), 296.

19. See Robert A. Neimeyer, "Narrative Strategies in Grief Therapy," *Journal of Constructivist Psychology* 12 (1999): 65–85; Robert A. Neimeyer, ed., *Meaning Reconstruction and the Experience of Loss* (Washington, DC: American Psychological Association, 2001).

20. Guthrie, *Christian Doctrine*, 297–98.

21. United States Conference of Catholic Bishops, *The Catechism of the Catholic Church*, 2nd ed. (Washington, DC: United States Conference of Catholic Bishops, 1994), no. 733, http://ccc.usccb.org/flipbooks/catechism/index.html #212.

Select Bibliography

Ambrose, Saint, Bishop of Milan. *On the Sacraments*. London: A.R. Mowbray, 1960.

Aponte, Edwin David. *¡Santo!: Varieties of Latino/a Spirituality*. Maryknoll, NY: Orbis Books, 2012.

Athanasius, Saint, Patriarch of Alexandria. *On the Incarnation*. London: David Nutt, 1891.

Barnette, Henlee H. "The Significance of the Holy Spirit for Christian Morality." *Review and Expositor* 52, no. 1 (1955): 5–20.

Bartlett, Robert. *Why Can the Dead Do Such Great Things? Saints and Worshippers from the Martyrs to the Reformation*. Princeton: Princeton University Press, 2013.

Bernard of Clairvaux. Sermons 8 and 18. In *On the Song of Songs I*, translated by Kilian Walsh. Kalamazoo, MI: Cistercian Publications, 1977.

Bouchet, Jean-René. "The Discernment of Spirits." In *Conflicts about the Holy Spirit*, edited by Hans Küng and Jürgen Moltmann, 103–6. New York: Seabury, 1979.

Brouillette, André. *Le lieu du salut: Une pneumatologie d'incarnation chez Thérèse d'Avila*. Paris: Cerf, 2014.

Brown, Peter. *The Body and Society: Men, Women, and Sexual Renunciation in Early Christianity*. New York: Columbia University, 1988.

Codina, Víctor. *Creo en el Espíritu Santo: Pneumatología Narrativa*. Santander, Spain: Sal Terrae, 1994.

Congar, Yves. *I Believe in the Holy Spirit*. 3 vols. in 1. New York: Crossroad, 2015. (Original published *Je crois en l'Esprit Saint*, 1979–1980.)

Cooke, Bernard. *Power and the Spirit of God: Toward an Experience-Based Pneumatology*. London: Oxford University Press, 2004.

Edwards, Denis. *Breath of Life: A Theology of the Creator Spirit*. Maryknoll, NY: Orbis Books, 2004.

Egan, Anthony. "Conscience, Spirit, Discernment: The Holy Spirit, the Spiritual Exercises and the Formation of Moral Conscience." *Journal of Theology for Southern Africa* 138 (2010): 57–70.

Elliott, Dyan. *Proving Woman: Female Spirituality and Inquisitional Culture in the Later Middle Ages*. Princeton: Princeton University Press, 2004.

Erikson, Erik. *Identity: Youth and Crisis*. New York: WW Norton and Co, 1968.

Faggioli, Massimo. *Sorting Out Catholicism: A Brief History of the New Ecclesial Movements*. Translated by Demetrio S. Yocum. Collegeville, MN: Michael Glazier/Liturgical Press, 2014.

Fowler, James W. *Stages of Faith: The Psychology of Human Development and the Quest for Meaning*. San Francisco: Harper & Row, 1981.

Francis, Pope. *Laudato Si'*. Papal encyclical of May 24, 2015. http://w2 .vatican.va/content/francesco/en/encyclicals/documents/papa -francesco_20150524_enciclica-laudato-si.html.

Freeman, Charles. *Holy Bones, Holy Dust: How Relics Shaped the History of Medieval Europe*. New Haven: Yale University Press, 2011.

Geary, Patrick J. *Furta Sacra: Thefts of Relics in the Central Middle Ages*. Rev. ed. Princeton: Princeton University Press, 1990.

Gonzalez, Justo. *The Story of Christianity*. Revised and updated. 2 vols. New York: Harper Collins, 2010.

Hahnenberg, Edward P. *Awakening Vocation: A Theology of Christian Call*. Collegeville, MN: Michael Glazier/Liturgical Press, 2010.

Hereford, Amy. *Religious Life at the Crossroads: A School for Mystics and Prophets*. Maryknoll, NY: Orbis Books, 2013.

John Paul II, Pope. *Dominum et Vivificantem*. Papal encyclical of May 18, 1986. http://w2.vatican.va/content/john-paul-ii/en/encyclicals/ documents/hf_jp-ii_enc_18051986_dominum-et-vivificantem .html.

Johnson, Elizabeth A. *Ask the Beasts: Darwin and the God of Love*. London: Bloomsbury Academic, 2014.

———. *She Who Is: The Mystery of God in Feminist Theological Discourse*. New York: Crossroad, 1993.

Kegan, Robert. *In Over Our Heads: The Mental Demands of Modern Life*. Cambridge, MA: Harvard University Press, 1994.

Kelsey, David. *Eccentric Existence: A Theological Anthropology*. Vol. 1. Louisville, Kentucky: Westminster John Knox Press, 2009.

Lennan, Richard and Nancy Pineda-Madrid, eds. *Hope: Promise, Possibility, and Fulfillment*. Mahwah, NJ: Paulist Press, 2013.

Levison, John R. *Inspired: The Holy Spirit and the Mind of Faith*. Grand Rapids, MI: Eerdmans, 2013.

Loyola, Ignatius. *Personal Writings*. London: Penguin Books, 1997.

"Martyrs of Lyon." In *The Acts of the Christian Martyrs*, translated by Herbert Musurillo. Oxford: The Clarendon Press, 1972.

Maslow, Abraham H. *A Theory of Human Motivation*. Mansfield Centre, CT: Martino Publishing, 2013.

Maurer, Susan A. *The Spirit of Enthusiasm: A History of the Catholic Charismatic Renewal, 1967–2000*. Lanham, MD: University Press of America, 2010.

Mazza, Enrico. *The Celebration of the Eucharist: The Origin of the Rite and the Development of Its Interpretation*. Collegeville, MN: Liturgical Press, 1999.

McGowan, Anne. *Eucharistic Epicleses, Ancient and Modern*. Collegeville, MN: Liturgical Press, 2014.

McGuire, Meredith B. *Lived Religion: Faith and Practice in Everyday Life*. Oxford: Oxford University Press, 2008.

McKenna, John. *Become What You Receive: A Systematic Study of the Eucharist*. Archdiocese of Chicago: Liturgy Training Publications, 2012.

Mezirow, Jack. *Transformative Dimensions of Adult Learning*. San Francisco: Jossey-Bass, 1991.

Moltmann, Jurgen. *The Spirit of Life*. Minneapolis, MN: Augsburg Press, 1992.

Monti, James. *A Sense of the Sacred: Roman Catholic Worship in the Middle Ages*. San Francisco: Ignatius Press, 2012.

Mooney, Catherine M. *Clare of Assisi and the Thirteenth-Century Church: Religious Women, Rules, and Resistance*. Philadelphia: University of Pennsylvania Press, 2016.

Neimeyer, Robert A., ed. *Meaning Reconstruction and the Experience of Loss*. Washington, DC: American Psychological Association, 2001.

Origen. *On First Principles*. Translated by G. W. Butterworth. Notre Dame, IN: Ave Maria Press, 2013.

Ospino, Hosffman. *Hispanic Ministry in Catholic Parishes: A Summary Report of Findings from the National Study of Catholic Parishes with Hispanic Ministry*. Huntington, IN: Our Sunday Visitor, 2017.

"The Passion of Perpetua and Felicitas." In *The Acts of the Christian Martyrs*, translated by Herbert Musurillo. Oxford: The Clarendon Press, 1972.

Russell, Norman. *The Doctrine of Deification in the Greek Patristic Tradition*. New York: Oxford University, 2004.

Schneiders, Sandra M. *Finding the Treasure: Locating Catholic Religious Life in a New Ecclesial and Cultural Context*. Mahwah, NJ: Paulist Press, 2000.

Schroeder, Joy A. "A Fiery Heat: Images of the Holy Spirit in the Writings of Hildegard of Bingen." *Mystics Quarterly* 30 (2004): 79–98.

Seitz, Christopher. "The Trinity in the Old Testament." In *The Oxford Handbook of the Trinity*, edited by G. Emery and M. Levering, 28–40. Oxford: Oxford University Press 2011.

Steigenga, Timothy J. and Edward L. Cleary, eds. *Conversion of a Continent: Contemporary Religious Change in Latin America*. New Brunswick, NJ: Rutgers University Press, 2007.

Synan, Vinson, ed. *The Century of the Holy Spirit: 100 Years of Pentecostal and Charismatic Renewal, 1901–2001*. Nashville: Thomas Nelson Publishers, 2001.

Tengström, S. "רוח *rûaḥ*." In *Theological Dictionary of the Old Testament*, edited by G. Botterweck, 65–96. Vol. 13. Grand Rapids, MI: Eerdmans, 1974.

Teresa of Avila. *Collected Works*. 3 vols. Washington: ICS Publications, 1976–85.

Thomasson-Rosingh, Anne Claar. *Searching for the Holy Spirit: Feminist Theology and Traditional Doctrine*. London: Routledge, 2015.

Toner, Jules. *Discerning God's Will*. St. Louis: Institute of Jesuit Sources, 1991.

Van Asseldonk, Optatus. "The Spirit of the Lord and Its Holy Activity in the Writings of Francis." Translated by Edward Hagman. *Greyfriars Review* 5 (1991): 105–58.

Vauchez, André. *Sainthood in the Later Middle Ages*. Translated by Jean Birrell. Cambridge: Cambridge University Press, 1997.

Vaughn, S. Bruce. "Recovering Grief in the Age of Grief Recovery." *Journal of Pastoral Theology* 13 (2003): 36–45.

Zizioulas, John. "The Doctrine of the Holy Trinity: The Significance of the Cappadocian Contribution." In *Trinitarian Theology Today: Essays on Divine Being and Act*, edited by Christoph Schwöbel. Edinburgh: T&T Clark, 1995.

Contributors

All the authors are members of the faculty of Boston College's School of Theology and Ministry.

John F. Baldovin, SJ, is professor of historical and liturgical theology. He has recently coedited *A Commentary on the Order of Mass of the Roman Missal* (Liturgical Press, 2011). He is a past president of the North American Academy of Liturgy and the international ecumenical Societas Liturgica; he has previously taught at Fordham University and the Jesuit School of Theology at Berkeley.

André Brouillette, SJ, is assistant professor of theology and a Jesuit priest from Quebec, Canada. He holds graduate degrees in philosophy, history, and theology. He earned a doctorate in sacred theology (STD) summa cum laude from the Institut Catholique de Paris, as well as a PhD from the Université Laval (Quebec City, Canada), specializing in systematic and spiritual theology. His latest book is titled *Le lieu du salut: Une pneumatologie d'incarnation chez Thérèse d'Avila* (Paris: Cerf, 2014).

Francine Cardman is associate professor of historical theology and church history. She teaches Christianity in late antiquity. She publishes and lectures on early Christian ethics, theology, and spirituality, with a focus on the development of Christian praxis in its cultural and political contexts. From these historical perspectives, she also writes on contemporary questions of gender, justice, and contemporary church practice. Recent essays have appeared in *Healing God's People: A Reconciliation Reader* (2013), and *Wealth and Poverty in Early Church and Society* (2008).

Andrew R. Davis, assistant professor of Old Testament, received his doctorate in Hebrew Bible from Johns Hopkins University. His research in ancient Israelite temples and religion led to his first book, *Tel Dan in Its Northern Cultic Context* (2013). His other interests include the intersection of the Bible's theology and literary style, especially in the Books of Genesis, Ruth, and Job. His commentary on Job will appear in the forthcoming *Paulist Biblical Commentary* published by Paulist Press.

Brian Dunkle, SJ, is assistant professor of patristics and historical theology and a member of the Northeast Province of the Society of Jesus. Author of *St. Gregory of Nazianzus: Poems on Scripture* (St. Vladimir's Seminary, 2013) and *Enchantment and Creed in the Hymns of Ambrose of Milan* (Oxford University, 2016), he also ministers at Boston-area parishes and the Massachusetts Correctional Institute.

Colleen M. Griffith, professor of the practice of theology, works at the intersection of theology and spirituality studies. She has research and writing interests in theological anthropology, historical and contemporary spirituality, and method in practical theology. Her most recent publication is *Catholic Spiritual Practices: A Treasury Old and New* (2014), coedited with Thomas H. Groome. Griffith's edited collection, *Prophetic Witness: Catholic Women's Strategies for Reform* (2009), received a 2010 first place award from the Catholic Press Association.

Margaret Eletta Guider, OSF, is associate professor of missiology. Her teaching and research interests focus on global Catholicism, world Christianity, consecrated life, and studies in religion and society. She is a member of the *Sisters of St. Francis of Mary Immaculate* and served as the congregation's vice president and Councilor for Mission 2008–12. She is past president of the American Society of Missiology.

Angela Kim Harkins is associate professor of New Testament. She uses integrative approaches to examine how prayers and ritual practices can bring about experiences of transformation. Her book *Reading with an "I" to the Heavens* (2012) takes a fresh look at the Thanksgiving Hymns from the Dead Sea Scrolls. Prior to arriving at Boston College's STM, Harkins was the Marie Curie International Incoming Fellow at the University of Birmingham, England, where she conducted several studies on texts from the Second Temple period.

Franklin T. Harkins, associate professor of historical theology, holds a PhD from the University of Notre Dame. He has published widely on medieval Scholastic theology. He is the author of *Reading and the Work of Restoration: History and Scripture in the Theology of Hugh of St. Victor* (PIMS, 2009) and editor of *Transforming Relations: Essays on Jews and Christians throughout History in Honor of Michael A. Signer* (University of Notre Dame Press, 2010).

Melissa M. Kelley is associate professor of pastoral care and counseling and earned a PhD from Boston University in pastoral psychology. She is a fellow and nationally certified pastoral counselor through the American Association of Pastoral Counselors. She is also a fellow in Thanatology: Death, Dying and Bereavement through the Association for Death Education and Counseling. Her teaching and research interests include loss, grief, resilience, and justice-centered pastoral care. She is the author of *Grief: Contemporary Theory and the Practice of Ministry* (Fortress Press, 2010).

Richard Lennan is professor of systematic theology and a priest of the diocese of Maitland–Newcastle (Australia). His publications include two monographs: *Risking the Church: The Challenges of Catholic Faith* (Oxford University Press, 2004); and *The Ecclesiology of Karl Rahner* (Oxford University Press, 1995). The books he has edited include *Hope: Promise, Possibility, and Fulfillment*, coedited with Nancy Pineda-Madrid (Paulist Press, 2013), and *An Introduction to Catholic Theology* (Paulist Press, 1998). He is a past president of the Australian Catholic Theological Association.

Catherine M. Mooney, associate professor of church history, focuses on Christian history, saints, and spirituality. She is the editor of *Gendered Voices: Medieval Saints and Their Interpreters* (University of Pennsylvania Press, 1999); author of *Philippine Duchesne: A Woman with the Poor* (Paulist Press, 1990), which has been translated into several languages; *Clare of Assisi and the Thirteenth-Century Church: Religious Women, Rules, and Resistance* (University of Pennsylvania Press, 2016); and articles on figures such as Francis of Assisi, Teresa of Avila, and Ignatius of Loyola.

Theresa O'Keefe is associate professor of the practice of youth and young adult faith. She works at the intersection of theology, sociology, and developmental psychology. She has published several articles, book chapters, and essays examining the transition from adolescence to adulthood from a Catholic theological perspective. She is a native of western

Massachusetts, with over a dozen years of education and ministry experience in Catholic secondary schools, diocesan groups, and parish settings. She holds a PhD in theology and education from Boston College.

Hosffman Ospino is associate professor of Hispanic ministry and religious education. His research and writings explore the relationship between faith and culture as well as the impact of this relationship on Christian ministerial and educational practices. He served as a principal investigator for the *National Study of Catholic Parishes with Hispanic Ministry* (2014) and the *National Survey of Catholic Schools Serving Hispanic Families* (2016). He has authored and edited nine books.

Nancy Pineda-Madrid is associate professor of theology and Latina/o ministry. Her work examines the nature of salvation, suffering, and religious symbols. Her book *Suffering and Salvation in Ciudad Juárez* (Fortress, 2011) is the first theological work on feminicide. She coedited (with Richard Lennan) *Hope: Promise, Possibility, and Fulfillment* (Paulist Press, 2013). She is past president of the Academy of Catholic Hispanic Theologians of the United States, and vice president of the International Network of Societies of Catholic Theology.

O. Ernesto Valiente is associate professor of systematic theology. He holds a PhD in systematic theology from the University of Notre Dame. His main areas of scholarly interest include political and liberation theology, and theologies of social reconciliation. He recently published *Liberation through Reconciliation: The Christological Spirituality of Jon Sobrino* (Fordham University Press, 2015). He is chair of the board of *Christians for Peace in El Salvador* (CRISPAZ). Ernesto lives with his wife and daughter in Watertown, Massachusetts.

Andrea Vicini, SJ, MD, is associate professor of moral theology. He holds a PhD and an STL from Boston College; an MD from the University of Bologna; and an STD from the Pontifical Faculty of Theology of Southern Italy. In 2015, he coedited two collections: *Just Sustainability: Technology, Ecology, and Resource Extraction*, with C. Z. Peppard (Orbis Books); and *The Legacy of Vatican II*, with M. Faggioli (Paulist Press). His forthcoming book is *Emerging Issues in Theological Bioethics* (Paulist Press).

Scripture Index

1 Corinthians

1:15	75
2:10	3
3:16	6
6:14–19	25
6:15	32
6:19	4, 5–7, 32
8:12	32
12:1–31	48
12:4–10	149
12:4–11	3
12:11	49
12:12	32
12:13	49
12:27	32
14	78
14:4–5	78
14:8–9	78
14:26	140

2 Corinthians

6:4–8	81–82
8:9	15

Galatians

2:11–14	46
3:28	87
5:16	11
5:16–26	81
5:22–23	3, 81, 109, 162

Ephesians

1:10	47
3:6	32
4:7–13	149

Philippians

2:5–11	113
2:14–15	80
3:21	29

1 Thessalonians

5:11	140
5:19–21	132

2 Peter

1:20–21	78–79

1 John

2:28—3:10	81
4:1	81, 132
4:2	81
4:5–6	81
4:13	16

Revelation

1:10	76
1:13–16	76
2:7	131
4:2	76
4:2—5:14	76
21	86
21:5	180

Subject and Author Index